W9-CIH-579

WITHDRAWN

Also by Jonathan Yardley

Out of Step: Notes from a Purple Decade
Our Kind of People: The Story of an American Family
Ring: A Biography of Ring Lardner

States of Mind

Warren Smethport Gale

Kane

OilCity Ridgway St Marys
Renovo
Clarion
Du Bois
West Branch
Philipsb
St
Kittanning
PENNS
Butler
Indiana Altoona
Aliquippa
Pittsburgh
Bethel McKeesport Johnstown
Park Clairton Greensburg
Washington Monessen Somerset Breezewo
Connellsville
Wheeling Uniontown Chambersbu
Moundsville

Morgantown Cumberland Hancock
Fairmont
Romney Martinsburg
Williamstown Grafton Harpers
Parkersburg Clarksburg Ferry
Winchester
Weston Strasbur
Elkins
ipley WEST Front Royal
Sutton
New Market
Harrisonburg Shenandoah
Cass Nat. Park Cu
Monterey
Charleston Staunton Gordonsvi
RGINIA Charlottes
Marmet Ansted Waynesboro

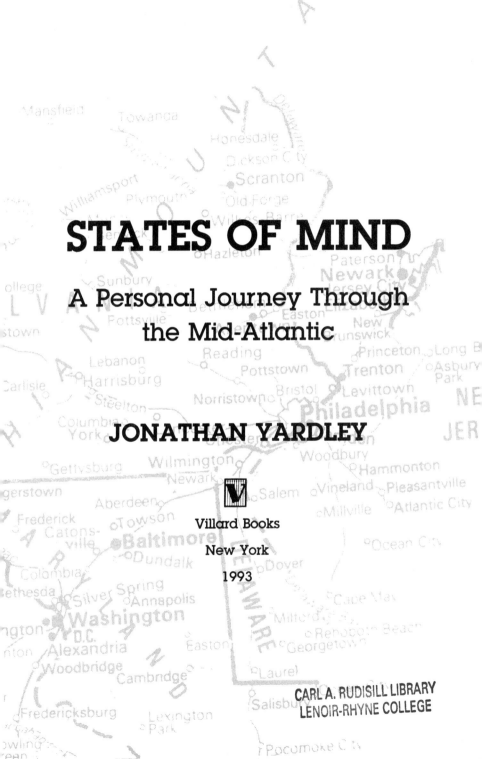

STATES OF MIND

A Personal Journey Through the Mid-Atlantic

JONATHAN YARDLEY

Villard Books

New York

1993

F
106
.Y35
1993
160392
Nov.1993

Library of Congress Cataloging-in-Publication Data
Yardley, Jonathan.
States of mind/by Jonathan Yardley.
p. cm.
Includes bibliographical references.
ISBN 0-394-58911-4
1. Middle Atlantic States—Civilization—20th century.
2. Yardley, Jonathan—Journeys—Middle Atlantic States. I. Title.
F106.Y35 1993
917.504′43—dc20   92-24690

For

Edwin M. Yoder, Jr.

Contents

States of Mind

1

MY MID-ATLANTIC

When I was a boy of nine my family moved from a suburb of New York City to a very small town in Southside Virginia. This was *terra incognita* for me, but what it took me a long time to understand was that, to my new neighbors, I was every bit as unknown and mysterious. Every time I opened my mouth I was in trouble: I was a "Yankee," and various characters in various schoolyards took immense pleasure in making me pay for it.

So you would think that I found sweet relief when my family drove north for summer vacations, but a funny thing—I didn't think it funny at all—had happened: Now people in the North thought I sounded like a Southerner, a Rebel, a mushmouth. If my tormenters in my new home loved to ride me for the way I pronounced *ball*—"bwal," they said in mimicry—my friends and kinfolk in my old one tried to tease me into blurting out the "y'all" that somehow had found its way into my vocabulary.

There I was, betwixt and between. Neither Yankee nor Rebel, yet a bit of both. Was I, as in my confused moments I believed myself to be, from nowhere at all? Southerners did nothing to disabuse me of the notion: If you aren't from the South, born and bred, then so far as they're concerned you're

from nothing worth mentioning. Ditto for New Englanders:
Good fences make good neighbors, is what they say, and their
fences are built to keep outsiders out.

So for half a century I wandered back and forth between
these polar opposites, coming to terms with both of them yet
never managing to develop a strong sense of my own regional
roots, a sense that all Americans instinctively long for, born
as we are into a vast and heterogeneous nation. Then, quite
by accident, an understanding of where I come from—and
thus, in no small degree, of who I am—came to me in the
summer of 1990, when the telephone rang and an invitation
was extended by an editor of a small magazine called *Mid-
Atlantic Country* to write an article about "the soul of the
Mid-Atlantic." Truth to tell the notion sounded fairly silly,
but the terms were adequate and I was in need of extra funds.
I accepted the offer, began to mull over its implications, and
in time came to an unanticipated bit of self-knowledge: I am
a son of the Mid-Atlantic.

This wasn't exactly an epiphany, but neither was it a
phony revelation conjured up for journalistic convenience.
Thinking some tentative, exploratory thoughts about this
amorphous, ill-defined piece of ground called the Mid-Atlantic, I suddenly was struck with the awareness that it is *my*
piece of ground. My favorite American writer, the great Mis-
sissippian William Faulkner, used to refer to his environs as
"my postage stamp of native soil." Well, the Mid-Atlantic is
my own little piece of America.

Consider the evidence. My mother grew up in New Jersey,
my father in Maryland. I was born in Pennsylvania, a state
settled early in the seventeenth century by members of my
family (after whom a town was subsequently named). I grew
up in Virginia. I went to college in North Carolina and subsequently lived there for a decade, during which one of my two
sons was born. I am now employed by a newspaper in the
District of Columbia, and I live in Maryland; one of my two
sisters lives in West Virginia.

What about Delaware? Here's about Delaware: Like everyone else who lives in the Mid-Atlantic, I have spent something
on the order of half my life on that ghastly 11.3-mile stretch
of Interstate 95 between the Maryland state line and the
Delaware Memorial Bridge. Over the years the road has had
different names and numbers, not to mention contours and
potholes and construction delays, but there has been one
constant: It is the bottleneck through which every resident of
the Mid-Atlantic must pass en route from almost every point
therein to almost every other. Delaware is to the Mid-Atlantic
as Hartsfield Airport in Atlanta is to the South: as inescapable
as death and taxes. To live anywhere in the Mid-Atlantic is to
hold honorary citizenship in the First State.

So there you have me: a true person of the Mid-Atlantic.
Which makes me a . . . what? A Middleman? A Middler? A
Mid-Atlanticker? A Midsectionite? It's a problem, isn't it?
Not merely does the resident of this region of ours have trou-
ble defining his region, he has just as much trouble giving
himself a name.

Say "Southerner" and you say worlds, conjuring up everything from Faulkner to football, Memphis to magnolia, juleps
to jazz. Ditto for "New Englander": Frost and frappes, Boston and beans, town meetings and Transcendentalism. But
say "resident of the Mid-Atlantic," and not merely have you
said a mouthful, you haven't evoked a single image, except
perhaps that of Interstate 95 making its noxious course from
Rowland in southeastern North Carolina to the town of—
yes!—Yardley in northeastern Pennsylvania. Say "Southerner," and in some places you've still said fighting words; say
"resident of the Mid-Atlantic," and you've put your audience
to sleep.

Maybe it has something to do with being in the middle, a
location that rarely arouses much in the way of passion. Good
old North Carolina, situated as it is between South Carolina
and Virginia, for generations has called itself "a vale of humility between two mountains of conceit." One could say much

the same for the Mid-Atlantic except that it contains the
District of Columbia, inside the Beltway of which humility is
in precious short supply.

Still, it's true all the same: The Mid-Atlantic is a middling
sort of place. There's nothing in its history to compare with
the legacy of slavery and defeat that still haunts the Deep
South, nor is there anything that so vividly reveals a distinctive regional character as did the religious fervors and witch
trials that swept through New England during its formative
years. "The Land of Pleasant Living" is what beer commer-
cials used to call the Chesapeake Bay, and the words suit our
part of the world just fine: not "passionate" or "puritanical,"
but "pleasant."

If you're looking for someone to say that this is bad, look
elsewhere. The pleasant atmosphere of the Mid-Atlantic—
pleasant climate, pleasant topography, pleasant people—
suits me just fine. But it certainly isn't an atmosphere
conducive to cultural or artistic upheaval. The great blues
singer Big Bill Broonzy once said: "The thing I think about
the blues is—it didn't start in the North—in Chicago, New
York, Philadelphia, Pennsylvania, wheresoever it is—it
didn't start in the East—neither in the North—it started in
the South, from what I'm thinkin'." He was thinking right:
Can you imagine the blues starting in the Mid-Atlantic?

No, the Mid-Atlantic isn't blues country and it isn't Yankee country. It's too diverse, too elusive of pat definition, to
have produced the kind of regional sensibility that in turn
produces distinctive artistic or cultural movements. Can you
imagine a coffee table book called *Great Country Houses: The
Mid-Atlantic Style*? Yet easy though it may be to laugh at the
very idea of the Mid-Atlantic, to make sport of its somewhat
artificial arrangement of seven states and one federal district,
the truth is that we have a real history and even, perhaps, a
real identity.

The first part of it is easy. If you accept the boundaries of
the Mid-Atlantic as charted by the editors of *Mid-Atlantic
Country*—and I most certainly do—then the first thing to be

said of the place is that it is the cradle of American history.
Go to the Outer Banks of North Carolina and the Tidewater
of Virginia, and you're in the places—Roanoke Island and
Jamestown—where the American adventure began. Many of
the great battles of the Revolution were fought in the Mid-
Atlantic—ditto for those of the Civil War—and it was in
Philadelphia that the colonies transformed themselves into a
nation.

Having done that, they then chose a capital city called
Washington and placed it squarely in the middle of the Mid-
Atlantic. Two of the new country's first important cities arose
in Philadelphia and Baltimore. It was in the latter that, a few
decades later, the terrible conflict between North and South
boiled down to a painfully divisive and in some respects incon-
clusive microcosm; torn between the Southern and Northern
parts of its identity, Baltimore was racked by divided loyalties just as, in other ways, the entire region was.

Indeed it's useful to think of the Mid-Atlantic as America
in microcosm. In the past the country's conflicts have been
fought out here in miniature just as, today, its prospects and
problems are all about us. In the Research Triangle of North
Carolina, bursting at the seams with new development—most
of it hideous—we have the Sunbelt in miniature. In the
steady defoliation of Maryland and Virginia countryside by
suburban developers, we have what seems to be a picture of
the American future. In the ruined urban hulks of Camden,
New Jersey, and the rotted slums of Philadelphia and Baltimore, we have the costly and explosive legacy of the industrial past.

In these characteristics as in others, the Mid-Atlantic is
distinctly and distinctively American; if there's another part
of the country in which is contained so much of what defines
us as a people, I am unaware of it. It's true that our landscape
has little of the West's melodrama or the Midwest's monotony, but the land that stretches from our beaches to our
mountains is in all other respects paradigmatically American:
You couldn't see it in any country except this one.

It is also, much of it, land of uncommon beauty and character. In the film adaptation of Edna Ferber's novel *Giant*, Rock
Hudson travels east from his bleak ranch in Texas to buy a
horse. Arriving by train in the Maryland horse country, he's
swept away not merely by the horse he will buy or the
woman—Elizabeth Taylor—he will marry, but by the countryside itself. The boy from the great state of Texas had never
seen anything so beautiful as that—the lush grass, the gentle
hills, the rich vegetation, the bright colors—and the memory
of it remained with him for the rest of his life.

There's not a place in the Mid-Atlantic that's gone un-
marked by beauty. New Jersey, with its hills to the north and
its shore to the south. Delaware, with its mighty river and its
Brandywine Valley. Pennsylvania, with mountains at both
ends and incomparable farmland in the middle. The District
of Columbia, with the great park that cuts through its heart.
Maryland and Virginia, with the bay they share and the hills
that roll away from it. West Virginia, with its steep, emerald
mountains. North Carolina, with its endless coastline and its
magnificent mountains.

We've done a good deal to ruin this landscape, and doubtless our heirs will do more, but so far its beauty and serenity
endure, touching our senses and shaping our character. For all
the bluster of the region's cities and the pushiness of its suburbs, this is still a quiet and modest place.

You can get a picture of it—a true picture, I think—if you
drive down U.S. 29 from northern Virginia to Piedmont
North Carolina. Yes, this means Charlottesville's gridlock and
Lynchburg's ghastly bypass and then the chaos of Greensboro, where the highway suddenly vanishes in an orgy of
interstates, but along the way you see the mountains of the
Blue Ridge and the comfortable small towns—be sure and
take a look at Lovingston—and the apple orchards and the
farms.

It is my favorite drive, one I make several times a year. It
takes me through places I know well and love deeply, which

is why for me Route 29, not I-95, is the main artery of the Mid-Atlantic, the road that takes me where I want to be.

What I wrote for *Mid-Atlantic Country* is, in the main, what you have just read. To my surprise and pleasure, I learned a lot more about myself in writing those words than I could possibly have anticipated, and I got a few things off my chest. But not everything. I sent the article in and went on to other matters, but I did not set the Mid-Atlantic aside. Instead I found myself musing about it often. I might pass a truck on the highway—Mid-Atlantic Tire Distributors, Mid-Atlantic Beverage Service, Mid-Atlantic Electrical Contractors—and there I'd go, thinking about my newfound roots again. The satisfactions I'd gained from writing that article may have been considerable, but obviously they hadn't closed the case. I had Mid-Atlantic on the mind.

The article had been written from memory and reflection—what some in the newspaper business call thumb-sucking—but in time I came to realize that wasn't going to be enough for me. I had to get out and have another look at the region, revisit some places I knew and loved, see others for the first time. Once having reached that conclusion, it didn't take much of a leap to reach the next: I wanted to write about it, at far greater length than a two-thousand-word magazine assignment permits. Writing is what I do, both to make a living and to try to make sense of the world; for me to take a protracted journey and then fail to come to grips with it on paper would be wholly out of character.

What was less clear to me was *how* I would write about it. At first I had visions of following in the tradition of writers who climb into their buggies or wagons or vans and venture forth to discover, or rediscover, America: Frederick Law Olmsted on the road in the antebellum South, Mark Twain roughing it along the fresh paths to the West, John Steinbeck traveling with Charley at the shank end of the Eisenhower years. It took only a day or two on the road for this to reveal itself as pure self-delusion. I am by nature reticent and shy, by professional habit an observer and critic rather than participant and reporter. I like people but am uneasy among those I do not know, and my efforts to achieve a state of bonhomie with strangers only rarely succeed. I like to look and listen, to make note of what I have seen and heard and then try to figure out what, if anything, it means.

So it did not take me long to realize that my trip, and the book in which it would eventually result, would be no *Travels With Charley* or *Blue Highways*. It would be *me*, for better or for worse. It would also, as in time it turned out, put me far more firmly at the center of things than I had at first suspected. The use of the first person singular has always given me pause, as it presumes an interest among readers in the writer's private affairs that often is wholly and deservedly nonexistent. But in traveling around the Mid-Atlantic I found myself being drawn repeatedly into my own past, until it dawned on me that what I was undertaking was truly, as this book's subtitle suggests, a "personal journey."

That is why there is just about as much in these pages about the past as about the present. I hope that I am not unduly afflicted by nostalgia, retreating from the hard present into a never-never land of the past, but I readily admit to believing that in certain important respects the past that I can recall from my own experience was a better place than the present in which I now live, and I have written about that. Some years ago I wrote a book about my parents, who were born in the early years of this century; theirs, I wrote, "was the last generation to have seen and known America before its despoliation by the quintuple pestilence of overpopulation, the automobile, the developers, the industrial polluters and television." Well, by the same token, as a son of that vintage year 1939 I am old enough to remember an America that in many respects is quite lost. I remember the day FDR died and the day the war ended. I remember two mail deliveries a day, cold milk in glass bottles at the back door, white napkins and red roses in the Pullman dining car, Mutual's "Game of the

Day" on the radio—and WHITES ONLY signs on public water
fountains and COLORED signs on gas station bathrooms.
You lose some, you win some. As I began to explore and
reexplore, over and over again I found myself confronted by
loss that was both personal and communal, much of it having
to do with unchecked growth and cynical exploitation: my
beloved Chapel Hill eaten up by high-rise dormitories and
sunset-years condominiums; the green spaces around Washington and Baltimore paved over for shopping centers and
quick-lube auto shops; the once-pristine upper Outer Banks
sinking under the weight of million-dollar weekend palaces;
Atlantic City's oddly sanitized casinos shutting out the sad
reality of the battered old resort beyond their doors. I found
such losses everywhere and I make no apologies for writing
about them so frequently; they are facts of my life, and of
ours.

But they must be weighed against the obvious: the remarkable improvements in the opportunities available to black
residents of the region and the somewhat less momentous
changes in personal relations between the races. When I was
a boy in Southside Virginia, segregation was rigidly uncom-
promising and utterly, implacably universal; when I was a
student at the University of North Carolina, other students
fifty miles away were sitting in at the lunch counter of Wool-
worth's; as a young father in Greensboro, I shared duties as
a "bus parent," trying to help ease the way for children into
the new world of desegregation; now, as a middle-aged adult,
I live in a city whose mayor is black, whose government and
school system are largely controlled by the black middle class,
whose future is inextricably bound to the fate of its black
residents.

To say that this is "change" barely hints at the way life has
altered in this region caught between abolitionist New England and the slave-holding South. There was evidence of it
at just about every stop along the way; I could not help but
take note of it and in time record it in these pages. I do so not
out of any urge to make public display of my correct posture

on matters of human and civil rights but out of the conviction
that one cannot hope to understand the Mid-Atlantic, much
less the United States itself, unless one faces the question of
race head-on. But as an old-fashioned integrationist I am
proud of what we have done in the three-plus decades of my
adulthood, and it was with self-evident pleasure that I observed the signs of it that I encountered in many, if not all,
of my stopping-off places.

I got to those places the same way most other Americans
do: on the road. As will quickly become clear, I love roads and
the odd constructs that man in his infinite peculiarity has
erected alongside them. You can tell a lot about a place from
whether its roads run flat or hilly, smooth or rough, wide or
narrow; from what is for sale in the establishments along the
way; from what signs urge the driver to buy or do or think;
from the manners—or, more usually, the lack of them—of
those who drive them. There's a modest amount of road talk
in these pages, again, with no apologies. This is what I find
interesting, what gives me pleasure, and my hope is that you
will agree.

In no way does this purport to be a definitive book on
the Mid-Atlantic; it is neither a conclusive statement of the
region's history and character nor a guide to its tourist attrac-
tions and roadside inns. The reader looking for comprehensiveness will be disappointed. There is a good deal here about
Pennsylvania and North Carolina, rather less about New Jersey and Delaware; Baltimore and Philadelphia are examined
at modest length, while Richmond and Charlotte get not a
glance; there is a fair amount about beaches, a bit less about
mountains. These are not deliberate slights, but reflections of
what happens when you let yourself go where the roads, and
your heart, take you.

What follows is, as I have suggested, primarily a work of
observation and memory, but I have attempted to catch a bit
of the flavor of the region's history. For this I relied heavily,
as is obvious from the text, on the American Guide series
undertaken during the Depression by the Work Projects Ad-

ministration as a make-work venture for writers and journalists. A half century after their original publication these books remain not merely the best of *vade mecums* for the traveler but also invaluable catalogues of local color and lore; I have quoted from them often, for the sheer pleasure of doing so.

The WPA guides were my principal traveling companions. My wife, Sue, accompanied me on a couple of long journeys as well as the very short one with which my story ends, but she is a busy person who can afford even less time away from her job than I can from mine. Thus for most of this account I am a solitary wayfarer, which may be the appropriate persona for the author of a book such as this to assume but is a distorted picture of my life as I actually live it. Beyond that, when Sue does appear it is as a somewhat shadowy and ill-defined presence. This is deliberate, for two reasons. The first is that it seems to me painfully difficult, and perhaps unseemly, to write in public about the living people whom one loves; I would have the same reticence were I writing about my sons. The other is that this book is redolent of my opinions, many of them flavorsome if not fetid; in no way do I wish to tar Sue with them.

Be all of that as it may, this book began as one notion and ended as quite another. There is nothing surprising about that. During what now threatens to become a fairly long writing career I have learned that words don't always do what one expects; sometimes a book can take a writer where it would never have occurred to him to go. Even in the workaday worlds of journalism and nonfiction, as opposed to the ostensibly more rarified ones of poetry and fiction, words can assume lives of their own and the imagination can come into play. Thus it is that a journey that began as a venture into the world became, in the end, something of an interior passage, an exercise in self-discovery as much as an exercise in the pure pleasure of travel.

Whatever the hell it was, let's get on with it.

2

HOME PLACES

Before I could climb into my car and begin my travels, I needed a proper car. To be sure, I had an automobile—by the mid-1980s Sue and I had succumbed to American reality and had become a two-car family—but it wasn't the right one. It was a Volvo 740 GLE, a handsome and stodgily comfortable vehicle that drove like the living room sofa, a defect for which it in part compensated by consuming surprisingly small amounts of fuel. But the problem with the car had nothing to do with any of that. The problem was that the Volvo radiated yuppie from every pore—not merely yuppie but import-buying yuppie: silver outside, black leather inside, looking overall considerably smugger and more self-confident than I'd ever managed to feel about myself. I'd lived with that for four years, but how people would feel about it out there in the Mid-Atlantic hinterlands struck me as another matter entirely. It was time, I thought, to buy American.

This, as every car buyer knows, was easier said than done. In the late summer of 1990, as new-car thoughts began dancing in my head, I thought more readily of Acura and Nissan than Chevrolet and Plymouth. The great leap forward in American auto quality was still in the future; pickings were still slim. But I did remember an article in *Car and Driver* that

had caught my eye, and scrounging around in the stack of
back issues I actually managed to find it. There on the cover
of the December 1989 issue was a photograph of an exceedingly sleek black automobile, and above it the headline:

AMERICA'S
BEST SEDAN!
220 hp, 143 mph, $20,000.
Ford Taurus SHO.
Ole!

Inside the magazine the hyperbole was if anything even
more extravagant. The writer, Csaba Csere, called the Taurus
SHO a "breakthrough," a vehicle that "turns the high-
performance four-door-sedan class on its head." He said that
the SHO outperformed celebrated models by Mercedes, Audi,
and Saab, and that the only cars "faster or quicker" were two
BMW models retailing at $51,000 and $71,000. He noted that
SHO means "Super High Output," explained (at least to
those who understand such things) the workings of its "remarkable" new V-6 engine built by (ssh!) Yamaha, rhapso-
dized about its "finely-tuned suspension," and ended with a
crescendo:

> Because the Taurus SHO can out-run any other four-door
> costing less than $50,000, it completely upsets the perfor-
> mance-sedan pecking order. The Taurus SHO is the first sedan
> to combine top-rank, autobahn-ready performance with great
> handling, everyday family utility, *and* a price within the reach
> of mere mortals. Those qualities make this dazzling car the
> most important automotive breakthrough in years.

Car and Driver was to repeat and embroider upon this
judgment in the coming months, including the SHO among its
annual "Ten Best Cars" in 1990 and 1991, and finally declaring it to be—inflation rears its ugly head—the "Best $25,000
Sedan in the World." But what was mainly on my mind was

that this sounded like just what I had been looking for: an American automobile—in name if not in all parts—that I could actually drive with pleasure. To be sure, what seemed to *Car and Driver* a reasonable price seemed to me exorbitant, but then my notions of auto prices are fixed back in 1972, when I drove away from the Datsun showroom with a 240Z for $4,200. Now I realized that if I wanted a good car, I was going to have to pay a 1990 price for it.

One day I had lunch with a friend and afterwards, my sales resistance perhaps slightly lowered by the wee martini I'd had an hour before, wandered onto a Ford dealer's lot. A scared young man stumbled in my direction—it was, I later learned, his first day on the job and I his first customer—and, when I inquired, steered me to an SHO occupying pride of place in the showroom. Like the Volvo it was silver on the outside— "light titanium," actually—and black on the inside, but it didn't look arrogant or smug, it just looked *fast,* and it *ran* fast when I took it out on the highway. I was sold; all of the caveats about car buying I'd boned up on in *Consumer Reports* went right out the window because I'd committed the cardinal error—I'd fallen in love with a car.

For a day I haggled with the sales manager, a sharpster who, I subsequently decided, took me for about $1,500. What with the sunroof and the leather and the top-of-the-line audio and the keyless entry system, not to mention the CD player I tossed in a week later, I was out $25,000. It had been an unpleasant experience—isn't it always?—but I didn't care, and in the event I got a small measure of revenge by taking my maintenance and repair business elsewhere. What mattered to me was that I had my very own "breakthrough" automobile, indeed the very first SHO I'd ever seen, and that it had a good old American nameplate.

Sue drove over to co-sign the papers. She made the appropriate noises of admiration.

"Isn't that a *beast?*" I said. "I think that's what I'll call it: The Beast. I'll get a license tag that says 'BEAST.' "

"No," she said. "That's a lousy idea. You get enough speeding tickets as it is. 'BEAST' would be waving a red flag at the state troopers."

She was right, of course. So I decided instead to honor both my alma mater and graduating class, and settled for "UNC 61," though my neighbor John Renner was quick to point out that all *this* did was tell people how old I was.

Right. Fifty years old and ready to roll.

With a mighty roar under the hood, I pulled off the Baltimore Beltway and onto Interstate 95, headed north. About that road there is little to be said. Unlike the others that connect Baltimore and Philadelphia, I-95 is strictly a working highway. The only real visual pleasure it offers during the drive between the two cities is so brief that in heavy traffic it can easily be missed: a majestic view of the Susquehanna River that can be seen from the Millard Tydings Bridge, just northeast of Havre de Grace in Maryland. Otherwise I-95 is a battle. When the northeastern Maryland segment of it opened on November 14, 1963—eight days before the death of the man who cut the ribbon, John F. Kennedy, for whom the highway was subsequently named—it seemed positively sylvan by contrast to its parallel route, old U.S. 40, but over the years traffic has expanded to fill the vacuum. Today's motorist thinks of I-95 primarily in terms of its bottlenecks, especially one just north of Baltimore at White Marsh and, of course, the notorious 11.3-mile stretch through northern Delaware.

The most sensible way to get from Baltimore to Philadelphia is not by car but by train, but give a boy a brand-new SHO and he certainly isn't going to be found on Amtrak. Besides, I had a side trip in mind. So the SHO got to show me its stuff for the first time at interstate speeds—fifty-five miles an hour in Maryland, Delaware, and Pennsylvania, so everyone goes seventy—and made me a very happy fellow.

Philadelphia. No members of my family have lived there for two decades, but Yardleys have been in and out of it for two centuries. They settled there sometime in the late eigh-

teenth century; the first about whom I know anything is my
great-great-grandfather, Thomas Howe Yardley, who was
born in 1800 and during his sixty years achieved an honorable
reputation as a physician and man of conscience. Thomas
begat Henry, who begat Thomas, who begat William, who
begat me. When you think of genealogy in such terms, the
years wither away and suddenly you understand how short is
the human thread that connects you to long-ago times and
vanished people: only three men between me and the presi-
dency of John Adams!

Thomas Howe Yardley spent his entire life in Philadelphia
and may perhaps have left a small mark there, though the
houses he inhabited on Fourth Street and then on Arch Street
were demolished years ago. His son Henry moved on to Connecticut, but Thomas Henry Yardley, my grandfather, began
and ended his life in the Episcopal ministry at Philadelphia
churches, and after his death in 1933 his widow, Eva Louise,
lived out the last four decades of her incredibly long existence
in a dark and gloomy apartment on Highland Avenue in
Chestnut Hill. My Uncle Harry went to the University of
Pennsylvania for a time; my Uncle Paul actually was graduated from it, as was, a generation later, Harry's daughter
Louise.

So Philadelphia is something of a hometown for my family;
the feelings it arouses in me are those of a slightly prodigal
son. As a teenager I visited it often. I had been shipped off to
preparatory school in Massachusetts, a venture that strained
my parents' budget to the point that they could not afford to
bring me all the way home to Virginia for every school holiday. Instead I took the New York, New Haven & Hartford
from Boston to New York, then switched to the Pennsylvania
Railroad and rode to the North Philadelphia station, from
which a commuter train took me to within walking distance
of my grandmother's apartment.

She was a kind and witty but prickly and implacable
woman; I was your garden-variety troubled teenager. Still, we
were fond of each other, in a Waspy sort of way, and we

passed those brief holidays happily; we worked together on the Sunday *New York Times* double crostic puzzle and read our separate books, and with a friend I went off to Army-Navy football games—in those days they really meant something, often the national championship—for which my father had wangled precious tickets through an acquaintance high up in the service.

Highland Avenue became part of the landscape of my youth, one that long ago receded into dim and unreliable memory. Except for one brief job-hunting trip, I had not been to Philadelphia since my grandmother's funeral in November 1971. I had kept up with its news, though, and the news was not good. The mayoral administration of W. Wilson Goode was on the verge of collapse and so too was the city itself. Quite literally, Philadelphia was within a whisker of bankruptcy; tax revenues had steadily declined, a predictable consequence of the depletion of heavy manufacturing and the flight to the suburbs of the white middle class with its tax dollars. Along with its desolate neighbor across the river in New Jersey, Camden, Philadelphia had become a nationally recognizable symbol of pessimism and decay in the old Rust Belt. It was still not merely the most populous city of the Mid-Atlantic but also the greatest, rich in many ways that don't show up on the public ledgers: its universities and medical institutions, its symphony and art museums, its irreplaceable location at the very heart of American history and culture. It was still all of that, but it was in desperate trouble.

Depending on your vantage point, it did or did not look that way. I checked in at my hotel, surrendered the SHO to the ministrations of its valet parkers, and set out to walk. My first stop was just blocks away at City Hall, a hulking granite structure of Victorian design, completed in the late nineteenth century after years of what an anonymous contributor to *The WPA Guide to Philadelphia* called "much bitter criticism and more than a hint of bribery and corruption." Its great tower, "of massive masonry, solid and tall, portrays the city's early growth and its part in the struggle for independence." Now, though, several entrances were shielded by high wire fences, and a glimpse within revealed nothing so plainly as the fruits of neglect.

The same was true a few blocks east on Market Street, at Independence Square. Business was brisk at the Liberty Bell, where schoolchildren were listening to an account of the bell's history by a young Park Service ranger whose passion about American liberty and justice seemed in no way diminished by the fact of his being black; *that,* it seemed to me, was in and of itself a lesson for the day.

A block away, at Independence Hall, the picture was quite different. There and in other places around what tourist brochures promote as "America's Most Historic Square Mile," rooms and in many cases entire buildings were closed, victims of the budgetary lunacy from which the national government had been suffering for a decade. "Closed Until Further Notice," "Enter At Your Own Risk"—the signs of Reaganite irresponsibility were all about. A year later the National Trust for Historic Preservation published a list of "America's eleven most endangered historic places"; Independence National Historical Park was among them, because it "lacks adequate resources to repair leaky roofs, replace archaic fire-sprinkler, plumbing, heating and air-conditioning systems or remove such potential hazards as asbestos and PCBs."

All of which was singularly depressing, yet a walk of only a few blocks took me into what might as well have been another world. This was central Philadelphia, the heart of the city's business community and the shops that service it. Wanamaker's, the city's great old department store, was closed for renovations—it reopened months later, considerably less great than it formerly had been—but its competitor, Strawbridge & Clothier, was very much in business, as crowded with customers as ever it had been in the years when Eva Louise Yardley used to come in by train to shop, though the trendy clothing on sale there now would certainly have startled that staunchly conservative old lady. She would have been no less taken aback by the crowds streaming along outside on Market Street, a racial and ethnic jumble that, I fear, would have given no pleasure to so adamant a Wasp as she. City Hall may have been rotting but all around it immense new skyscrapers were in place or under construction, a few of them buildings of real architectural distinction. More than any other city of the Mid-Atlantic, central Philadelphia *looks* like a city, with its narrow streets and tall buildings; a New Yorker or a Chicagoan would have no trouble being at home here. Along Chestnut and Broad and all the other famous old streets, crowds bustled down the sidewalks, wielding bulky shopping bags, clad in the attire of the prosperous.

Some no doubt were headed for the Shops at the Bellevue, a quietly ostentatious shopping center carved out of what had once been the Bellevue Stratford Hotel—"One of Philadelphia's oldest and most important hostelries," according to the WPA guide; since its opening in 1904, "its construction and arrangement have been copied by many other leading hotels in the country, including five of the best known in New York City." Now the Bellevue was copying New York, transforming its lower floors into an emporium in the tradition not of John Wanamaker but of Donald Trump. I took a look. Polo/Ralph Lauren, Pierre Deux, Gucci, Alfred Dunhill, Neuchatel Chocolates, Avant-Garde Paris—these and others displayed the wares most in favor among the conspicuously self-indulgent, with Tiffany's soon to join their number.

Shops at the Bellevue, City Hall: these are the two Philadelphias. The first is rich, self-satisfied, self-protective. A few months after my visit the merchants and businessmen of downtown formed something called Center City District, a cooperative the purpose of which was to provide unto the prosperous the services the city itself could not afford: private sidewalk sweepers, private security guards, private trash collectors. Their motives were not unreasonable—the protection of their investments and their selves—but by throwing up an invisible fence around their enclave they separated it still further from the second Philadelphia, the one that is poor or lower middle class, underpaid or unemployed, sometimes homeless, often black. The money they disburse on their private services is for their own benefit, not the city's; in spending it they increase the distance between rich and poor, divert funds from public to private purposes, leave untouched the basic difficulties that produced the conditions they so rightly fear and deplore.

What I needed after all that was a drink and a meal. I cleaned up and took a cab to Old Original Bookbinder's, the city's most famous restaurant; I had eaten there years before and had pleasant memories of its swordfish. But either Bookbinder's had changed or I had. What I entered wasn't a restaurant but a tourist trap. At the door I was greeted not by a welcoming smile but by a vast display of T-shirts, sweatshirts, and souvenir gimcracks. Scarcely a customer was in the place and I had a reservation to boot, but that didn't prevent the maitre d' from proving Yardley's Law: No matter how many good tables may be free, Yardley will always be given the worst available. I found myself in a second-floor Siberia, at the mercy of a waiter whose interest in me was both perfunctory and dismissive. The swordfish was ample and fresh and unimaginatively prepared, accompanied by the most ordinary array of vegetables; the instant I took my last bite the waiter rushed in with the check, the size of which fair took my breath away. I went back to the hotel, collapsed on my bed, and eventually drifted off into an uneasy sleep; I was glad to be in Philadelphia, but troubled by too much of what I had seen.

The next morning I fetched the SHO from the garage and headed out of town. I was off to Yardley, forty-five minutes away on I-95, and Harvest Day, its annual fair. Once Sue and I had driven up for the occasion, but had arrived in a heavy rainstorm that stubbornly declined to abate, eventually resulting in cancellation of the day's activities; in the intervening time my curiosity about this tribal rite of the old family town had greatly increased, and I was determined to see just what strange affairs transpired.

That's no joke. Yardley really is the old family town. Its origins lie in a grant of five hundred nineteen acres of prime Delaware River frontage from William Penn to his loyal Quaker co-religionist William Yardley, whose nephew, Thomas, eventually acquired control of the property and established the family's permanent presence in the colonies. Over the years the settlement was known as Yardley's Ferry, then as Yardleyville, and since 1883—at the instigation of the United States Post Office, which kept getting it mixed up with Yardville, across the river in New Jersey—simply as Yardley. Though it has been accessible to Philadelphia by rail and auto for many years, only recently has it become an exurban haunt for commuters. Until its outlying lands began to convert from agriculture to development it was almost exclusively a farming community, hence Harvest Day.

I go to Yardley rarely, but always with delight. Were I a Smith and were I to visit Smithfield, I might take some pleasure in the juxtaposition but not much or for very long; there are, after all, many Smiths and many Smithfields, and the novelty surely would long ago have worn off. But there are very few Yardleys and the name is scarcely on the public's lips, save that part of the public loyal to the soaps and shaving lotions manufactured by Yardley of London, a firm with which unfortunately I enjoy no financial relationship at all.

So if your name is Yardley and you find yourself in Yardley, Pennsylvania, you are in for a shock: Yardley is everywhere. At the Yardley Shopping Center you can buy pastry, film, jewelry; nearby is Yardley Pizza. Family practice is offered at the Yardley Medical Center, wherein can also be found Yardley X-Ray. R. Brian Struck, R.P.T., offers Yardley Physical Therapy. Yardley Hardware (next door to the Yardley Chiropractic Centre) sells Pittsburgh Paints and the Yardley Bank hands out money. The Yardley Manufacturing Company, located in a small white building just off South Main Street, manufactures God knows what. The Yardley Birth Center brings new residents into Yardley, if not new Yardleys. You can read all about it in the *Yardley News*. The

Yardley Post Office proclaims, above its front windows, the family's very own Zip Code: 19067.

I'd just as well admit it: A trip to Yardley is an ego trip. Not merely that, but it's a lovely little town. The developments on its fringes are hideous, with names like Hidden Oaks and Yardley Estates and Bexley Orchards, not to mention graceless, overpriced "tract mansions" such as are to be found in the less attractive new suburbs of Washington and Baltimore. But the little old town on the Delaware still retains much of its character. There are some handsome old buildings, one of the oldest and unquestionably the most handsome being Lakeside, the house constructed in 1728 by the first Thomas Yardley—who spelled it, as the family then did, Yeardley—across the street from the jewel-like Lake Afton right in the heart of town. Like much American architecture of the period, Lakeside is in the Georgian style; no doubt it evoked for the émigré Yardleys memories of the native land they had chosen to leave for reasons of religious conviction, but it is of stone rather than brick, with stucco overlay. The current owners have painted it a handsome shade of yellow; I wish it were mine.

On the morning of Harvest Day I got to town before nine, having been warned on a previous visit that the occasion brought the local folk out early. It was good advice. I managed to slip into a parking spot across from the Yardley Historical Association, but fifteen minutes later there wasn't a place to be found within half a mile of Main Street. I locked the car and followed the crowds, and in a matter of minutes found myself on Canal Street, sampling the local wares.

There were, according to the *News*, some three hundred merchants selling them. There wasn't a farmer in the lot. If what was for sale along Canal and Main streets is any guide, what is now harvested in Yardley isn't food but junk. Rarely have I seen so much of it in one place. "Baskets-n-Bows": that set the tone. Table after table was cluttered with what now passes for craftwork: baskets, papier-mâché jewelry,

toy animals, wooden ducks, clay dwarfs, plastic pumpkins—
thingamabobs and gizmos and whatnots. At the "Jaycees'
Entertainment Area" a rock band plunked noisily if purpose-
lessly, while the Makefield Women's Association sold pizza,
Diet Coke, nachos, and other native dishes. In the "Spirit of
Yardley Area," the Bucks County Homeless Shelter and the
Yardley Republican party coexisted unnaturally. The
crowd—it really *was* a crowd—was happy and busy, browsing
the merchandise and, incredibly enough, buying it.

After a couple of hours I wandered over to the Yardley
Women's Exchange, in hopes of purchasing some of its elusive
sweatshirts. Word of these wondrous garments had found its
way to various far-flung Yardleys whose longings I had been
unable to satisfy due to insufficient supply at the source. But
now, on a table in front of the exchange, stood a substantial
stack of them: none of the first-choice "Historic Yardley"
shirts, alas, but enough of the plain "Yardley" variety to
meet my family's needs. I picked out a half dozen and went
inside to pay for them. The pleasant lady at the cash register
said an out-of-town check would be fine. I handed one over
and headed for the car.

"Mr. Yardley! Mr. Yardley!"

The woman at the cash register was running across the
lawn. What on earth had I done? Was it really possible that
my check had *already* bounced? In *two minutes?*

"Mr. Yardley!" She stopped and caught her breath. "Mr.
Yardley, I'm Anne Yardley. Ralph Yardley's wife."

So it had happened at last. I had found Yardleys in Yardley. Family.

A few years before I had corresponded with Ralph Yardley,
a gentleman of my parents' generation about whom I knew
little except that he had long practiced law in Philadelphia
and that he had a lively interest in the family's genealogy. It
was in search of help in this latter category, while doing
research on my book about my parents, that I had written to
Ralph Yardley. Our letters had become friendly and I had

taken to calling him "Cousin Ralph"—what our precise relationship is I cannot say, except that it is real—but we had
never met.

Now, an hour later, thanks to Anne's immediately proffered
invitation, I was sitting in the Yardleys' ample, comfortable,
unpretentious old house on North Main Street, sipping a glass
of wine and eating a ham-and-cheese sandwich.

Anne was talkative and bouncy; Ralph was understated
and wry. I liked them both, and was comfortable with them.
For more than an hour we talked. It was for me an immensely
happy occasion, yet an unsettling one as well; suddenly finding oneself in the company of relatives who are not merely
long-lost but never-met is an eerie experience. We talked
about our own families, retraced common family history, tried
halfheartedly to figure out the precise nature of our kinship.
We talked as well about this place called Yardley, this old
town in this old state from which over the generations our
ancestors and contemporaries had fanned out in an ever-
widening pattern: first to the states of the Mid-Atlantic and
Northeast, then to those of the far and middle West. Anne,
who during the 1980s worked as a real estate agent, told me
how in those years virtually the entire stock of local farmland
was relinquished to developers, who built the pretentious—
and expensive—residences I had noticed in ever-increasing
numbers on each of my previous visits. The little old town had
been swallowed up by the big world, she said; this had not
been without profit to her household, but there was far more
sorrow than satisfaction in her voice.

It was time for me to go; I had an appointment back in
Philadelphia. I said good-bye to Ralph and Anne, then
pointed the SHO back toward I-95. Over the years I had made
the return trip several times, but never before with the emotions that now washed over me. Until this day my trips to
Yardley, much though I had enjoyed them, had been excursions to a strange place that merely happened to bear my
family's name. Now, though, I had found family there, and
had felt at home.

. . .

My appointment was with the rector of the Church of St. James the Less. I had not been there since the day in late November of 1971 when the Yardley clan gathered to observe the last rites for my grandmother, who had died in Chestnut Hill in her ninety-third year.

The funeral was one of the more peculiar and unsettling experiences of my life. I was then living in Greensboro and thus was closer physically to Philadelphia than any of the other eight grandchildren. My father asked me to attend the funeral and of course I agreed. I drove the central arteries so familiar to residents of the Mid-Atlantic, I-85 from Greensboro to Petersburg, Virginia; I-95 the rest of the way. Upon reaching Chestnut Hill I found only my Uncle Harry in the dark old apartment; my father, Bill, had yet to arrive from Rhode Island, and the youngest of the brothers, Paul, was flying in from Hawaii. In my suitcase I had a bottle of Scotch, arms against the gloom that seemed likely to descend. I put it on the kitchen table. That was a major mistake.

Harry, a dear man and a terrible sot, lit up like a Christmas tree. He brought out a couple of glasses and we hunkered down. By the time Bill and Paul drove up a couple of hours later, we were sloshed. My recollections of the rest of the evening are dim—the three brothers were vexed with each other, though that was nothing new—but the next day I remember as clearly as the most ghastly nightmare.

It was chilly and bright. Much, much too bright. Somehow we patched together breakfast, though I could get little down. Then we made our way to the residence of Betty and Martin Kneedler, my grandmother's dear friends, where my mother had wisely taken shelter, as far as possible from the stinking fen of masculine grievances on Highland Avenue. A limousine was soon forthcoming; when it arrived we all piled in, my father holding on his lap the tiny box in which rested his mother's ashes—making, as was his wont, irreverent jokes about its contents and final destination. The air inside the car was humid and woolly; gasping against the embarrassment of

sudden illness, I cracked open a window and inhaled great
gulps of late-autumnal air. By the time we reached St. James
the Less I was desperate.

Somehow I made it through the service, though I barely
glanced at the interior of the historic stone church to which
my grandfather, Tom Yardley, had turned in the last months
of his life. He had lost, through a series of disputes—the
precise nature of which is now a mystery—his own church in
a suburb of Baltimore; he had suffered through a siege of
mental illness; he was grateful beyond measure for the tiny
part-time job as vicar that he was able to find at St. James the
Less. He had been buried there in 1933, and now his wife was
to join him. It was an occasion of considerable familial weight,
but I was in no condition to appreciate or understand it.

Not wanting to participate further in family argument, I
rushed back to Greensboro soon after the funeral, relieved at
my escape but burdened by a sense of incompleteness. Heart-
ily though I dislike the self-serving notion of funerals as feel-
good exercises in "saying good-bye," I did sense that I had
not paid proper respects to my grandmother. Twenty years
later, I thought I might be able in some measure to make
atonement by visiting the church that had meant so much to
her and by visiting her grave. I also had a more mundane
mission: I wondered how what was once an old-line Wasp
Episcopal church had managed to survive in a neighborhood
that, like so many others in North Philadelphia, had turned
black and poor.

The Reverend Father David Ousley met me at the door of
the rectory. He was a tall young man with a brusque, reddish
beard and a deliberate manner. The church, he told me, had
been built in the 1840s at the instigation of Robert Ralston,
"a merchant in the China trade who wanted a church
nearby." It was modeled upon St. Michael's Church, Long
Stanton, Cambridgeshire, England, an edifice dating to the
1230s and a minor classic of medieval Gothic. Completed in
1849, with a bell tower added in 1909 by Rodman Wanamaker
(John Wanamaker is buried in the St. James cemetery), the

church at first was "mainly for the wealthy." After the Civil
War the church "began to receive bequests that were the
beginning of its endowment, principally in the form of real
estate," an endowment that even now enables the church to
survive with no support from its diocese and a congregation
of only a hundred communicants.

The church began to change in the late nineteenth century,
when a large mill nearby brought in worshipers from the lower
ends of the social order; the workers came to the early services
and the wealthy to eleven o'clock morning prayer. But it was
not until the late 1960s that the really radical changes occurred. Then whites began their escape to the suburbs and poor
blacks supplanted them; now the neighborhood is to all intents and purposes entirely black, a reality the church has
attempted to meet with various "outreach" programs, including a Sunday School that, Ousley said, "is almost all from the
neighborhood."

It is, in its current incarnation, an uncommonly interesting church. On the one hand it engages in what could fairly
be called social activism; on the other it is ecclesiastically
and liturgically old-fashioned. Indeed, Ousley described it,
proudly, as a "conservative Anglo-Catholic parish." Its parishioners "want biblical rather than political preaching," a
preference tolerated by the Diocese of Pennsylvania, "which
has a history of being diverse and unruly; it is historically low
church but it tolerates high." Though there are many distinc-
tions between "low" and "high" in the Episcopal church, an
oversimplified definition would be that low prefers a plain
service of worship while high goes for elaborate, Romanesque
ritual, replete with incense and bells. David Ousley is a bells
man; so was Tom Yardley.

St. James the Less sits near the eastern point of a triangular
plot of about three acres; Clearfield Street and Hunting Park
Avenue, the latter a major artery, intersect at that point. The
modest row houses in the surrounding streets are in various
stages of upkeep, from tidy to disheveled. As Ousley sees it,
any difficulties the church may now face in its neighborhood

have relatively little to do with race and everything to do with drugs, which since the late 1980s have become endemic. But to the motorist passing by, the stumpy stone church with its great trees and old gravestones, surrounded by its thick stone wall, looks like nothing so much as a fortress, holding out against whatever it is Out There that has so changed Philadelphia.

I thanked Ousley for his kindness and promised to return in the morning for a sampling of his liturgy. Then I set out on one more gesture to the memory of Eva Louise Yardley. I pointed the SHO to the northwest and began to drive out Germantown Avenue, to Chestnut Hill and Highland Avenue.

My memories of Germantown Avenue in the years when I knew it best, the 1950s, are not surprisingly somewhat vague, but I feel certain in recalling an atmosphere of bustle and a prosperity that was modest at the street's southeastern end near the heart of the city and more substantial as it approached Chestnut Hill and the suburbs beyond. I remembered the trolley cars that ran down the middle of the street, and the cobblestones over which automobile tires crashed and banged, and the neat stores that lined the street all along the way.

Never in my experience has a clash between memory and present reality been more dramatic or disheartening. The trolley cars were still there, and the cobblestones, but from Hunting Park Avenue to Chestnut Hill all else was a war zone. Beirut. Dresden. Saigon. Storefronts were battered, boarded up; those that were open presented a wary eye to the world, while those that were closed hid behind protective layers of wire. The day was bright yet almost all the colors seemed bleak, defeated, faded; weeds overran empty lots, graffiti soiled walls and doors.

For three or four miles this grim procession continued; at its end I was heartsick, in this instance not so much because of my own sense of loss but because of what we as a community have abandoned and destroyed in our rush to the bland lawns of suburbia.

At last I reached Chestnut Hill, I am sorry to say with a
considerable sense of relief. Except for change of the most
superficial nature—a Banana Republic on Germantown Avenue, and a Bombay Company, and a Laura Ashley, relics all
of the 1980s—it was as I remembered it. Caruso's Market,
Kilian's Hardware, Hilton Drug—these and others struck familiar chords, as did the prevailing atmosphere of old-shoe
leafiness. Chestnut Hill is home to the rich, to be sure, but it
also has room along streets like Highland Avenue for those of
more limited means.

Eva Louise Yardley was one of these. Were it not for gifts
from wealthy relatives and her own astonishing parsimonious-
ness she almost certainly would have been at the edge of
poverty upon her husband's death, but she had enough
money to take the five-room apartment at 212 West Highland
and to pay the rent on it for nearly forty years. The street
itself was a bit shabbier than I'd remembered it, but the
apartment house looked exactly the same: grandmotherly.
There it stood, three stories high, its brownish orange brick
dulled yet further by the years, the little courtyard between
its two wings still only glancingly touched by sunlight. The
windows of my grandmother's apartment still looked out on
it from the first floor on the right.

I drove back to town feeling better. Change may be exciting
and interesting; stability is reassuring. What I found when I
got back to the center city was a bit of both. I wanted to see
the house at 100 Pine Street, the first place my grandparents
had lived after their marriage in 1905. Tom, then new in the
ministry, had an appointment as vicar at Old St. Peter's, a
historic church in the heart of Society Hill, the equally historic urban neighborhood right at the edge of the Delaware
River. In those days it was a rough place; I wondered what it
looked like now.

It looked beautiful. Society Hill, with its red-brick Federal
row houses and its narrow streets lined with trees, has become
in its years of restoration a place of exemplary urban beauty.
As at Georgetown, or Federal Hill in Baltimore, what has

happened there is gentrification, but in the stony climate of the 1980s that was the price to be paid for urban renewal. In the event, Society Hill did not seem so dominated by the likes of Laura Ashley and Ralph Lauren as to have completely abandoned all traces of urban funkiness. I found my way to South Street, which teemed with counterculturites of all races and sexual persuasions; I went shoulder to shoulder with jazz lovers at a decidedly anti-cute Tower Records, and I had a beer at a bar that surely would have given pause to anyone of the thirtysomething culture.

In time I got around to 100 Pine Street, but it was not the building in which my grandparents had lived. Instead it was a red-brick row house of relatively recent vintage, far from ugly but clearly constructed with an eye to defense against the madding crowd outside. The river was in clear view, but fences and the daunting barriers of Delaware Avenue and I-95 made it all but inaccessible; I think the fetid, grimy waterfront of my grandparents' day would have been a better neighbor.

But standing at 100 Pine Street and looking inland, it wasn't hard to conjure up images of their surroundings. Apart from the autos and a few newer buildings, the houses along Pine were the same ones past which they had walked every day; just to the west was Head House Square, the handsome old market at which Louise presumably did much of her shopping, now selling pizza and redolent of potpourri yet retaining the essence of its airy and intimate character; another block to the west St. Peter's still stood, its tall white spire still a landmark of the neighborhood, its pews still welcoming worshipers.

I returned in the morning to St. James the Less. Not really for worship, for the church long ago receded from my life after too many years of too much exposure to it, but to hear once again the majestic language of the Book of Common Prayer, language compromised by the Episcopal church in its headlong plunge toward terminal trendiness but still used by

David Ousley and his loyal parishioners, "not only as a common liturgy, but as a standard of doctrine and a bond of fellowship, allowing prudent revision and diverse forms and usages, provided that the substance of the Faith be kept alive."

Thus read the "Declaration of Principles" on the back of the bulletin that I picked up at St. James early that Sunday morning. There were, in the cramped, medievally uncomfortable pews, some fifteen of us. I was, at fifty, by some years the youngest; all except three of us were white. The nave was small and dark, beautiful in its unconventional way but suggesting a parish huddled together rather than one reaching up toward God.

The service began. The old words washed over me as in a dream, the words from which I had unwittingly learned how the language is put together, the words of my boyhood. Bells tinkled; incense rose. We were summoned to the rail and given communion. More words were said over us, and we were released into the day. I shook the rector's hand and that of a parishioner who seemed to have appropriated the role of official greeter, then went about the last of my familial Philadelphia missions.

I wanted to find my grandparents' graves. The church secretary had told me the location of my grandmother's, but could find no mention of my grandfather's in her records. I wanted to see both; I felt that a chapter was closing and that this last word of it was necessary.

For a long time I walked slowly about, peering at gravestones but finding no mention of Yardleys. A sense of urgency that bordered on anxiety began to take hold of me: Had my grandparents quite literally vanished into the earth? Back and forth I moved across the small plot where I had been assured my grandmother lay.

Frustrated, I wandered more speedily through the rest of the cemetery. I was ready to leave, then decided to take one more look. As I walked through the thick ivy along the wall my foot struck something hard. I brushed the vines with my shoe. Something lay below it. I got on my knees and pulled the ivy away. There it was, a flat white stone:

> THOMAS HENRY YARDLEY. A PRIEST.
> BORN JULY 8, 1869.
> DIED JUNE 12, 1933.
> EVA LOUISE THORNE YARDLEY.
> BORN JANUARY 27, 1878.
> DIED NOVEMBER 26, 1971.

An inexpressible feeling swept over me, part relief, part gratitude, part pure peace. Here were my grandparents. Here was my family. Here was *my* Philadelphia.

3

SHOP. SHOP. SHOP.

It was early in November. The fog was so thick on U.S. 3, just south of Baltimore, that I could barely see beyond the hood of the SHO, which strained against the leash the weather had placed on it. Traffic was heavy, headed south toward Annapolis or Prince Georges County in the late minutes of the rush hour. My own destinations were in Virginia and North Carolina, on the first long haul of this venture in regional inquiry.

At last the fog eased, though it was some time in lifting. I hadn't been down here in ages, not since construction had been undertaken to alleviate the incredible automotive crush that in recent years had threatened to suffocate this section of Maryland. I was on a great slash of concrete, six lanes in some stretches, eight in others. Trucks were everywhere, most of them hurtling along through the fog in blissful confidence of their power to transcend whatever obstacles man or nature might throw in their way. In the far left lane one rumbled along at fifty miles an hour, utterly oblivious to the honks of the other trucks and automobiles backed up behind him. The car magazines call drivers like that "left-lane bandits," because they steal your speed; what I think is, six miles down the road he's going to make a left turn, and he wants to be ready for it.

All of a sudden U.S. 3 turned into U.S. 301. No road signs
warned of the change, but 301 was what I wanted. I could
have gotten where I was going on I-95, a few miles to the west,
but I hadn't been on 301 for more than thirty years and I
wanted to see what it looked like now.

I first rode it in the early 1950s, in the back seat of the Ford
sedan and, later, Pontiac station wagon that my parents had
in those years; it was one of the main routes we used on our
trips between Chatham, Virginia, where we lived, and Middle-
town, Rhode Island, where we stayed each year from June
until August.

The summer of 1958 is particularly clear in my memory.
There were four of us in a car, driving from Virginia to a
little town outside Baltimore named Stevenson, where—odd
though this may seem to those who know Baltimore's steamy
summers—my girlfriend's parents had a summer house. She
and I were in the front seat, another couple in the back. The
road was being widened, as Lord knows it needed to be, but
the result was a traffic jam of genuinely stupendous dimensions. It seemed to me I spent half my life on 301 that afternoon.

In the summer of 1959, I had a job on a little railroad in
western Pennsylvania and was headed there with a couple of
friends. First we had to stop in Philadelphia, where one of
them had to pick up some gear at his parents' house. So there
we were, cruising along 301 early of an evening, when we
thought to stop at one of the slot machine parlors that lined
certain stretches of the highway in those days. My mother had
given me perhaps $20 or $30 to tide me over until the first
paycheck—that seemed a lot of money to a teenager in those
days—but when I walked out of the clip joint it was gone.
Right down the slots. I got to Pennsylvania broke and
scrounged for a week.

That was, to the best of my recollection, the last time that
I had been on 301. The road that I was on thirty years later
was four-lane, pretty much unlimited access, dotted with
stoplights. It wasn't pretty: good old American strip develop-

ment, most of it of relatively recent vintage. A sign beckoned me to something named Wild World, an invitation I would have resisted even had it been late enough in the day for the place to be open. But in a state so tame and placid as Maryland, how on earth could there be anything called "Wild World"? The answer is simple: On the American roadside, incongruity is a constant.

Now I was in Prince Georges County. If North Philadelphia is the gloomy side of racial change in the postwar years, P. G. County is the bright side. Just east of Washington, the county for most of its history had been a quiet backwater of farmers, fishermen, and a few commuters, but in the 1980s it suddenly became the residence of choice for members of the black middle class, many of them moving there from streets in the District of Columbia that had turned mean. According to the 1990 census, Prince Georges' black population grew from 37.3 per cent in 1980 to 50.7 per cent a decade later. A demographer interviewed by the *Washington Post* said, "It is the premier black suburban county in the nation. It's a middle-class black suburb. Just as middle-class as the white suburbs. . . . It is unique."

The signs of the county's prosperity were all about, not least on the highway itself. Both I-95 and the Baltimore–Washington Parkway run parallel to 301, and both offer drivers the convenience and safety of limited access, yet 301 was jammed with trucks, obviously doing local rather than long-distance business. Many of the traffic signs and signals were accompanied by warnings that they were "new," clear evidence of the haste of the county's growth and its helter-skelter response to that growth. Shopping centers were on all sides, prominently featuring establishments familiar to Washington suburbanites: Giant Food, Blockbuster Video, People's Drug, Circuit City, Sears, Ward's, Penney's. From time to time a remnant of an older 301 hove into view: the Bragg Motel, Cleo's Motel, the Drift Inn, this last selling "Patuxent Crabs."

An hour out of Baltimore the sign said, WELCOME TO CHARLES COUNTY, but it was just a continuation of the Prince

Georges strip development, Anywhere, U.S.A.: more shopping centers, bare office buildings, Hardee's, a gas station with Food Mart attached, Sandy's Sandwich Shop, Bob-Lu Dairy Mart carryout, the Martha Washington Motel, Whispers Restaurant, Fairlanes, Firestone, Mr. Muffler. Then an anachronism: the Diamond Club, "Closed for Renovation"— a roadhouse, a place to get tanked up for the drive home. A bit farther along, another: REB'S FIREPLACE, the sign said; LET'S DO IT TONIGHT. They must have done it right, because the place had burned to the ground.

By now I was at the southern end of the county and hallmarks of the old ways became more frequent: battered houses leaning toward the road, some inhabited and some not. A sign called this the SCENIC ROUTE, against all the evidence. Just like that there was a profusion of liquor stores. Why? A sign at one gave the answer: LAST LIQUOR STORE BEFORE VIRGINIA. DRIVE-IN LIQUOR. VA. LIQUOR SOLD BY STATE. When the state is the vendor, no bargains are to be had; if you want cheap booze on U.S. 301, buy it in Maryland.

In the near distance, Virginia loomed. To get there I had to go over a bridge. NICE BRIDGE, the sign said, but it didn't seem especially nice to me, at least such of it as I could see through the fog that had in an instant reappeared. Later I looked it up: the Harry W. Nice Bridge, named for a governor of Maryland during the late 1930s whose administration took preliminary steps toward construction of a bridge across the Chesapeake Bay.

Now I was in King George County, Virginia, but Developer Heaven would have been more like it. WATERFRONT PROPERTY, WATER ACCESS LOTS—the signs of ruination were everywhere, even if for the most part the digging hadn't actually gotten under way. Then, in a trice, the world of suburbs and exurbs vanished and there I was in pure country, a stretch of flat coastal plain between the Potomac and Rappahannock rivers known as the Northern Neck. The landscape was absolutely spectacular; no other word will do. Open fields, breaks of trees, barns, tobacco shacks.

Over the Rappahannock via a quick little bridge—the river was very narrow here—and then a farewell to 301. The rest of the way I drove along the southern shore of the Rappahannock on U.S. 17, the famous old highway that comes to this point from the northwest and winds along the coast the rest of the way, breathing its last lungful of carbon dioxide in Punta Gorda, Florida. HISTORYLAND HIGHWAY it was called here: light traffic and rural views until, at Tappahannock, water reappeared on my left and, between me and it, a gaggle of showy tract mansions.

The remaining sixty miles were a breeze. For most of them there was nothing to look at except the occasional farmhouse or country church. Not until the southern end of the peninsula did the clutter of strip development begin to reappear, and by then my drive was over. At the town of Gloucester Point I crossed the York River and made my way along the Colonial Parkway to what, in the minds of untold millions, is the chief shrine of the American civil religion to be found in the Mid-Atlantic. I was back. I was going to give Williamsburg another try.

When I was a boy Williamsburg seemed a romantic and exotic place. Once each year during the 1950s and 1960s my parents climbed aboard a bus and rode there with the senior class of Chatham Hall, the girls' preparatory school in Chatham, Virginia, of which my father became rector, or headmaster, in 1949. The trip covered about two hundred miles and cannot have been much fun for them, surrounded as they were by fifty teenagers in need of twenty-four-hour supervision, yet clearly they looked forward to it. They were happy in Chatham but it was something of a prison for them, isolated both physically and culturally from the upper Mid-Atlantic in which they had lived most of their lives. Williamsburg provided a break in their routine as well as a chance to shop. Both of them liked Craft House, which produced antique reproductions that they found authentic and well-made—if for the

most part priced well beyond their means—and both were
history buffs, my father most particularly.

The first time I went there myself was in the 1960s, driving
over from Greensboro with Rosemary, my first wife. The
place made no particular impression on me one way or the
other, though I recall a certain annoyance at the ladies and
gentlemen dressed up in eighteenth-century garb and masquerading as gracious hosts, all the while shoving us purpose-
fully from one room or building to the next. Then Sue and I
went there in the early 1980s, and my upper lip went into full
curl. I was appalled by the pervasive phoniness and artificial-
ity; "every time you turn around there's someone's hand in
your pocketbook," I later wrote, "though in Williamsburg the
hand is at least soft and agreeably scented." From Williamsburg we drove over to Jamestown, where the contrast struck
me as both stark and revealing; while the former was all
commercialism in the guise of historic re-creation, the latter
was bare and real and—in the emphatic sense it conveyed of
the world the colonists must actually have known—powerfully moving.

I held Williamsburg in contempt, yet I couldn't quite dis-
miss it out of hand. More than a million people visit it every
year. Could all of them really be all that wrong? Was there
something in Williamsburg that somehow I had missed?
Shouldn't I give it another try?

That is what I was there to do. But I had something else in
mind as well. For reasons presumably having to do precisely
with those million-plus tourists pouring into the southern end
of what Virginians call "The Peninsula"—they also call their
state university "The University"—a peculiarity of the 1980s
had asserted itself on Williamsburg's outskirts. The colonial
capital of Virginia had become a contemporary capital of
shopping plazas specializing in outlet stores, phenomena that
had made their first significant Mid-Atlantic appearance, at
least to the best of my knowledge, in Reading, Pennsylvania.
Now they were creeping all over the map; according to numerous tourist brochures, Williamsburg was the place to be. As

the flyer for the Williamsburg Outlet Mall put it: "SHOP. SHOP. SHOP."

So I made a reservation not at the Williamsburg Inn, the expensive hostelry right in the heart of what is reverently called the "Historic Area," but at the Best Western Williamsburg Outlet Inn, where the real action was. The place was a dump: long, narrow, several stories high, its hallways redolent of a mustiness usually associated with old seaside resorts, its indoor pool so tiny that I needed more than two hundred lengths to get in a mile. The confidence of its management in the scruples of outlet store customers did not seem unduly high: The hangers were hookless; the remote control was bolted to the bedside table; the clock radio was built in. "Includes Belgian Waffle Breakfast," its advertisement had noted, and indeed as I drove to the motel along Richmond Road I couldn't help noticing that Belgian waffles were omnipresent. Was this the chosen breakfast of the colonial governor?

It certainly was the choice of the clientele at the Outlet Inn. Early the next morning the restaurant in the motel's basement was jammed with women of various ages—there was only one other man—all of them bellying up to the buffet for Belgian waffles and heaps o' the fixin's: jellies, jams, creamed chipped beef, apples, melted butter, maple syrup, hash browns, grits, bacon, sausages, biscuits. Sitting off in my corner with my orange juice and English muffin and decaffeinated coffee, I felt an absolute ascetic, the evidence of my self-mortification all too plainly before me. Not with pity but with envy I looked at the jolly, bouncy testaments to the astonishing abundance of American agriculture seated all about, stuffing themselves to the full before venturing out to have one hell of a ball in the outlet stores. I envied them but I did not emulate them; however priggishly, I stayed faithful to nutritional common sense and kept away from the buffet.

At breakfast's end the ladies headed for the vans with which they'd jammed the motel's parking lot, but no Governor's Palace for *these* gals! They were off for a day of "SHOP.

SHOP. SHOP." So too was I. Not, I hasten to add, reluctantly. It is perhaps a peculiar confession for one who spends
his working days reading and writing books and otherwise
living what might be called, if with excessive self-flattery, the
life of the mind, but the truth of it is that I love to shop. The
age of recreational shopping came along just in time to accommodate me. Some may sing that they love a parade, but me,
I love a mall.

The first to which I went in Williamsburg wasn't a mall at
all but what may well be the weirdest place in the whole
Mid-Atlantic. It is called the Williamsburg Pottery Factory
and, the *AAA Mid-Atlantic Tourbook* reports, it "offers
woven baskets, brass pieces, china and crystal as well as pottery." Sounds good, doesn't it? Local arts and crafts, redolent
no doubt of the particular skills acquired over the centuries by
craftsmen at Williamsburg and other citadels of The Peninsula.

Dream on. The Williamsburg Pottery Factory is Harvest
Day writ large, a collection of junk so stupendous as to knock
the mind for a loop. It spreads over one hundred and thirty
acres, consists of something on the order of thirty buildings,
and hauls in the gullible from everywhere; next to the SHO in
the parking lot was a small bus from the Dover Baptist
Church, Orlando, Florida. Its buildings are ramshackle, tin-
roofed. Some look like the Quonset huts that were thrown up
overnight during World War II to serve as anything from
barracks to classrooms to storehouses and then were left,
undemolished, to survive into the 1950s and even 1960s. Others look like tobacco shacks or farm outbuildings indigenous
to the Virginia Tidewater. All are surrounded by parking lots
that seem to go on forever.

I grabbed a shopping cart—it seemed the thing to do—and
plunged right in. Ahead of me a woman was leaning on her
cart, nudging it along through the endless aisles, poking and
prodding the merchandise. At the kitchenware section temptation at last got the best of her. She reached onto a display
counter, grabbed a pot holder and tossed it into her cart. Then

she turned to her companion and uttered the outlet shopper's most plaintive words: "I don't really need it, can't you see? The price is just too good."

Oh? It seemed to me the prices weren't any better than what you could expect at your friendly neighborhood K Mart or Giant Food and nowhere nearly so good as those at Price Club and similar warehouse stores. Thinking I might find a bargain, I prowled the wine section, but no bargains were to be had; I could do far better at Eddie's Supermarket in Baltimore. Otherwise, the Pottery Factory was nothing so much as testimony to *de gustibus*: a universe of kitsch. At the cement and gardenware department were garish elephant plant stands, more reminiscent of Las Vegas than India, and Mexican planters of a distinctly non-Latino character. The glass-etching workshop had elaborate glassware of all descriptions, any of it sure to please the tastes of Leona Helmsley or Dolly Parton.

As for the ceramic factory, you might have expected to see some examples of fine local work there, but none was to be found. This was pure schlock Americana, heavy and artless stuff that you could find at any roadside stand in Florida or California. But it fit right in at the Pottery Factory, which wasn't at all what its name promised but an Arabian bazaar, a glorious never-never land of the undesirable, the unimaginable, and—or so at least one might think—the unsalable. Almost nothing there, save the odd country-cured ham or bag of peanuts, gave off a clue as to where the bazaar happened to be. It could be in Chattanooga or Istanbul; but Williamsburg is where it is.

It and a whole lot more. The Pottery Factory may be mother of them all, but its babies are everywhere, and they give it pretty stiff competition. The West Point Pepperell Mill Store, the Lenox Factory Outlet, Corning Revere Factory Store, Kitchen Collection Factory Outlet Stores, Dansk Factory Outlet, Book Warehouse, Villeroy & Boch Factory Outlet, Rolane No Nonsense Factory Store, Berkeley Commons Outlet Center, Williamsburg Outlet Mall—by contrast with the Pottery Factory they're mostly clean and modern, but that's about as far as differences go. Otherwise they're all in the same business: selling mediocre merchandise at prices that aren't half so good as you're likely to walk in the door looking for.

What can I say? I spent a whole day wandering through these places and didn't buy a thing. That, in my life as a shopper, may well be without precedent. But what was there to buy? "Second-quality" porcelain that would have been every bit as ugly had it been "first-quality"? Shoes either a size too large or a size too small? Books that looked as if they'd already been remaindered twice? Levis that didn't fit? Thanks a lot but no thanks.

What I thought was, I'd better get to Williamsburg itself, to the "Historic Area." Surely things would be better there. So promptly at eight-thirty the next morning I was in line at the Visitor Center (located on the alluringly named Information Drive), the chilly modern building through which all must pass en route to the eighteenth century. Forced to choose among a Basic Admission Ticket ($19), a Royal Governor's Pass ($22.50), and a Patriot's Pass ($26), I decided to be a good citizen of the Mid-Atlantic and took the middle course. I climbed aboard the bus that plies around and around the sacred ground, and hopped off at the Governor's Palace. I aimed to start at the top.

Eight others had made the same choice. We were outnumbered at the entrance by ladies and gentlemen in waiting, all of them got up in period costume and none of them apparently feeling in the least bit foolish about it. "Good morning," one of them said, "my name is Mrs. Arthur," and right away she got ten points in my ledger for not saying, "Hi, I'm Kimberly and I'll be your special hostess this morning." With no small amount of dignity she ushered us in, and the tour began.

To my considerable surprise, it was just fine, at least as tours go. The display of swords and firearms in the entrance hall was positively brilliant, and a canopied bed in one of the upstairs rooms was as handsome an example of that particular species as ever it has been my pleasure to see. Mrs. Arthur was amiable but reserved, just as a proper colonial dame should be. She spoke in a soft voice about the slaves whose labor had helped so much in the assembly of all this glory, and she was downright jolly when we got to the dining room. After her interminable recital of the spirituous liquors tossed down by the governor and his cronies at a typical midday meal, I asked if perhaps they spent much of the time in a state of tipsiness. "Oh, yes," she said, then paused a moment and added, "But of course the water was *very* bad!"

Mrs. Arthur on the other hand was very good. She made a convert of me, and I headed out toward the rest of the show in high spirits. I walked down the Palace Green, made a left on Duke of Gloucester Street, and reveled in what had turned into a perfect Mid-Atlantic autumn day: bright, crisp, clear. Ahead lay the Capitol, and disenchantment.

Here the crowd was far larger than it had been at the Governor's Palace, a mixture of bored retirees determined to get their full tickets' worth and edgy schoolchildren eager to get on with it; all in the group of about forty were white. No friendly Mrs. Arthur awaited us at the door. Instead it was barred by a sour young woman who wore her colonial cape and apron as though they had been boiled in starch. We were required to stay outside until the witching hour, at which time the witch appeared: a prim, censorious, condescending middle-aged woman who was clearly determined to display her superiority at every turn.

In a singsong voice the woman recited her lines, pausing from time to time to advise us of her wisdom. In the legislative chamber she interrupted herself to remark, "Compromise was a very effective tool," a pearl all of us savored; a few minutes later, in the courtroom, she topped herself by noting, "It's more fun to be a spectator than to be the accused," and then tossed off a merry little laugh, complimenting herself on her wit.

I couldn't get out of there fast enough. However hoked up

the Governor's Palace may have been—the more I thought
about it, the more its spanking-new appearance bothered
me—it had nonetheless had its own dignity and authenticity.
But the Capitol had been reduced to just another pit stop on
a theme park ride. By the time we got to the end of the tour
I felt released from prison—sorry, about that, *gaol*—and so,
by the looks on their faces, did my fellow inmates.

It was nearly noon now, time for lunch; more specifically,
after what I'd just gone through, time for a martini. The
choices were all thick as hominy with ye-olde quaintness:
Christiana Campbell's Tavern, the King's Arms Tavern,
Chowning's Tavern—each no doubt filled with stout fellows
downing their yards of ale and toasting—God bless him!—the
king. The mere thought of it so set me to salivating that I
ducked into the very first that presented itself, the King's
Arms.

Yardley's Law was of course honored at once—I got a far
table in a far room on the second floor—and in time a young
woman appeared all got up in the usual. Her mission was
plainly to run me and everybody else in and out as fast as
possible, these eating establishments being in fact ye olde
assembly lines. I'd scarcely taken a sip of my martini when
the bowl of soup arrived, and hard upon it came the salad.
Mercifully I eat too fast anyway, so this was just my ticket;
if I'd had my wits about me I'd have lingered as long as
possible, reading my brochures, ordering up a refill of coffee,
generally making them pay for hustling me through in the
express lane. But my wits weren't about me; good boy that I
am, I ate up and cleared away for another customer.

Besides, it was time to get back to Williamsburg's favorite
pastime, shopping. Stroll along Duke of Gloucester Street and
you're quietly, politely, gently assaulted by shop after shop:
the printer and bookbinder, the milliner, the silversmith, the
baker, the apothecary, the blacksmith. Enter any of these and
you'll see a jolly smithy or an apple-cheeked milliner or who-
ever it may be, plying his or her trade as once it was in the
days of yore. You'll also find a cash register and a credit card

machine and a person who will be just as happy as can be to take your money in exchange for one "authentic" trinket or another.

Wander across North Henry Street and you've left the hallowed ground, but you're still in the heart of sales central. Now you're in Market Square, a cozy nest of "almost fifty shops and services"; there you will find Beecroft & Bull, Ltd., "Retailers & Importers of Gentlemen's Clothing," and R. Bryant, Ltd., "Traditional Apparel for Men and Boys," and Scotland House, Ltd.—yes, Americans really *are* suckers for the "Ltd." scam—not to mention the Christmas Shop and the Sign of the Rooster and Baskin-Robbins. I managed to escape with only a couple of turtleneck shirts, and blessed my good fortune for that as I watched my fellow tourists shoot the national consumer debt up a couple of points.

I'd had two days of it and I was shopped out. It was time to move along. I didn't make it to Water Country USA or Busch Gardens: The Old Country, both of which were closed for the season, but there was no need to; it was transparently obvious that both were merely extensions of "SHOP. SHOP. SHOP." I know I would have been especially infuriated by Busch Gardens, which broadcasts ads on television that say, "How to get to Europe from Baltimore," and, "It's all the fun of Europe—but closer," and thus reinforce Americans in the Disneyesque conviction that the ersatz is better than the actual. I'd had enough of the ersatz already, in the "Historic Area"; I didn't need any more.

So the next morning I rose early, bid a relieved farewell to the Outlet Inn, and headed for Jamestown. I got there too early for a trip through the national park, but I'd done it before and well knew the quiet satisfactions it offered. A decade earlier I wrote: "Jamestown, in its permanent state of excavation, is the real thing: a tiny spot, desolate but beautiful, the foundations of its mean houses huddled together against the Indians and the weather and the unknown—the place where America began." I knew that it remained essentially unchanged, and

saw no reason to make what could only be a perfunctory
return visit.

Instead I went past it a few yards and into the line for the
ferry that crosses the James River between Jamestown and
Scotland. I was on my way to North Carolina, to hang out at
Democratic Headquarters in Raleigh as the votes came in for
the big senatorial race between Jesse Helms and Harvey
Gantt, but the voting wouldn't take place until the next day.
I hadn't terribly far to go and I had all day to do it in, so I
aimed to take the ferry and ride the back roads.

A few minutes later the ferry rattled into its slip, discharged
its vehicular and pedestrian passengers, and took us aboard.
By the time it pulled away it was about two-thirds full,
mostly cars and pickups, but with one extraordinary exception. This was a battered old gray van with Virginia plates; its
driver was a bearded, burly guy in a Harley-Davidson T-shirt,
alongside him was a stringy woman with tattoos on both
shoulders, and in the back were two immense brown dogs that
looked in equal measures lean, hungry, and mean. On each of
the rear windows was a decal of a screaming eagle, under it the
legend GET YOUR CLAWS INTO SOMETHING. My first inclination
was to leap off the ferry and swim to shore, but soon enough
my fellow passengers started poking their heads into the van
and asking questions about the dogs that were met with civil,
if not exactly articulate, replies. Live and learn, I said to
myself, and settled back for the ride.

Fifteen minutes later—well, twenty, actually, because it
took Harley about five minutes to get his rig rolling and let
the rest of us off—I was tooling comfortably along on State
Road 10, watching the scenery pass by, when suddenly traffic
came to a halt. A state police roadblock had been set up; all
drivers and their passengers were being asked to show their
licenses. Perhaps drugs were passing through this impoverished part of the Tidewater. I didn't ask and wasn't all that
interested. What really caught my eye, and jolted my memory into gear, was that both of the troopers running the
roadblock were black.

Thirty-two years earlier, I returned to Chatham from that trip up 301 with my girlfriend via what was my customary vehicle in those days, my thumb. I managed to hitch all the way from Baltimore to Lynchburg when I got what proved to be the ride that took me the last fifty miles home. The driver was a black man in his early thirties; it turned out he was going to Chatham too, though not by choice. On his way north he'd been stopped there for what he said was a nonexistent violation, a matter about which he had ample reason to know; he was one of the first black policemen in his hometown in North Carolina. But however unfair the charges against him may have been, he had to return to Chatham for resolution of them.

He was half angry and half hurt. "I'm a *police officer*," he said, "and they're treating me like a *nigger*." I nodded sympathetically and expressed my own indignation, which was very real and utterly pointless. Here it was the summer of 1958 in the heart of Southside Virginia and this pleasant, intelligent man was being treated like a field hand by the gendarmes of Chatham—all of whom in that day were white, some of whom were louts and oafs possessing neither his dignity nor his brains.

He dropped me off in front of the Pittsylvania County Courthouse, on Main Street in Chatham. We shook hands. I walked the mile or so to my family's house; he went into the courthouse to get his punishment. What it was I do not know. It never occurred to me to look for news of his case in the local paper, much less to inquire about it at the courthouse. But I never forgot about it, and when I saw those two black troopers telling white drivers to pull over and show their licenses, it leaped immediately to mind. A little justice was being doled out here; it gave me more pleasure than had anything in Williamsburg.

So my mood was high as I headed south toward Smithfield, and it got higher as I drove along. The road was two-lane and I was making a steady fifty-five; the big, smug Lexus in front kept me from pushing it up to sixty, but I didn't care. The scenery was lovely; most of the way trees hugged the road, just beginning to turn yellow and red. A sign beckoned: FOR SALE: SWEET POTATOES, PUMPKINS, COLLARDS. Another sign: ELECTRIC GUITAR AND BASS LESSONS. A few miles farther along I had a pickup in front of me: gun rack, good old boy in sunglasses at the wheel, tall and slender companion nestled next to him; passing, I snuck a look and saw that his companion was his dog.

Pulling onto Business 10 to enter Smithfield, I was assaulted by the smell of salt and pork fat; country ham was one of the first local institutions my parents learned about when they came to Virginia, and I quickly acquired their love for it. It is true that the quality of country ham has declined as demand for it has increased; the ham is not aged so long as it once was, with the result that it is almost impossible to find one now that has been cured the slow, old-fashioned way. But the pretensions of Georgia, Tennessee, and Kentucky to the contrary notwithstanding, the hams of Virginia and North Carolina are still the only ones that really live up to the name "country ham." The Mid-Atlantic is the universe of ham, and Smithfield is its capital.

The town was a bit on the ramshackle side but had some lovely Victorian houses in varying states of repair. If I'd needed a haircut I could have stopped at the Hamtown Barber. Instead I pulled in at the Joyner Country Ham Store and laid in some provisions: peanuts, bacon, half a ham—enough cholesterol to last me past Christmas. You could slice the ham-country atmosphere with a knife and I wanted a piece of it.

Outside Smithfield I was on U.S. 258 South for a blink, then turned onto State Road 620. This wasn't a blue highway, it was a thin gray one; you could barely see it on the map and the road itself wasn't much bigger. The countryside was flat; tree breaks made it seem less coastal than it really was. The trees along the road were tall, scrawny pines with long trunks and thin tops; at times they came right up to the edge of the road, at others they were far in the distance, past arable fields now dry and brown. The Virginia highway department must assume that the only people who drive this road know it intimately; I went through a sharp S-curve that on any other road would have been marked with signs and flashing lights. If you've read *The Confessions of Nat Turner* you know what this country is like; William Styron got its forbidding, barren beauty exactly right.

Off 620 and onto 616. More of the same. A farmhouse stood in the middle of acres and acres of flat, brown land; I could have been in Texas or Oklahoma. The road curved this way and that. The SHO loved it; the temptation to take it up to seventy-five or eighty was extreme, but what was the rush? I came to the hamlet of Courtland and realized I was now in the heart of peanut country; a few miles later a sign read, WELCOME TO BOYKINS VA., HOME OF ASTER NUT PRODUCTS.

By now I'd worked my way onto Route 730, headed for Emporia. All of a sudden it turned into the most desolate road I'd ever seen. A couple of guys were working on a car—right in the middle of the road. An old party leaning against a mailbox pointed his index finger at me in a fashion that I didn't take as welcoming. I passed a small white frame house with a satellite dish in the yard; it was the first dish I'd seen all day, an indication no doubt of the general poverty of the area, since if people had the wherewithal to buy dishes and cut down the wall between themselves and the world, presumably they would.

It was hard to realize that I was driving through the same region of the United States that also includes Philadelphia and Pittsburgh, Baltimore and Washington, Richmond and Charlotte. This wasn't my Mid-Atlantic, it was *Deliverance* country. It was also an instructive reminder that those of us who live in cities and think we understand the country don't know the half of it.

I was mulling this over when, almost before I knew it, I was in Emporia. It was the first Monday in November and the SHO's outside-temperature gauge had rolled over eighty. I saw a sign for I-95 and said the hell with it, let's go to Raleigh. It was time to count the votes.

4

ELECTION NIGHT

The issue was decided long before anyone in the room had anticipated. In Democratic Headquarters at the North Raleigh Hilton the word from the outset had been, "It's going to be a long night," but the voters of North Carolina were having none of that. Shortly after ten on the evening of November 6, 1990, with barely half the votes counted, CBS News "declared" Jesse Helms the victor in his campaign against the Democratic nominee, Harvey Gantt, for reelection to the United States Senate. There were a few hisses and a few shouts of protest, but everyone in the room seemed to know that the network's projection was on the mark: The improbable campaign of Harvey Gantt had come to its inevitable end.

This was a pity, but—the feelings of many in that crowded, sweaty room to the contrary notwithstanding—it was neither the end of the world nor a return to the discredited racial politics of the not-so-distant past. To be sure, a black man running as a liberal had been defeated by a white man running as an arch-conservative, and by a wider margin than the polls had predicted; not only that, but this margin seemed to have been shaped by an eleventh-hour advertising campaign in which Helms, not for the first time in his long, sordid career, had played with cynical virtuosity on racial tensions.

All of that was true, yet the final particulars of the 1990 senatorial election—which man won and by how many votes—seemed to me of considerably less consequence than the very fact of the Gantt candidacy and the support it had attracted. The reelection of Helms may have been a last-gasp reaffirmation of the old, but the Gantt phenomenon struck me as of greater interest and importance: a light, however thin and unclear, shining on the future. It was this that I wanted to see and to participate in; it was this that had me in the Hilton that night.

It was also more than that. As a young man I had cut my political eye teeth in North Carolina; politics had long since lost much of its appeal for me, but I retained a sentimental affection for those old days and discovered, quite to my surprise, a longing to relive them. That of course was foolish fancy, for the North Carolina to which I returned in the 1990s was so different from the North Carolina I had left in 1974— not to mention the North Carolina I first knew in the 1950s— as to be almost literally unrecognizable.

It was in North Carolina that I made my first and only venture into elective politics. By my sophomore year at Chapel Hill I realized that I urgently wanted to become editor of the *Daily Tar Heel*, the student newspaper. It published six days a week, had a circulation of about ten thousand, and was in many respects a wholly professional newspaper—the best possible training for a career in journalism's real world. The problem for me, given my innate shyness, was that the editorship was an elective position; the newspaper earned its keep by a combination of advertising revenues and student fees, and those who paid the fees understandably believed that they were entitled to a voice in the newspaper's management.

So in the late winter of my junior year I summoned up such limited gregariousness as I possess and hit Chapel Hill's equivalent of the hustings: the dormitories, sororities, fraternities, and private apartments where the students lived. I talked to hundreds of them, not merely pressing my own case but hearing theirs, most particularly their complaints about their student newspaper. I won the election by a decent if not over-whelming margin, and retreated into the editor's office for the year of my term. But though the daily responsibilities of the job put me at least partway into an ivory tower, the lessons I learned remained with me; I had been taught something about the people who read newspapers as well as those who write and edit them, and I like to think—no, I pray to think—that I have remembered that ever since. Thus it will come as no surprise that I was appalled to learn that beginning in 1993 the editorship of the *DTH* will be chosen by an "impartial" committee, in order to get the "politics" out of the process; the politics, dear Tar Heels, was the point of it all.

My editorship began in the spring of 1960, which meant that I held the job through the riveting presidential and gubernatorial campaigns of that year. I followed John Kennedy in what I unoriginally called a "whirlwind" tour of the state; I was one of several journalists who interviewed Adlai Stevenson and Luther Hodges, stumping the state for Kennedy, on a television broadcast; after it was over I sat in a small room with Stevenson, Hodges, and Terry Sanford, watching the second Kennedy-Nixon debate and eavesdropping on their devastating dissection of the Republican candidate; I covered the Jefferson-Jackson Day dinner in Raleigh and was introduced to Harry Truman, in town to arouse the party faithful—in the photograph from his news conference that still hangs on my office wall I'm seated right in front of Truman and next to my *DTH* managing editor, Wayne King, who went on to a long and distinguished career as a reporter for the *New York Times*.

When my editorship ended I went off for my own brief and undistinguished career on the *Times*, then returned to North Carolina in 1964, as an editorial writer for the *Greensboro Daily News*. I stayed there for a decade of political turmoil and wrote about it with fascination and glee: the rise of the Republican party, the emergence of the black vote, the bitter controversies over free speech on campus, the expansion of the state's public university system. I covered legislative meetings in Raleigh, hung around with state legislators and other ne'er-do-wells at the coffee shop of the Sir Walter Hotel, interviewed candidates who came hat in hand in hopes of the endorsement of the *Daily News*. Over that decade my professional interests gradually shifted from the editorial page to the book page, but my enthusiasm for Tar Heel politics never entirely evaporated; one of the last signed pieces I wrote for the *Daily News* before moving off to the *Miami Herald* was a tart commentary on North Carolina's political hypocrisy on the issue of over-the-bar sales of alcoholic beverages, and in the two decades since leaving the state I've always looked up North Carolina first when election returns are published.

Which explains why I was in a state of some excitement as I registered at the Velvet Cloak Inn, hard by the campus of North Carolina State University. This alone was a mark of change. In my day everybody stayed at the Sir Walter Hotel, and both political parties had their headquarters in the heart of town; in that time, though, nobody paid any attention to the Republicans, the Democratic nomination being, as we journalists insisted upon putting it, "tantamount to victory." Now the Sir Walter had been transformed into a high-rise old folks home and the politicians, like everybody else, had moved to the suburbs; the North Raleigh Hilton, where the Democrats were to gather on election night, was off Interstate 64, part of the beltway that encircles the city.

Downtown Raleigh was, if not exactly dead, pretty well moribund. On election day I strolled around it, and I didn't find much to see. In my student days it was the center of the region; Rosemary Roberts and I drove over there from Chapel Hill to buy her engagement ring, and even as late as the 1970s it was something of a commercial magnet. But now everybody goes to Crabtree Valley Mall, out in the suburbs, and the numerous clones thereof; downtown Raleigh is left to the government workers, the lawyers and lobbyists, and the few customers who can still be lured to the stores that urban renewal has failed to transform into real competition for the shopping plazas lining the beltway.

Like everybody else, I left downtown too. I hopped onto
U.S. 264 East and drove the forty miles to Wilson for lunch.
My interest in Wilson had nothing to do with politics and
everything to do with barbecue, which in North Carolina is
above politics and everything else. But barbecue has its own
version of politics. Though North Carolinians would not for a
moment dream of acknowledging that barbecue prepared in
Tennessee, Texas, Georgia, or anywhere else even deserves the
name *barbecue,* they are of two minds—two violently disputa-
tious minds—as to the relative virtues of the barbecues produced in North Carolina.

One side holds that the barbecue cooked in the eastern part
of the state, wherein the pork tends to be relatively tasty and
dry and to be chopped relatively fine, is the only true barbecue; the other side holds that the barbecue of the Piedmont,
wherein grease is accorded its true place in the scheme of
things and the chopping is coarser, is God's barbecue.

Everything is relative: grease is grease and fat is fat, and
barbecue in any guise has its full share of both. My old friend
Walt Rand, a native of the East who now practices law in the
Piedmont, once passed along to me some wit's remark that
barbecue has killed more white males in North Carolina than
tobacco ever has. Be that as it may, my own experience with
barbecue had been primarily of the Piedmont variety. I ate it
first at Stamey's in Greensboro, a deservedly celebrated bis-
tro, and then as often as possible at Allen & Son's near Graham, midway between Greensboro and Chapel Hill and reason
enough to travel between the two cities.

Now I was to have a taste of the eastern version. Walt,
whose wife, Mary Christian, comes from Wilson, had partaken
of many a barbecue platter at Bill's, and urged that I go out
of my way to do the same. After getting lost for a while in the
streets of Wilson, I found it on the city's outskirts, surrounded
by enough parking lots to do the Williamsburg Pottery Factory proud, many of the spaces filled with pickups and Trans-
Ams and other good-ole-boy cars of choice.

It didn't take me long to realize that Bill's—Bill Ellis Barbecue, actually: "Pig Picking Our Specialty"—is a considerable undertaking. It has seven private dining rooms, a seating capacity of eight hundred fifty, banquet and party catering (1-800-68-BILLS) with twenty-four catering trucks on call, a substantial souvenir shop, and its very own stock car replete with racing colors and STP emblem. Somehow in the midst of all this it even manages to serve a platter of barbecue.

I ordered one: a heaping pile of finely chopped pork, a big scoop of cole slaw, corn sticks, and the *sine qua non* of any self-respecting Tar Heel eatery, sweetened iced tea. The barbecue was good, well worth a forty-five-minute drive when you consider that the alternative was Burger King, but at the risk of giving shooting offense to some trigger-happy citizen of the East, I have to admit that when it comes to barbecue, I'm a Piedmont man. I guess I just need that grease.

Even when it's light on the grease, a big meal of barbecue tends to sit on the stomach for quite a while. The pleasures of Bill's were still making themselves known to me at six forty-five that evening, when I lumbered into the large room at the Hilton that the Democrats had commandeered for the evening. In the old days it would have been a ballroom in a downtown hotel, with a big blackboard on stage for recording the results and with everyone milling around on the floor. But this was the age of television. A podium had been set up on one of the long sides of the rectangular room; across from it, the best location in the house, was a small grandstand upon which were arranged cameras from all the networks and the major North Carolina stations, while the ladies and gentlemen of the newspapers were relegated to seats off to the side from which their view was blocked by cameras and those wielding them.

There were still forty-five minutes before the polls closed. Suddenly a flack from the Gantt campaign rushed in to announce that in Durham a number of voting machines had broken down and closing time had been extended until ten. Four buses were outside to take workers there. "We need your

help in Durham," he shouted, "or there's not going to be a
party here tonight!" It wasn't clear whether this summons
included members of the press, but it seemed to me that
things were likely to be a lot more interesting in Raleigh than
on a bus en route to Durham, so I stayed put.

The night was young. The television people were still setting up. A reporter for one of the networks, a no-nonsense
woman with an unenviable complexion, rummaged around in
her notes and fiddled with her fire-engine-red dress; off to the
side a far younger and far prettier correspondent for one of the
local stations, wearing a dress of similar hue, eyed her with an
envy that struck me as entirely unwarranted. Gradually the
room began to fill up. I ran into a few old acquaintances who
were still fighting the North Carolina political wars, and then
into one from the national press corps.

He looked at me in surprise. "What on earth are *you* doing
here?" he asked.

"What are *you* doing here?" I replied.

"That's easy," he said. "I wouldn't have missed it. It's a
big night. I had to be here."

"Well," I said, "that's exactly how I feel."

This was true. The candidacy of Harvey Gantt was a mile-
stone in North Carolina politics and possibly a watershed as
well. His was the first serious race by a black candidate in any
statewide contest in North Carolina. Though L. Douglas
Wilder had already been elected as the first black governor of
Virginia, Gantt's candidacy was more momentous not only
because the South lays as much claim to North Carolina as
does the Mid-Atlantic but because he was running against
Jesse Helms, the very embodiment of New South Republican-
ism with its not especially subliminal appeals to racial preju-
dices and fears.

I'd watched Gantt from afar since my days at Chapel Hill,
when he had become the first black student at Clemson University in South Carolina, an institution with a long history
of racial intolerance. Gantt had carried out this unpleasant
undertaking with admirable cool and, in the circumstances,

extraordinary good humor. After graduation he settled in Charlotte, practiced as an architect, and eventually added another first to his escutcheon: He served two terms as Charlotte's first black mayor. He was defeated after his constituents decided he'd lost interest in his job, but he learned his lesson and remained ever after an attentive politician. His candidacy for the Democratic senatorial nomination in 1990 had at first been regarded as a joke, but he pieced together a coalition of blacks, white liberals, and just enough discontented white workers to win the primary.

In the general election he was again at first taken lightly, but that was a mistake: The anti-Helms constituency is so adamant that you could run Mike Tyson against Helms and he'd still start out with close to 40 per cent of the vote; Helms himself, of course, starts out against any opponent with about the same percentage squarely in *his* pocket. The battle has always been over the swing voters; this is the battle that Gantt eventually lost. Since the results are now ancient history I won't dwell on postelection analysis, save to note that like innumerable politicians before him—Terry Sanford not least among them—Gantt underestimated the conservatism, or overrated the liberalism, of the North Carolina electorate.

Ever since the eminent political scientist V. O. Key called North Carolina the "Progressive Plutocracy," in his influential book, *Southern Politics in State and Nation*, the myth of North Carolina liberalism has had numerous true believers. They focus on "Progressive" and overlook "Plutocracy." Although Helms is something of an aberration in being so far to the right as he is, his deep conservatism is far closer to the dominant sentiments of North Carolina than was the liberalism of the much-mythologized former senator, Frank Porter Graham. A liberal has to move to the middle to be elected statewide in North Carolina, as Graham learned to his grief in 1950's famous senatorial race against Willis Smith and as Terry Sanford recognized when he returned to politics in 1986 and ran successfully for the state's other Senate seat.

This was the lesson that Harvey Gantt failed to learn. He

had the black vote and the moderate white vote sewed up. In order to win he had to appeal to the inherently conservative swing vote, and this he almost belligerently refused to do. He laid himself open to the affirmative action attack with which Helms predictably assaulted him, and he welcomed the support of fringe groups—militant feminists, animal rights activists, homosexuals—whose causes are anathema to mill workers in Kannapolis and farmers in Rocky Mount. That, far more than the color of his own skin, is why he lost.

But nobody was thinking such thoughts in the Hilton in the early hours of election night. To the contrary, most were thinking victory. All the polls indicated that the race would be very close, and some suggested that Gantt could win; even though it was by then a truism that voters often mislead pollsters in political contests where race is a consideration, there seemed every reason to believe that it would be a long, taut night.

The first whiff of tension arose at seven-fifteen, when another Gantt functionary rushed in and declared, "It's a one per cent election!" That was not borne out by the television monitors scattered about the room in lieu of the trusty old blackboard; WBTV in Charlotte, with 1 per cent of the votes in, showed Helms with 53 per cent and Gantt with 47.

At that hour there wasn't much to watch. Most of the monitors were still tuned to "Family Feud," then to "Rescue 911." Not until eight o'clock did rumors begin to spread with anything like the intensity of a real political struggle. "Not just *one* machine down in Durham?" one black woman said to another. "*All* of them? That can't be *entirely* coincidental!"

I'd never been to a North Carolina political rally at which so many blacks were present. Back in the 1950s and early 1960s you might see an occasional old black gentleman off in a corner, dignified and wary, but the truth is that in those days neither the people who ran the state's politics nor those who wrote about it paid much attention to black voters; they were invisible. But on this night they were everywhere; they gave off no air of gratitude at being let into the white man's party, and by the same token there was no sense of white condescension or patronization. My favorite sight of the evening was of a fat old white man with a huge whiskey schnozzola, his buttocks spilling over the sides of the folding chair on which he was perched—the very caricature of the old Southern politician, Bilbo or Vardaman or Watkins. He was talking animatedly with a reporter, and on his lapel was a button with the smiling black face of Harvey Gantt.

Some of the chatter on the floor:

· "My *word*," a white woman said to a black man. "The press is *definitely* here."

· A guy who looked like a public policy wonk whispered to another of the breed: "That's Hodding Carter! He's one of the regulars on 'This Week With David Brinkley'!"

· An older white woman, walking out of the room in sorrow and anger: "I can't think of *anything* worse than Jesse Helms!"

· One black man to another: "The rural whites who voted for Jim Hunt against Helms six years ago aren't voting for Gantt. It's as simple as that."

· A white man, reacting to a report that 6 per cent of black voters had cast their ballots for Helms: "How could any black person in his right mind vote for Jesse Helms?"

As the evening progressed the totals mounted but the percentages stayed steady. At eight forty-five P.M., with 19 per cent of the votes counted, Helms was at 55 per cent to Gantt's 45. An hour later, with 46 per cent in, the margin was the same. The mood was upbeat—"Durham will make up those votes all by itself," one man claimed as the Helms lead rose to twenty-five thousand—but more and more people were talking about other races. A congressman named David Price was roundly applauded when he came in to speak to the television cameras. A loud roar went up when Ann Richards took the lead in the gubernatorial race in Texas.

That roar reflected, no doubt, the feminist presence in the room. Other presences were noteworthy, if less populous. A white couple looking very much as if they'd just left the

English Department faculty meeting wandered by, sporting buttons that read, ANIMAL RIGHTS ACTIVISTS FOR GANTT; off in a corner four young men of conspicuous homosexual preference chatted busily. That Gantt's following numbered among its members these rainbow coalition activists may in some eyes have been a refreshing comment on its diversity; but their prominence in a North Carolina campaign was also in large measure why his race was just about run.

At 10:05 CBS gave its decision. "Not yet!" one woman yelled, but the tide of resignation was beginning to wash over the floor. In hopes of luring the candidate down for a pep talk a chant of "Harvey! Harvey!" started, but it was halfhearted and soon petered out. At 10:30, with 68 per cent of the vote tabulated, Helms's lead was over a hundred thousand votes and he was up by 54 per cent to 46. "It's over," I wrote in my notebook. I closed its cover, slipped it into my pocket, and took an elevator upstairs.

I went to the small suite that had been taken for the night by James Gooden Exum. At Chapel Hill we'd just missed each other—he is four years older than I—but in Greensboro, where he practiced law in the 1960s, we became good friends; we could tell some war stories on each other, but that, alas, was a long time ago.

When I stepped off the elevator, Jim was talking with his son and namesake. He saw me and immediately said, "Why, James, do you remember Jon Yardley? Why, he wrote my first political speech!"

This unfortunately is true. I shudder to imagine how my boss, Leonard Downie, the executive editor of the *Washington Post*, would react should I behave thus now; his sense of the proper separation between journalists and politics is so firm that he doesn't even vote, and though I wouldn't go that far, in essence I think he's right. But back in 1966, when I wasn't telling the world what to do via the editorial columns of the *Greensboro Daily News*, I moonlighted as speechwriter and *éminence grise* in Exum's first political venture. He was running for the state legislature in Guilford County, of which

Greensboro is county seat, and I was working behind the scenes on his behalf. I wrote what he used as his standard stump speech—I remember not a word of it, but it must have been riddled with clichés—and I offered incessant counsel, all of it surely useless, on political strategy.

Jim won that election. It didn't take long for him to establish himself in Raleigh and for speculation to begin stirring about his political future. Then, only months after taking office, he was offered a seat on the state's superior court. He served there for eight years, then was appointed to the state supreme court. In 1986, after the incumbent Republican governor declined to do the right thing and name him chief justice, Jim ran for the position statewide and won it handily. He really ought to be on the United States Supreme Court— this isn't just friendship speaking, but admiration for Jim's fine legal mind, his ability to see all sides of a complicated question, and his implacable fairness—but that won't happen unless a Democrat arrives at the White House with either a debt to North Carolina or a willingness to choose Supreme Court justices solely on the basis of qualification: in all events, a most unlikely possibility.

Now Jim was running for reelection, along with two of his associate justices. All three were Democrats, but "tantamount" had long since made its departure from North Carolina's political vocabulary. The races were very, very tight. Though by the time I got to Jim's suite he had begun to put a little daylight between himself and his challenger, it was obvious that the huge turnout inspired by the Helms-Gantt race had brought a lot of Republicans out of the woodwork.

I hung around Exum headquarters for about an hour, drinking a couple of beers and talking politics with other old friends. As midnight neared, fatigue began to set in—to think that on election night 1960 I'd stayed up until five in the morning!—and I decided to head back to the motel. Gantt still hadn't shown up and I no longer felt any need to be on hand when he did; if you've heard one concession speech, you've heard them all. So I said good-night to Jim and Judy

Exum, went down on the elevator, walked past what was now a quiet, dispirited headquarters, and drove to the Velvet Cloak.

I got to my room and flipped on the television just in time to hear Gantt's gracious and self-effacing remarks. It would have been easy to be sad, particularly at the thought of six more years of Jesse Helms, but I felt otherwise. As one whose sense of the political order had in large measure been shaped by the North Carolina of the 1950s and 1960s, I was both startled and delighted that a massive turnout of Tar Heels had given fully 46 per cent of its votes to a black man; the progress that this represented seemed to me vastly more important than the lingering old habits and attitudes represented by Jesse Helms.

The North Carolina in which I came of age was rigidly fixed in those old ways. At Chapel Hill in the 1950s and Greensboro in the 1960s, racial separation bordered on the absolute. Blacks sat in separate sections in movie theaters, attended separate schools, used separate public bathrooms and water fountains, ate at separate restaurants. Many stores refused to permit black customers to try on clothing; utility service in black sections of town was spotty and streets were often unpaved; relatively few blacks were registered to vote, and no politician with any hope of a prominent career courted their good opinion with anything other than indirect and condescending attention.

Now all of that had changed. The racial millennium had no more arrived in North Carolina than it had in any other state of this troubled country, but the contrast between past and present as illustrated by the campaign of Harvey Gantt seemed to me so great as to assume historic dimensions. Socially and politically as well as geographically, North Carolina was now beyond dispute a state of the Mid-Atlantic; to put it another way, its race relations could now be seen as characteristic of the country's rather than of those of the Old South.

Obviously this is a mixed blessing. We now know all too well that the Old South had no more monopoly on intolerance than the rest of the country had on righteousness; to say that any state has become "American" in its race relations is not, alas, as much of a compliment as it should be. Yet in race as in other matters of history, our memories are too short; we despair too much of how far we have to go and take too little pride in how far we have come.

For me North Carolina is a measure of that progress. I knew it well as a youth and return to it with some frequency in middle age. Each time I do I am struck anew by how many once-insuperable barriers have been demolished, by how many opportunities are open to those once denied them, by how much the old obdurate bigotry of the white majority has melted away into tolerance at the least and open acceptance at the most.

Forty-six per cent of the vote for a black man? A quarter century ago it would have been, in the most literal sense of the word, unthinkable. But that night in Raleigh it had come to pass, and no one seemed to think it in the least remarkable. If that isn't progress, there is no such thing.

5

FLOWERDEW

The next day I had a lunch date with Jim Exum. We met at the offices of the North Carolina Supreme Court. Once again, however unlikely it may seem, my past leaped out at me. One of the associate justices who had survived the previous evening's scare was Bill Whitchard, who had been a year behind me at Chapel Hill and whom I had known slightly as a consequence of our mutual interest in student politics; we said a cordial hello.

Another member of the court was Henry Frye. We too said hello. I didn't think he remembered me and I decided not to bother him with explanations, but I remembered him very clearly. Twenty-five or so years earlier, he had been a young lawyer in Greensboro and I an even younger journalist. He was in the news because of his involvement in various local civil rights matters and because he was gearing up to run for legislative office. I invited him to talk about these undertakings over lunch at what was in those days just about the only tolerable eating place in Greensboro, the S&W Cafeteria. It was a polite if somewhat awkward occasion; whites and blacks simply did not eat together then, and many of the S&W's regulars regarded us with icy distance. But they were the past

and Frye was the future; Guilford County elected him to the
State House in 1968 and to the State Senate in 1980, and in
1983 Governor Jim Hunt put him on the state supreme court,
thus making him the first—and still only—black to serve
thereon.

Exum and I had lunch at a lively restaurant within walking
distance of the court. We were joined by George Ragsdale,
who'd been president of the student body at Chapel Hill while
I was there; it was from his family's jewelry store that Rosemary and I bought that engagement ring. Now he was a
prominent and successful lawyer, traveling the nation and
world much of the time, plugged into politics and business and
the press.

We sat down. "So!" George said at once. "What does Washington have to say about Luther?"

I looked at him in utter bewilderment. "Washington?" I
said. "Luther?" I said. "What on earth are you talking
about?"

"Why, Luther Hodges, Junior," he said, and went on to
explain a controversy in which the son of the former governor
had managed to become involved. It was all Greek to me, and
I could in no way enlighten George as to how "Washington"
felt about any of it. No doubt this was to some degree a
reflection of my firm standing as a Washington outsider, but
it also, I thought, was pure and wonderful North Caroliniana
in its fascination with the peccadilloes of local personages and
its assumption that the rest of the world shares that fascination. George Ragsdale may wear the subdued suits and striped
shirts that are the hallmarks of international high style, but
he's Tar Heel to the marrow.

After lunch Jim walked me to my car. Being a man of taste
and discernment, he immediately expressed admiration for
the SHO as it sat coiled by the curb, eager to leap onto the
highway and get about its business; I popped open the hood
and gave him a look at its extraordinary twenty-four-valve
engine, a thing not merely of immense power but also of

surprising beauty. Then we shook hands, made mutual vows that it wouldn't be another dozen years before we saw each other again, and I was off.

I was headed back to Virginia, so I left Raleigh on New Bern Avenue, a four-lane road divided by a grassy median and lined with pleasant red-brick houses. It evolved into U.S. 64 and the view took a turn for the worse: strip development such as I'd already seen all too much of along Richmond Road in Williamsburg. But that didn't last long. Soon 64 became a four-lane, semilimited-access road, one I knew well from numerous trips to the Outer Banks. Traffic was light, the day was lovely—this November heat wave was one for the books—and the temptation to push the speedometer well over sixty was well-nigh irresistible. I resisted, however, because the North Carolina Highway Patrol regards me as a source of assured income.

Near Rocky Mount the road passed over I-95, but I declined the invitation to get back to Virginia the fast way. Instead I headed east a bit more and went north on U.S. 301, which soon became a straight, two-lane shoot through cotton country. I stuck with it for about thirty miles, then swung to the east on U.S. 158, another pleasant two-lane country road.

I was rolling along, minding my own business, though the day was darkening faster than I'd anticipated; I didn't want to arrive too late at the inn, so I nudged the speedometer into the low sixties. There was scarcely a car on the road, except for a sporty black Ford Escort coming from the other direction. I looked at it with interest—was this the high-performance Escort I'd read about somewhere?—and followed it through the rearview mirror with my eyes as we passed.

That wasn't an Escort, that was a Trojan horse. Suddenly it did a sliding U-turn that even the great North Carolinian stock car racer and moonshine runner Junior Johnson would have envied, and a little red light atop its dashboard started flashing violently. "God *damn!*" I pulled onto the shoulder and waited. A Uriah Heepish trooper—name withheld, to protect the guilty—claimed that he'd clocked me at sixty-seven; the SHO had said sixty-four, but you can't argue with a cop. He handed me a citation—the second I'd racked up in North Carolina in two years, though the SHO's first—and then had the audacity to say, as I pulled away, "Have a nice day."

A bit later I turned north on State Road 35, crossed into Virginia, and in a matter of minutes was back in Boykins, HOME OF ASTER NUT PRODUCTS. From there I retraced my route of two days previous, and in a couple of hours was back on The Peninsula. My business there wasn't until the next day, so I headed right for the place at which I'd made a reservation.

I'd gotten the impression from the tour book where I'd found it listed that the place was a historic inn, though my alarms should have been set off when the proprietress told me, over the phone, that she'd give me a room "where there isn't much froufrou." This wasn't an inn, it was a bed-and-breakfast. If there is one thing I am not, it is a bed-and-breakfast kind of guy. The only thing I like less than second-rate Victorian furniture is a proprietor who insists on being my friend and, even worse, exercises his or her God-given right to talk to me as I try to eat breakfast. But I was stuck; the night's lodging had already been rung up on my Visa card.

So I pulled into the place, the "historic" interest of which turned out to be marginal at best. I opened the front door and was assaulted—no other word can describe it—by the ghastly aroma of potpourri. I felt as if I'd been plunged into the largest, most pungent Christmas shop on earth. Though one or two handsome pieces could be discerned through the clutter, what greeted me was a public room jammed to the rafters with what appeared to be all the rejects from Harvest Day: curios and bric-a-brac and bibelots, each attempting to outdo the other in ugliness and artificial quaintness.

The lady of the house came forth to greet me. She was all that I had feared she would be: a cameo from *Gone With the*

Wind, reeking of that insincere cordiality that is the Southern belle's stock in trade. Gasping through the potpourri, I followed her upstairs to the froufrou-free room. When she opened the door, the sight I beheld fairly knocked me down: a bed whose mattress reached almost to the ceiling—was there a pea underneath?—lamps dripping with lace, stuffed animals, vases, ungodly paintings, and a bathroom the size of a broom closet. If this was froufrou-free, what on earth did the real thing look like?

I didn't hang around to find out. Night was upon us, so I snuck away to a nearby restaurant for a meal that turned out to be better than I'd expected. I drove back to the B&B, put on my pajamas, pole-vaulted onto the bed—and slept the sleep of the innocent. Never have I been so surrounded, in the privacy of my chambers, by so much ugliness; rarely have I slept so soundly or awakened so refreshed. Perhaps there is a moral there, but I know not what it might be.

Still, there was breakfast to be gotten through. Madame was up and about, supervising the labors of the cook, a black woman with whom she appeared to be on easy, friendly terms. None of the other customers had arisen—at least I didn't have to talk to *them*, too—so Madame had me all to herself. She took it grievously that I declined the freight car of cholesterol that the kitchen was prepared to ship my way, but that did not prevent her from sitting directly across from me.

Somehow the subject of historic preservation came up. We agreed that it was hard to persuade people to restore their houses to the original condition. She leaned across the table, looked me in the eye, and whispered, "It's the blacks. They just won't pay to do it. It's the blacks."

I had come back to the James River thanks to my cousin, Louise Yardley Braunschweiger, who lives in San Francisco and works at the University of California at Berkeley, where she is on staff at the Lowie Museum of Anthropology. Knowing that I was wandering around the Mid-Atlantic in search

of interesting and perhaps familial things, she called one day
to ask if I was aware of the important historical archaeology
under way at Flowerdew Hundred in Hopewell, Virginia.

Not only was I totally unaware of it, I had never heard of
Flowerdew Hundred. I knew Flowerdew as the surname of the
wife of my distant kinsman, Sir George Yeardley, the first
colonial governor of Virginia; but if ever the name of Flowerdew Hundred had passed before me, it somehow had not
registered. I most certainly was unaware, as Lolly set about
telling me, not merely that Sir George's plantation on the
south bank of the James still existed but that it had become
the site of archaeological digs of great scholarly significance.
I expressed immediate and enthusiastic interest; she promised
to send me some articles about what was going on there, much
of it under the direction of her colleague at Berkeley, James
Deetz.

I wrote at some slight length about Sir George in my book
about the lives of my parents and do not propose to repeat
myself. In the mythology of my own family, his interest lies
not in blood—we are descended not from him but from his
older brother, Ralph—but in the uses my father made of this
connection when we moved from New York to Virginia in
1949. Dad was both a snob and an ancestor cultist, and he
played Sir George for all he was worth among his fellow
totemists in the First Families of Virginia. Since Bill Yardley's children almost always knew what he was up to in such
antics, I tended to regard Sir George as a figure of fun and to
give him little thought.

He was, in truth, a figure of substance. His colonial service
to his king had much to do with the establishment of the
rights and liberties we now enjoy. That he was a slaveholder
gives me no pleasure, but then so were many others whose
contributions to the nation cannot be gainsaid. In his tiny
little world he was for a time the sun around which all else
revolved, as is suggested by this inscription on a monument
near the historic church in Jamestown:

> Sir George Yeardley, the Governour, being sett down in his
> accustomed place, those of the Counsel of Estate sat next to
> him on both handes, except onely the Secretary, then ap-
> pointed Speaker, who sat right before him. And forasmuche as
> men's affaires doe little prosper where God's service is ne-
> glected, all the Burgesses took their places in the quire till a
> prayer was said by Mr. Bucke, the Minister, that it would
> please God to guide and to sanctifie all our proceedings to his
> owne glory and to the good of this plantation.

Jamestown was where Sir George conducted much of his
business. Directly across the river was Flowerdew Hundred, a
one-thousand-acre tract granted to him in 1618 by the Virginia Company, much as those five hundred acres on the shore
of the Delaware had been granted to William Yardley by
William Penn. There Sir George settled the members of his
plantation and built the first windmill in English North
America. His land was in a protected area and his settlement
was thus able to survive the terrible Indian massacre of 1622
relatively unscathed; that can be inferred from a "muster"
done in 1625 in which were listed on the plantation fifty-seven
people, twelve houses, forty-four cattle, thirty-one hogs, six
cannon, and the aforesaid windmill.

The year previous Sir George had sold the plantation to one
Abraham Piersey, the first of several owners. The last of them
was named David Harrison. He was a son of the Tidewater
who had managed to do quite well as an investment banker
in New York but never lost his feeling for his home country.
By the 1960s the Flowerdew acreage was once again on the
market; as a young man he had hunted there and felt a
familial connection to it, so he bought it. His notion was to
become a gentleman farmer, growing the principal crops of
the region: corn, soybeans, peanuts.

But then a funny thing happened to David Harrison: He
got into archaeology. Artifacts began to pop out of the ground
in the course of tilling and other work, and in time the archaeology department at William and Mary got interested. The

college saw the land as a potential teaching tool, while Harrison now saw it as a historic area that should be open to all, children in particular. Eventually it became clear that the college and the gentleman farmer had enough in common that a partnership of sorts should be struck. In 1977 the Flowerdew Hundred Foundation was set up, and thereafter Harrison devoted himself—not to mention much of his money—to the exploration and preservation of this treasure upon which he had all unwittingly chanced.

I was told about this by Elizabeth Myrick of the Flowerdew staff; I'd made my getaway from the froufrou as soon as possible after breakfast and driven to the plantation in the first sunny minutes of yet another stupendously beautiful day. A historic marker sped me on my way:

FLOWERDEW HUNDRED

Four miles north. Sir George Yeardley patented land there in 1619, and in 1621 built at Windmill Point the first windmill in English America. The place was named for Temperance Flowerdew, Yeardley's wife. Near there Grant's Army crossed the James in June, 1864.

I'd spoken to Elizabeth Myrick by phone and, after explaining my mission, had set a date for eight in the morning. When I arrived not merely was she waiting for me, but she handed over a file of material about the Yeardley/Yardley family that, unsolicited, she had put together on my behalf; all of it was immensely fascinating to me but not, perhaps, to you, so we shall let it lie.

Libbie Myrick turned out to be short, friendly, energetic, and eager to give me as much time as I liked for a close look at Flowerdew Hundred and its mission. We spent a full morning together. At the tiny Anderson House Archaeological Exhibit in Williamsburg I'd made note of an inscription that read: "Care and common sense are the archaeologists' most important attributes, and their techniques are the product of both." Now, at Flowerdew, I was to be given instruction in just how "care and common sense" are put to work and just how much archaeologists can do for the public good when they are free of the commercial considerations with which a theme park such as Colonial Williamsburg is encumbered.

James Deetz, who in the view of many is the leading figure in American historical archaeology, has written an engaging and informative introduction to his discipline in a little book called *In Small Things Forgotten*. If, as he says, archaeology itself is "the study of past peoples based on the things they left behind and the ways they left their imprint on the world," then historical archaeology adds "to our understanding of the American experience in a unique way, by looking not at the written record alone but at the almost countless objects left behind by Americans for three and a half centuries." It is, to oversimplify just about as far as possible, a form of extrapolation: Presented with an object unearthed from the past, usually a mundane one and almost always a very small part of its entire, original self, the historical archaeologist attempts to deduce from it whatever he can about how it was used, who used it, and what sort of world it came from.

That, in essence, is what goes on at Flowerdew Hundred. If Williamsburg is the sanitized past as entertainment and revisionism, Flowerdew is the past incomplete and unvarnished and, so far as possible, true. It is a chipped, faded shard of Blue Willow porcelain; the bowl of an old tobacco pipe; a rusty, battered hinge; the firing mechanism of a musket; a glass bead; a pottery bowl meticulously reassembled from pieces painstakingly dug up from the buried remains of an old kitchen.

"Flowerdew Hundred is one of the best preserved early seventeenth-century English settlements yet to be discovered in America," according to a brochure released by the foundation. "Its size, preservation and history make it a major source of information about the early colonization period and the transformation of Englishmen into Americans." It is all of this far less because of what meets the visitor's eyes than because of what lies under the ground, still untouched by the tools of the archaeologists who come there each year to dig.

You can walk around Flowerdew, as I did with Libbie Myrick, and what you mostly see—if it's early November and the trees are beginning to turn bare—is a flat, somewhat bleak landscape hard by the shore of the James, indeed so low by that shore as almost to vanish into the water. The trees are a mixture of the grand and the scruffy. Here and there were clusters of low posts arranged in what turned out to be orderly patterns; they were the outlines of houses and other structures that once stood during Flowerdew's four centuries of Anglo-American occupation. In other places were large sheets of black plastic, anchored to the ground by nothing more elegant than old, dead auto tires, covering digs still in progress but halted for the winter.

Only a couple of buildings intrude between the visitor and Sir George Yeardley's America: a reproduction of an eighteenth-century windmill constructed by David Harrison in tribute to the plantation's history, and a small visitor center with a museum and picnic areas. A power line crosses the James and modern boats ply it, but those are small distractions; it takes no immense effort of the will or the imagination to leap back in time and get some sense of how hard and precarious life was at that time and in that place. One person who made that effort was an anonymous writer for, of all things, *Your Virginia State Trooper Magazine*, in an article published in 1987 and included among those my cousin Lolly sent to me. That writer said:

> It is difficult for us in this day and age to imagine life at Flowerdew in the early 1600s. Living conditions cannot fail to shock us, if indeed we can fully appreciate them. A circa-1635 sunken-floored hut currently under excavation at Flowerdew tests our understanding of the way our forefathers lived. Diggers found more than twice the usual number of vessels and implements on the site, which indicates that the inhabitants were fairly well-to-do. The hut also contains a built-in clay

bake-oven. Yet it strikes our modern minds as incredible that
perhaps four people lived in what amounts to a ten-foot square
shallow pit in the ground and that they were well off in comparison to their neighbors.

Incredible isn't the half of it. The pit therein described had
been filled in or covered over by the time I got to Flowerdew,
but the sense of precariousness and vulnerability that this
writer had detected was everywhere about me. One clump of
posts, only a few feet from the river's edge, represented the
outline of a major building of Sir George's time—a fort, to all
intents and purposes, in which residents of Flowerdew huddled together for everything from companionship to protection from the Indians and the elements. It could not have
been larger than twenty feet by ten. On this brisk November
day it was easy to imagine what it must have been like inside
that building when icy water blew off the river in February or
rain cascaded down in July. Survival to the next day must
have seemed a miracle; England and all they had known there
must have seemed a universe away.

But if the risks and terrors of seventeenth-century life were
open to the imagination that morning, the beauty of the place
was self-evident to the eye. If on the one hand there is much
that is flat and bleak, there is also the bright blue of the river
and the faint roll of the countryside as it begins to reach
inland; the brisk, cold air seemed, to one whose senses have
been corrupted by the air of the late twentieth century, almost unbelievably clear and pure. It was easy to see why,
having made the arduous crossing to this tiny spot of land and
having labored mightily to make themselves a habitation
there, these people were so determined to stay.

No effort has been made, at Flowerdew, to reconstruct or
resurrect their world. Flowerdew over its long life has been
many things to many people, from the Algonquin Indians to
the colonists to many generations of farmers to, now, the
scholars who have set up camp there. The guardians of Flowerdew understand that to "restore" it to its condition at any

one time would be to deny the validity of all its other times, as well as to create an inherently artificial, prettified fairyland such as the millions enjoy at Williamsburg.

No doubt there is a place for the likes of Williamsburg; there must be, given the determination we Americans share to view our hard past through the rosy wistfulness of fancy and to make contact with it through the artifacts vended at gift shops. But if what you want is not to play in the past but to try to understand it, come not to Williamsburg but to Jamestown. Come to Flowerdew.

I crossed the James River once more, this time via the bridge near Hopewell. I turned right at State Road 5 and began the long, lovely drive down the north shore of the James, location of many of the great houses of the Mid-Atlantic. Most of them still stand, some in states of elegant repair. I stopped in the store at one of the most famous, Carter's Grove, to look for some books about the area. I found several and took them to the cash register, where an exceptionally gracious and courteous woman rang up the sale. In one of my fits of eco-freakiness I told her that I really did not need a bag. She gave me a reproachful look and said, as I left, "I am just *so* sorry that I cannot give you a bag."

A room in Norfolk awaited me, and rest before the next day's drive home through the Eastern Shores of Virginia and Maryland. It was another Best Western, an improvement over the one in Williamsburg in interior amenities but not in location. It lurked beside a horrendous thoroughfare called Military Highway, over which a stream of pugnacious traffic poured almost without cessation. Access to Military Highway from the motel was an elaborate undertaking, but I managed to pull it off and slip onto I-264 for a quick trip downtown in search of a *New York Times* and *Washington Post*. I found both in vending boxes, took a quick spin around a downtown that clearly was very much in the process of rejuvenating itself, and went back to the motel.

At six forty-five the next morning I pulled back onto Mili-

tary Highway, headed for U.S. 13 and the Chesapeake Bay
Bridge. It opened on April 15, 1964, long after I'd left my
parents' nest in Chatham and stopped making the regular run
to and from New England, with the result that I'd never
before been on it. I was genuinely excited about driving its
twenty-three miles but also slightly apprehensive; some years
before, driving from Miami to Key West with Sue, I'd been
witness to the bloody aftermath of a ghastly accident that had
left me with certain apprehensions about low, long, two-lane
bridges.

There was nothing to be apprehensive about this morning.
The weather system that would at last break up the week's
ethereal weather was beginning to roll in and there were a few
clouds in the sky, but the day was clear and so was the road.
I found that driving over dull water can be just as soporific as
driving over dull land. The view was beautiful, all right, but
it was also utterly unvarying; the tunnels actually provided a
bit of relief. My progress was efficient: Less than an hour after
leaving the motel, I was off the bridge and onto land.

WELCOME TO THE EASTERN SHORE OF VIRGINIA, A CERTIFIED
BUSINESS LOCATION. What I saw for the next several miles was
a motley, if far from unlovely, procession of small farms, junk
shops, modest houses, signs advertising PEA-NUTS and 100
YARDS: FIREWORKS, CIGARETTES, VIRGINIA HAMS—the four
staple products, it seems, of this little corner of the world.

At this point U.S. 13 calls itself THE OCEAN HIGHWAY,
though in fact it moves right up the middle of the peninsula
and gets farther from the Atlantic the farther north it pro-
gresses. It's a four-lane, unlimited-access road, flat and
straight, the kind that makes you want to go faster than you
really should. I kept the speed down because I was having a
good time looking, but there wasn't much to see: the occasional farmhouse, a sign boosting COUNTRY HAMS AND VIDEO
RENTALS. When I was a boy the centerpiece of any Mid-
Atlantic crossroads was the general store; now it's the video
store.

I was drawn off the road in a rage of curiosity by a sign that

said ONANCOCK. Pardon my dirty mind, but does anyone in
Onancock know what that means—or, more accurately, what
it sounds as if it means? Obviously not, because the name is
plastered all around the town as if it only meant what it really
does, which, according to *Virginia: A Guide to the Old Dominion*, is nothing more salacious than Indian for "foggy place."
In any event I pulled off the road to see this place with this
bizarre name, and was amply rewarded: a pretty little town,
with an exceptionally handsome Market Street United Methodist Church, a tuxedo and bridal rental shop advertising
WE TRANSFER HOME MOVIES TO VIDEOTAPE, and the irresistible Bonnie's Boutique (COME AS A STRANGER, LEAVE AS A
FRIEND). All in all, a place where I could easily imagine spending some time, though I couldn't help thinking that if they
moved it north, to Pennsylvania Dutch country, it could add
a fourth point to the celebrated Pubic Delta of Intercourse,
Paradise, and Bird-in-Hand.

I swung back onto 13, now more than halfway up the
Virginia leg of the Eastern Shore. On my left was a huge
Perdue plant; I shuddered to think what was happening right
at that moment to the poor chickens inside, not to mention to
the people butchering them. A few minutes later I passed an
immense truck, laden to the gills with crated chickens, all
squawking away in a cacophonous fury. Presumably the birds
were headed north for another plant in Salisbury and rude
treatment at the hands of some other manufacturer's minions.
No doubt when I wandered into Giant Food to pick up the
evening meal a couple of days later, some of them were on
display, nesting in their beds of yellow Styrofoam under blan-
kets of Saran Wrap.

A sign warned that Stuckey's lay six miles ahead: BIG REST
ROOMS AND OLD-FASHIONED CLAXTON FRUITCAKES, a weird
combination at best, though those who consume the latter
certainly will in time have urgent need of the former. At this
hour of the day the thought of fruitcake, never high on my
fantasy list, was downright revolting. The next Stuckey's sign
advertised cigarettes, in so doing unwittingly making the

point that tobacco country was now pretty much behind us,
though there are bits and pieces of it on the Maryland Eastern
Shore. Then, a couple of miles later, there stood Stuckey's
itself: attached to a Texaco station, looking more like a station than the station itself—like every other Stuckey's all
over the map, far less than its advertisements would lead you
to believe, or hope.

Now there were signs for State Road 175: turn right for
Chincoteague and Assateague. I'd been there before: beautiful
place, bad memories. A decade earlier Sue and I were at
Chincoteague with my sons, Jim and Bill, when the manager
of our no-frills motel came to the door to ask that I call Jack
Schnedler, in my office at the *Washington Star*. Jack wasted
no words: Time, Incorporated, as it was then still called, had
announced that it would close the *Star* in three weeks unless—
the odds against it were prohibitive—a legitimate buyer came
along. I was about to be out of a job. We threw our stuff into
the car and hustled back to Baltimore, there to try to make
some sense of our future. *That* was a part of my past I hadn't
the slightest urge to revisit.

Ninety-eight miles and two hours out of Norfolk, I crossed
into Maryland. I stopped off at a "Welcome Center" to pick
up a couple of state maps. The woman at the desk said that
one was enough; I said that my wife needed one for her car,
too; the woman forked one over, but with an expression on her
face that would have made any potential tourist do a U-turn
and go right back to Virginia.

A billboard for something called Carvel Hall promoted it as
a GENUINE FACTORY OUTLET—as opposed to all the fraudulent
ones I'd visited in Williamsburg? The thought of stopping
didn't even flit through my mind; I'd been cured of outlet
stores for a long time to come. Nor did the next billboard
entice me: COUNTRY HOUSE: LARGEST COUNTRY STORE IN THE
EAST—I'd had enough of that at the bed-and-breakfast to last
me a lifetime.

Thirty-five miles into Maryland, in the small rural city of
Salisbury, I left 13 and picked up 50, it too a federal highway.

Route 50, so far as Baltimoreans are concerned, exists solely
to transport them between home and Ocean City, the state's
chief beach resort and a place, I am sorry to say, not at all to
my liking: high-rise vacation, Miami Beach North. But I am
distinctly in the minority. Baltimoreans go "down the
ocean," as the distinctive local phrase has it, in astonishing
numbers, causing Route 50 to become gridlocked each Friday
and Sunday afternoon from May to December. A sign read:
REACH THE BEACH WEEKEND TRAFFIC MESSAGE SIGNS AHEAD;
those messages were shut down for the off-season, but in
summer they blink busily, warning motorists of the vast and
inescapable roadblocks ahead.

Right now traffic was light and the scenery was pleasant if
generally unremarkable; we were still far enough from Baltimore so that the predominant impression was of country.
Truth to tell all this coastal scenery in Maryland and Virginia
is pretty much the same; I like the way it looks, but it *does* get
dull after a while. Speaking of country, I passed a dog walking
along the road looking very much as though he meant to try
to cross it and get himself killed in the process. Years ago
Rosemary and the boys and I were driving from Greensboro
to Alabama when a dog ran out of a field and into our right
rear tire. There was a sickening thud; out the rear window I
could see the dog trying to haul itself along on its front legs,
its rear ones having been crushed. We were heartsick, and
made sicker when a pickup full of good ole boys hauled past
us, its inhabitants pointing merrily at us and jeering at the
stricken looks on our faces.

No, I don't mention that unpleasant encounter as further
evidence of the differences between city and country folk;
most country people surely would have been as upset as we
were. But there *are* differences—in this case, the pertinent one
being that country people tend to take a fatalistic view of
animal mortality—and city people would do well not to assume that their own views of the world can be exported very
far past the boundaries of the cities they inhabit.

The road by this point had stopped its northwestward

course and, near the bayside town of Cambridge and over the
Choptank River, had turned due north; the sky was bright,
the water was deep blue and looked unspoiled, boats were out
on it even in this forty-five-degree weather. The scene was
beautiful almost beyond words, but I couldn't help recalling
that in the 1960s Cambridge had been the scene of racial
tensions and violence just about as nasty as any the Deep
South was undergoing during the same period. In 1963 civil
rights marches were staged in Cambridge and quickly led to
violence between blacks and whites; then, in 1967, an incendi-
ary speech by the young radical leader H. Rap Brown was
followed by rioting and arson, an outbreak that helped transform the governor of Maryland, Spiro Agnew, from moderate
to reactionary so far as racial matters were concerned.

Fifteen more miles and I passed by—more accurately,
bypassed—the town of Easton. Back in the 1950s the Yardley
family occasionally stopped there en route to and from New
England to spend a night with Francis and Alice Murray,
older friends who had been instrumental in the marriage of
Bill Yardley and Chatham Hall School. They had money, at
least by our relatively impecunious standards, and a summer
house on the bay near Easton. By my calculations it was out
of their way for my parents to stop there, but from the way
they talked in anticipation of each visit to Easton, I grew to
have some sense of just how much the Murrays meant to them
and how privileged they felt to be their friends.

Twenty miles farther: the brand-new Kent Narrows Bridge
between the Eastern Shore and Kent Island. It had been in
the making for years; it was wide, fast, and, for anyone familiar with the bottleneck it replaced, an instrument of heavenly
mercy. In five or ten years, though, it surely will be outdated
as still more and more Baltimoreans and Washingtonians race
to the Eastern Shore, lured there in part by the illusion that
the new bridge will make the trip easier and faster, now and
forever.

From Kent Narrows to the Bay Bridge itself was only a
couple of miles. Everybody in Maryland and Washington

knows the Bay Bridge. It stretches into the sky, curves a
couple of times, invites vertigo and acrophobia. Not many are
indifferent to it; you either love it or hate it. My old friend
Joan Sylvester Wise hates it so much that her husband,
David, did her the favor of writing a novel, *Spectrum*, that
ends with the bridge under attack by a squadron of Phantom
jets:

> For a long moment, the roadway hung there. Then the
> second main cable snapped. The bridge began to creak and
> make a moaning noise. Slowly, very slowly, the concrete and
> steel roadway collapsed into the bay. The strain on the east
> tower was too much. A moment before, its great steel beams
> had stood 354 feet above the surface of the bay. Now, pulled
> down by the weight of the shattered roadway, the tower buck-
> led and folded into the bay like a child's erector set.

Mercifully, I got across unscathed, grateful as ever for a safe
landing. I pulled through the tollbooths and into the heaviest
traffic I'd seen since leaving Baltimore. A sign warned of
construction between Annapolis and Washington: PREPARE
FOR SUDDEN AGGRAVATION. What I thought was: That's
news? Bumper to bumper, we were a sea of rolling metal. I
broke away from it at I-97, the new road that gets halfway to
Baltimore before hooking up with the old Route 3 that I'd
been on a week before.

The rest was a piece of cake. As I approached Baltimore I
could see the skeleton of the new baseball park rising just
south of downtown: an unfamiliar but welcome sign of home.
My first prolonged trip through part of the Mid-Atlantic was
at an end, and already I'd been taught a lesson: However
much I may love the region, I don't love everything about it.
I looked forward to getting on the road again, but with a more
realistic sense of what awaited me. I hoped to find more such
as Flowerdew, but I had to be prepared for more Williamsburg; even in the Mid-Atlantic, perfection—or, more accurately, my notion of it—had not yet been achieved.

6

MEGALOPOLIS

If this is Monday it must be Washington.

At quarter of six on a January morning it was cold and dark; getting out of bed was hard. On Mondays I haven't any choice. On Mondays I leave my ivory tower in Baltimore and venture out into the real world—if, that is, the District of Columbia can be said to bear any resemblance to such a place.

In the nearly one and a half decades since I moved to Baltimore, I've been asked two questions far more often than any others. Baltimoreans invariably ask, "Are you related to the Yardley who used to draw cartoons for the *Baltimore Sun?*" Richard Q. Yardley was his name; though newspaper readers elsewhere were bewildered by his jolly, cluttered, rococo drawings, in Baltimore, where he was universally known by his nickname, "Moco," he was adored. The period of his greatest fame, if that is the word for it, coincided with my family's residence in Chatham, into which the *Sun* from time to time penetrated. My father tried hard to conjure up some form of kinship—all Yardleys are almost certainly related in one way or another—but he was never able to come up with anything that sounded very convincing to me, so when asked I generally just shrug and say, "We were kin somehow, but I don't know how."

In Washington, the stock question is: "But why do you live in *Baltimore?*" More often than not it is asked with a distinct undertone of incredulity or condescension, as if the person asking it finds the very notion quite impossible to believe. Even though the rejuvenation of Baltimore's Inner Harbor has raised the city in the esteem of some Washingtonians, it remains that in the eyes of many—especially those who fancy themselves to be "in the loop"—the old city on the Patapsco River is a disreputable place notable primarily for the disagreeable views of exhausted slums that it presents to those passing swiftly through aboard the Metroliner.

My answer to the question can be simple or complicated. The one-minute version has to do with money. In the fall of 1978, when I accepted the book editorship of the *Washington Star*, Sue and I had no resources beyond our small equity in the house we'd bought a year before in South Miami. We needed a fair amount of space to accommodate my home office and regular visits by my sons; we couldn't afford a substantial house in the District of Columbia, which was then heading toward the peak of its real estate boom, and for various reasons the suburbs of Maryland and Virginia held limited appeal. A friend who had already taken the Miami-to-Baltimore route suggested that we follow his example. We came up for a look, found a pleasant house in an old neighborhood at a third the price of a comparable place in Washington, and bought it.

The longer version takes into account other matters, some of them rather ambiguous. One was my sense that Washington is a company town, and a company whose business I dislike; politics interests and amuses me, but the forms it takes in Washington—influence peddling, back scratching, pervasive insincerity, high-octane vanity—do not. Baltimore seemed to me a real city, Washington inherently unreal, and to my way of thinking that counted for a lot. Another consideration was my fear that proximity to Washington's innumerable journalists and free-lance writers, many of them grinding out books certain to cross my desk, would compromise me

both as editor and reviewer. Yet another—it counted for little
at first, but gained increasing weight over the years—was a
family connection: My father grew up right outside Baltimore
in Catonsville, attended the Johns Hopkins University, and
always spoke of Baltimore with deep affection. Finally, and in
no respect trivially, Baltimore had a major-league baseball
team; to be sure it was not then *my* team, but the prospect of
regularly attending games meant a lot to me and to Sue as
well, she having grown up in Connecticut as a fan of the
Boston Red Sox.

But to say this is in no way to diminish the importance of
Washington in my life. It was there that I had my first
full-time, grown-up job; there that Sue and I had our first
date, an evening that rapidly ripened into our engagement;
there that each of my sons came to live upon his graduation
from Chapel Hill; there that I now enjoy the job I'd yearned
for much of my life.

As is no doubt true of most Americans, I first saw Washington as a youngster, brought there to take in its historic sights.
I came not on a school tour but with my father, on one of our
relatively infrequent—and thus by me all the more trea-
sured—father-and-son excursions. We stayed in a motel just
over the Potomac in Arlington, and one night we went to see
the newly released film *Captain Horatio Hornblower*, based on
the books by C. S. Forester that both of us loved. That is how
I know the trip was made in 1951, when I was eleven years
old.

We toured the obligatory monuments, but my most vivid
memory is one that will be familiar to countless others: the
rockets and airplanes at the Smithsonian Institution. There
was a crucial difference between then and now. This was well
before the Smithsonian's incredible growth of recent years.
There was no Air and Space Museum. The entire collection
was housed in, or immediately outside, the old Smithsonian
Castle. You entered the building and there, hanging directly
before you, was the *Spirit of St. Louis*, surrounded by a riot
of historic relics and technological marvels; if you wanted to

see rockets and other outsized objects, you left the building
and roamed its periphery.

Almost exactly a decade later I came to Washington to live.
As was true of many members of my generation, within a
couple of weeks I'd graduated from college, gotten married,
and reported for my first job. It was in the Washington bureau of the *New York Times*, where I had the incredible luck
to have been awarded a year's internship. I reported directly
to its chief, James Reston, then the most famous and respected journalist in the United States; I was to answer mail
related to the three columns he somehow wrote each week in
addition to his administrative duties, assist him with research,
and do odd jobs around the bureau.

It was an extraordinary time to be young and in Washington. John Fitzgerald Kennedy had been inaugurated six
months before. Although I have long since lost the illusions
about him and his administration to which I was then cap-
tive, it would be a disservice to the truth to say other than
that I held him in respect bordering on veneration and that I
was happy beyond expression to be at work in the city whose
mood he had so profoundly altered. Excitement was all
around me. One day I saw Pierre Salinger eating lunch at a
restaurant on 17th Street; another time I nearly smacked into
Edward R. Murrow at a bookstore on Pennsylvania Avenue;
once Mr. Reston let me go to Capitol Hill and interview Estes
Kefauver about the issues of the day; a couple of other times
I was allowed to tag along with the bureau's star reporters at
presidential press conferences in the State Department auditorium. The reporters at the *Times* were kind to me. They
invited me to their parties, talked to me about their work, let
me feel a part of their world. Some of them—Russell Baker,
Tom Wicker, David Halberstam, Anthony Lewis, Max Fran-
kel—in time became deservedly famous; I am grateful to, and
fond of, all of them.

Rosemary and I lived in a one-bedroom apartment on Porter Street, Northwest, just off Connecticut Avenue, near the
Uptown Theater and the Roma Restaurant and one of the

city's oldest shopping centers. She found a job on the staff of
a congressman from the Deep South who insisted that letters
to white constituents be addressed to "Mr. and Mrs.," but that
the conventional titles of courtesy be eliminated in those to
blacks, or "colored" as they were then called; incredibly
enough, as these words are written the man still serves, if
serves is the word, in Congress. But however antediluvian his
attitudes on race may seem, they were entirely in place in the
Washington of the early 1960s. Amusingly, and memorably,
Kennedy called it "a city of Southern efficiency and Northern
charm," but there was no joke about its rigid adherence to
Southern norms so far as race relations were concerned.

Surely there must have been black Washingtonians in
white-collar jobs in those days, but I cannot remember a
single one. There was none in the Washington bureau of the
Times, but then it was during my year's tenure that the
bureau appointed its first woman to the reportorial staff,
the estimable Marjorie Hunter. In those days, as had been
true for many years before, there was a substantial black
middle class, but it inhabited its own separate, segregated
world; only rarely was it noticed, and then usually with condescension, in the white corridors of power. Blacks didn't eat
at restaurants in downtown Washington, didn't walk its sidewalks in suits and ties, didn't send their children to St.
Alban's or Sidwell Friends. They worked as janitors and
maids and unskilled laborers—certainly not as clerks in stores
where whites might take offense—and in the eyes of whites
were largely, if not entirely, invisible.

I hope that I was offended by this, but I do not recall; I had
been persuaded to the civil rights cause at Chapel Hill, but
foremost on my mind were my new job and new marriage.
Washington hadn't yet gotten around to questioning its ways.
By the time it had, in 1963, I was in the New York office of
the *Times*. When I returned, in December of 1978, it was to
an entirely different place.

.   .   .

This was the place to which I was now en route. I struggled out of bed, shaved and dressed, ate a stand-up breakfast while skimming the *Sun* and the *Wall Street Journal*, put the *Times* in my briefcase, and at quarter of seven headed three and a half miles due south to Pennsylvania Station. I parked at a lot nearby, picked up the *Post* at a vending box, bought a one-day round-trip commuter ticket, and boarded the 7:05 "local express" as it pulled in from Baltimore's northern suburbs. Forty-five minutes later, having scarcely raised my head from the *Post* and *Times*, I was at Union Station in Washington.

Had I bothered to look out the window I would have seen the burgeoning evidence of what may well be the central fact of life at this moment in the history of this part of the Mid-Atlantic: the growth of Washington and Baltimore into a single vast entity, what is often called a "megalopolis." In the fall of 1992 the Federal Office of Management and Budget designated Washington-Baltimore as a CMSA, or "combined metropolitan statistical area," which it had long been in fact; now that it is one in name as well, it is, as the *Wall Street Journal* has reported, "the nation's fourth-largest market and, its backers hope, a marketing bonanza."

As the commuter train of Maryland's state-operated MARC system passes from Baltimore to Washington along the Penn Line—another, more westerly, route between the cities is the Camden Line—it makes stops at Baltimore-Washington International Airport, which is everything that its rather grandiose name suggests; Odenton, a small town that is rapidly turning into a substantial suburb; Bowie, where Bowie State University, historically but no longer exclusively black, enrolls three thousand students; Seabrook, a bedroom community just outside the Washington Beltway; and New Carrollton, which replaced the old Beltway station during the 1980s and connects the railroad line to Washington's Metrorail.

There are still many green spaces between these stations, but they are shrinking. Parking lots have been expanded, and the depots themselves improved, in order to meet increased commuter demand. When I first started riding the route in 1978, commuter trains were run by Conrail and operated only in rush hours, often haphazardly. Now there are more than twenty a day each way, the first leaving Baltimore at 5:20 A.M. and the last leaving Washington at 9:50 P.M. Trains run hourly during off-peak periods; the ones I ride back from Washington in late morning or early afternoon don't do much business, but it clearly is the state's expectation that demand will steadily grow—indeed it is hoped that eventually the two cities, or the two major parts of the one big city, will be connected by a high-speed rail system making the trip in fifteen minutes.

There is clear reason for this hope. Ridership on all MARC lines (a third connects Washington with points west in Maryland and West Virginia) rose from sixty-four hundred people a day in 1986 to seventeen thousand in 1991, a startling increase of more than 250 per cent; increases of 10 to 15 per cent a year are predicted for the 1990s, and Maryland officials tend to talk of MARC in terms of "enormous" potential and "a very bright future."

But rail is only a small part of the transportation network that binds the two cities. The brunt of the burden continues to be carried by the two limited-access highways, I-95 and the Balto-Wash Parkway, and the two local ones, U.S. 1 and U.S. 29, that connect them. From time to time I make the commute by car, but not often and not with much enthusiasm, even though the payoff is an hour at the wheel of the SHO. When I moved to Baltimore, I-95 between the two cities was new and underused; now it is a rolling zoo, soon to be a nightmare. As for the parkway, it is a lovely old road— opened in 1954, it was long considered a model of its kind— and because trucks are excluded it seems relatively bucolic, but construction is a constant headache and the approach to Washington on New York Avenue is riddled with potholes and ill-timed traffic lights.

So I ride the train. On the morning in question it pulled into

Union Station right on time, for a change, at 7:50 A.M. I
walked through the terminal in my usual hurry, scarcely looking about me and thus missing the spectacular interior vistas
of the great old station. In the 1970s it, and the railroads
serving it, came close to extinction; the station was just about
swallowed up into something called the National Visitor Center, which rarely had any visitors. But in the early 1980s
Elizabeth Dole, then serving as secretary of transportation,
decided not merely to save the station but to restore its original grandeur. This was done with a degree of compromise—
part of the station became a shopping mall, with the usual
fast-food and yuppie-trinket shops—but that was a small
price to pay for the salvation and refurbishment of the immense main room, a stunning evocation of the glory that was
Greece and the grandeur that was Rome.

I kept right on walking, down the escalator and into the
subterranean world of Metrorail. I pulled out the farecard
that I keep in my briefcase, passed through the turnstile, and
in a couple of minutes elbowed my way aboard the Red Line
train that six and a half minutes later deposited me two and
a half blocks from the offices of the *Washington Post*. The
door-to-door travel time was an hour and twenty minutes; the
round-trip cost was $17—$9 for the train ticket, $6 for park-
ing in Baltimore, and $2 for Metro.

There are any number of differences between the Washington that I knew in 1961–62 and the Washington that I know
now, but none of them except the change in race relations is
more dramatic or pervasive than Metro. In 1961, to get from
2740 Porter Street to the offices of the *New York Times* at
1701 K Street, I had to take a bus that ambled down Connecticut Avenue in the most leisurely and inefficient fashion; the
journey took at least half an hour, often much more. But now
the people living in my old apartment building can simply
walk about a hundred yards to the Metro stop and board a
train that deposits them at Connecticut and K four minutes
later.

Metro was born in 1967. Its full name is Washington Metro-

politan Area Transit Authority; its members are the District
of Columbia, Montgomery and Prince Georges counties in
Maryland, Arlington and Fairfax counties in Virginia, and the
Virginia cities of Alexandria, Fairfax, and Falls Church. On
the January day that I am describing its trains served sixty-
three stations over seventy-three miles of track, carrying
more than a half million passengers, as many as one hundred
and seventy-five of them to a car. Its five lines—Red, Blue,
Yellow, Orange, Green—crisscross in the district itself, then
fan out in ten different directions through the suburbs, in
some instances past the notorious Beltway that Washington,
as popular mythology has it, is "inside."

Speeding along underground from Union Station to Farragut North, I happened to notice a poster on the inside wall
of the sleek, semicylindrical car. It was an advertisement for
the George Washington University Health Plan. "You moved
to the suburbs for the kids," it read. "So did we." It is a move
that Washingtonians by the tens of thousands have made,
and one that has been greatly facilitated by the trains of
Metro. To be sure, Washington commuters still love their cars,
not least because many employers in the district subsidize
auto travel by offering free or reduced-price parking. But
Metro has become the glue that holds the Washington metropolitan area together. It is as difficult to imagine Washington
without Metro today as it was, three decades ago, to imagine
how a clean, safe, efficient mass-transit system could help
transform the old Southern city into a—for better *and* for
worse—sleek, rich, modern one.

Emerging from the dark of the Farragut North Metro station into the relatively bright light of the still-early morning,
I looked east and west on L Street. In either direction the view
was bleak. Washington is both beneficiary and victim of a
municipal ordinance limiting the height of buildings; the intent is to prevent skyscrapers from obscuring the Capitol
dome as the city's dominant architectural presence. This has
had the happy effect of keeping the city's scale relatively low

and thus its streets relatively sunlit, but it has also induced a uniformity of size and design that is soporific at best. Look down L Street or K Street or I Street and what you see is a row of boxes, each of them thirteen stories high, most of them sheathed in glass or some other cold, forbidding surface, almost all of them shut off from the outside by tight climate controls that eliminate fresh air and seasonal nuances.

Were it not for the parks and monuments and great federal buildings that break up the monotony, downtown Washington would be a visual and architectural disaster. These green spaces and historic shrines provide relief, but they cannot disguise the reality of Washington, which is that it is a city of indistinguishable boxes into which are crammed people whose principal business, directly or indirectly, is politics. Washington is as much a company town as Kannapolis, North Carolina, save that its business is not textiles but influence. Its white-collar work force, outfitted in cookie cutter raiment retailed at Brooks Brothers and Talbot's, dashes back and forth among the boxes, shuffling paper from one office to the next, doing not the people's business but its own. Many able and public-spirited people work among them, but they are distinctly in the minority; it is the cynical and self-interested majority that too often sets the city's tone, which explains why "Inside the Beltway" has become so pejorative an expression.

I turned left and walked east. Along L Street's wide sidewalks the street vendors already were open for business, beating their competition behind the storefronts by an hour or more. One sold purses, sunglasses, and neckties, these last of a most astonishingly kaleidoscopic nature; a few paces along another was putting into place the hot dogs and cold drinks that she would sell at lunchtime, while next to her the owner of a fruit stand sold bananas and oranges to on-the-run breakfasters; a bit farther along, still another was setting out displays of cheap watches, wallets, and Redskins souvenirs. For any number of reasons (some entirely legitimate) the merchants behind their glass facades don't like these interlopers, but for the pedestrian they bring life and variety to streets sorely in need of both.

Midway between 16th and 15th streets I turned into the L Street entrance of the *Washington Post*. It is an odd building, patched together over the years with little even remotely approximating rhyme or reason. Offices within move hither and yon at the whim of the building's tutelary gods. When I came to work at the *Post* in 1981, Book World, to which I report, was in a tiny nest on the first floor, worlds away from the rest of the news operation on the fifth; as these words were written Book World was in a Siberian corner of the newsroom made famous by the book and film *All the President's Men*; as these words are published Book World is down on the fourth floor along with a couple of other departments whose editorial missions are equally lacking in news urgency.

To some inside the building these strange comings and goings are evidence of bureaucratic incompetence at various places within the *Post*. I am inclined to view them as mere amusing eccentricities, though as one who works at home all week except Monday morning I probably am not entitled to pass judgment. I like to think of these and other oddities as signs that the paper is considerably closer to ordinary human reality than many outside the building believe it to be. The *Post* is big, rich, and powerful, and many within its circulation area resent it deeply; since it acquired, in the early 1970s, a reputation for tough and purposeful investigative reporting, it has been feared by many; inasmuch as the most notorious victim of its attentions was Richard Milhous Nixon, it is assumed by many to be implacably, monolithically "liberal."

My experience of more than a decade at the *Post* lends little support to any of these notions. Apart from the quite obvious truth that the paper *is* big, rich, and powerful, the rest seem to me more the products of fantasy than of actual evidence. Not having been on staff during Watergate I cannot testify to the presence or absence of excessive persecutorial zeal in that time, but I have seen little during my own tenure. Nor have

I seen any sign of the "party line" that writers for the newspaper allegedly toe on ideological matters. As it happens I am somewhat to the right of center on most cultural and social issues and on some political ones. In my first eleven years at the *Post* I expressed my opinions in its pages something on the order of one thousand five hundred times. On not a single occasion was any attempt made to influence or alter my opinion, though I cannot imagine that every person in newsroom management or higher office found all of those opinions congenial or sensible.

Obviously I cannot write objectively about the *Washington Post*, nor would I presume to comment on matters of policy that are the province of its owners and chief executives. But I am writing about my life in the Mid-Atlantic, and the *Post* is an integral part of that life. Not merely that, but the *Post* is by far the largest and most influential newspaper in the Mid-Atlantic, indeed it is the largest and most influential of any of the region's institutions of mass communication. With no television "superstation" in the region, no broadcaster has a reach so far and wide as that of the *Post*; although it as a matter of choice is a local rather than a national paper—Baltimore is only forty-five miles away, but the *Post* does not offer home delivery there—the range of its influence far exceeds the range of its circulation. The region has other fine newspapers—I think in particular of the *Philadelphia Inquirer*, the *Baltimore Sun*, and the *Raleigh News and Observer*—but the *Post* outdoes all in influence and prestige.

My own part in this is so small as to be undetectable; as one who came to the paper in mid-career, I am a beneficiary of the *Post*'s high position rather than a contributor to it. By the time I joined the *Post* in August 1981, not merely was Watergate nearly a decade in the past but the protracted internal competition to succeed Benjamin Bradlee, the legendary executive editor, was in its final hours. The "creative tension" for which the *Post* had been famous, or notorious, had calmed to a buzz not much more intense than is to be found in any office where smart and ambitious people work. Bradlee himself, I

am sorry to say, was never a vivid presence in my professional
life; I regret that my acquaintance with him was so slight, but
am grateful that he shaped the newspaper into an institution
in which I feel entirely at home.

There is no other newspaper in the country for which I
would rather write. In part this is simply because the *Post* is
what it is and because it gives me such extraordinary freedom
to speak my piece, but in great measure it is because of the
people who read the *Post*. I write about matters pertaining to
books and literature, social issues, cultural affairs, ideas.
These are of deep interest to many who read the *Post*, but
there are no self-infatuated literary or intellectual cliques
among them. They are smart, engaged, serious readers. I hear
from many of them, sometimes in sharp rejoinder to pieces I
have written, sometimes in agreement. Whatever the case,
this ongoing conversation with these people is the greatest
pleasure of my work, and says a great deal about the high
levels of literacy and intelligence enjoyed by many in Washington and its farflung suburbs who do not stroll the corridors
of power.

So. I waved my ID card at the guard and took the elevator—today, it happened to be working—up to the fifth floor.
By ten the rest of Book World's staff had arrived and we went
into our weekly meeting, the reason for my trip to Washington each Monday. In it we discussed the contents of the
forthcoming issue on which the staff would soon be at work
and the assignment of books for review. The meeting was, as
is invariably the case, lively, productive, and funny; if God
has ordained that I must attend one meeting each week, then
thanks be to Him that this is the one. It lasts a little more
than an hour—beyond which my tolerance for meetings
vanishes—and it consists, apart from the routine business at
hand, of running commentary by all involved on personages
and phenomena of the literary and journalistic worlds. The
door to the meeting room is kept closed, as well it should be:
The ears of many a litterateur would go up in flames at the

remarks made therein about current books and those who write them.

On this particular morning the bound galley proofs of a new novel by a prominent practitioner of that genre were the principal subject of discussion; inasmuch as its author is well known as an adroit player of literary politics, we spent nearly fifteen minutes trying to come up with the names of potential reviewers who are neither her friends nor her enemies, a task that exhausted us to the point of slapstick humor. Another book about the CIA was put on the table; we moaned in resigned submission to the reality that certain people in Washington like to read such books, and came up with a couple of names from the tiny circle of reviewers who know enough about such matters to pass reasonably competent judgment. Then we droned off into what seemed an interminable procession of first novels from the writing school assembly lines, "true crime" hack journalism, and public-policy books that, like CIA histories, have an inexplicable appeal to certain Washingtonians.

The meeting ended at eleven-fifteen. Some Mondays I stay in Washington for lunch, but this was not one of them. By taking the MARC local that leaves Union Station just before noon, I can be back at home shortly after one and back at work soon thereafter. That is what I did.

This is a life that I love, but I do not pretend that it is an unmixed blessing. The forty-five-mile barrier between me and the writers of Washington may serve a useful purpose, but I have many good friends in Washington—some of whom, not surprisingly, are writers—and I do not see them as often as I would like. I am at a considerable remove from the daily life of my office; its gossip is slow to reach me, I have only the most irregular contact with editors and writers whom I wish I knew better than I do, and I cannot duck into its library and morgue whenever I need that stray fact or reference.

Beyond all of this, I must admit that I have come to like Washington a great deal more than once I did. The violence with which it became afflicted during the 1980s, violence that seems on an ever-escalating path to calamity, is a terrible stain upon both its reputation and its daily life, but we have violence in Baltimore, too, and ours is not discernibly prettier. Washington is now a far more cosmopolitan place than it was three decades ago; though relations between black and white still leave much to be desired, the contrast between now and then is almost beyond description. The sheer physical beauty of the place is undeniable; though there may be no neighborhood in Washington that has quite the combination of leafy charm and beguiling architecture to be found in the one where I live, by the same token not even the most elegant of Baltimore's row house sections can rival the best of Georgetown or Capital Hill.

I remain confident, though, that in choosing to live in Baltimore I did what was best for me. I get my Washington fix once a week, and several times each year Sue and I drive over for dinner parties or other engagements. Nowhere else in the United States could I do the same; nowhere else—though residents of Dallas and Fort Worth or Minneapolis and St. Paul may disagree—are there two major cities of such contrasting character, economy, and culture so close and so accessible to each other by so many forms of transportation. As one who long ago decided that the best life of all is city life, I have, as I cross back and forth between the twin centers of this great megalopolis, the best of all possible worlds.

7

OPEN, SESAME!

I was back at Penn Station, not as a MARC commuter but as a passenger on Amtrak. It was time to have a look at New Jersey. I'd thought for a while about my connections to that state and the tenuousness of most of them, and had decided that I should take a break from chasing my own phantoms. It was time to get completely out of character. It was time to go to Atlantic City.

Until I boarded the Atlantic City Express that morning, this is how New Jersey had figured in my life: Like millions of other residents of the Mid-Atlantic, I had spent far more time than I cared to remember on the New Jersey Turnpike; my mother grew up just west of Newark, in Maplewood, from which my grandfather commuted to New York; during the 1980s Sue and I spent several vacation weeks at Stone Harbor, a few miles north of Cape May; in the spring of 1957 Princeton University declined to accept me as a member of its class of 1961.

It did not seem to me, upon careful reflection, that any of this lent itself to much in the way of fruitful reconsideration. I could have gone to Princeton, I suppose, to find out what I had missed, but I already know the answer to that: a superb education and further immersion in a prep school world I badly needed to escape. I regret the former but not the latter and, in any event, in rejecting me Princeton inadvertently steered me toward Chapel Hill, for which I am grateful beyond measure.

Stone Harbor is a lovely little place. Just to its south are the three funky Wildwood beaches, with their various honky-tonk bars and penny arcades, but Stone Harbor is a family beach—a summer place, not a resort. It has only a few small motels, no high rises much above four or five stories, and houses packed closely together that rent for a lot more than you'd expect. Much though we like it there we are not regulars and have no claim to intimacy with it.

My mother, Helen Marie Gregory, was very happy in Maplewood, to which her family moved in 1915, when she was seven years old. Her father, Alfred Gregory, was a self-made man of Scots ancestry who had risen to a partnership in one of New York's most respected law firms. Every weekday he rode to New York on the Lackawanna Railroad. It occurred to me to follow his old route on one of the commuter trains that still travel it, and I went so far as to finagle an invitation to stay with a friend who lived nearby. But though my friend is interesting, a commuter train ride is not; and in any case we have just taken a long one on MARC.

As for the New Jersey Turnpike, I well remember its opening in the early 1950s. Until then auto travel between the central Mid-Atlantic and the Northeast had been exceptionally unpleasant, entailing as it did driving directly through both Wilmington and Philadelphia. When the Delaware Memorial Bridge opened in 1951, and the turnpike thereafter, the trip suddenly became vastly more direct, safe and quick. Both of my parents were tight with a dollar, but neither of them resented paying the tolls for the bridge and the turnpike; these dramatic alterations in the infrastructure of the Mid-Atlantic saved them many hours of travel and incalculable road fatigue.

Now we take it for granted, and are more likely to curse than to praise it. It may still be safe and efficient, but we tend to think of it in terms of accidents undergone or avoided or merely witnessed. The closest I ever came was a few years ago when Sue and I were driving back from a vacation at Cape Cod. We were driving the southern end of the turnpike, no more than two hours from Baltimore, when suddenly a vehicle in the northbound lane lost a tire. It took one fierce bounce on that side of the road, soared high in a parabola that would have been majestic had it not been so scary, then headed down toward us. The whole thing probably took three seconds, but it seemed to happen in slow motion. At last the tire hit the side of the road, doing no harm to anyone, and we drove safely home.

Not exactly the stuff of legend, is it?

No, what New Jersey offered me was the chance to travel for a change as a mere tourist, bringing no baggage to the trip save what I carried in my hand. So I called the 800 number I found on an Amtrak schedule and talked with a representative of something called Amtrak's Great American Vacations. She offered me a one-night package at the Sands, train and hotel included, for $89, but that wasn't what I had in mind. I wanted to go whole-hog. I wanted to do my share in the great Donald Trump bailout. I wanted to stay at the Taj Mahal.

She let me do it for $109 plus $4.50 to send the ticket to me overnight. Inasmuch as I'd seen published room rates at the Taj floating around the $200 level, and inasmuch as round-trip travel between Baltimore and Atlantic City varied between $34 and $43, that seemed a pretty good deal: give Trump a helping hand, but not a very big one.

So at nine thirty-five on a breezy, chilly February morning, I climbed aboard Amtrak train number 663. There weren't many other high rollers heading to the shore that weekend, so I was able to seize control of a couple of seats and keep them to myself for the duration of the two-hour-and-forty-minute trip. The train had four cars, three of which were open; they were the standard, semicylindrical Amtrak cars, though a bit the worse for wear.

We pulled out of Baltimore, headed northeast to Philadelphia on the main Amtrak line. It's a route I know just about as well as any I've ever traveled; what with boyhood trips between home and school and more recent ones for work or pleasure, I must have made this run at least a hundred times. I'm so familiar with it that I can read intently, looking up when the rhythm of the train somehow tells me that it's passing something I like to see: the crossings in Maryland over the Gunpowder River, the Bush River and the Susquehanna; the sprint through northern Delaware parallel to I-95; the Philadelphia Museum of Art, the Philadelphia Zoo, the Schuylkill River and the boat houses lining its shore.

The Atlantic City Express passed all of these landmarks, but a few miles north of Philadelphia it took a hard right, crossed the Delaware River, and headed southeast into New Jersey on the old Pennsylvania Railroad tracks. For a while the scenery was standard-issue industrial clutter and waste, but twenty miles out of Philadelphia at Lindenwold, the only stop between there and Atlantic City, the countryside turned suburban and soon thereafter was pure farmland. It made me think of our drives to Stone Harbor along State Roads 49 and 47. You leave the southernmost end of the turnpike just before the tollbooths, and in no time you're in truck farm country. Perhaps there is a place in the United States where a better tomato is grown than southern New Jersey, but I am unaware of it. It's worth a week's rental in Stone Harbor just to have the excuse to stop at the vegetable stands along the way, picking up bushels of the fattest, juiciest, sweetest tomatoes you'll ever taste.

This is the side of New Jersey that most people know nothing about. Say "New Jersey" to most Americans and they'll think immediately of the slums of Newark, the immense gasoline storage tanks lining the turnpike at its northern end, the stink of the air there. But, in the words of the anonymous authors of the WPA guide, *New Jersey: A Guide to Its Present and Past*, writing more than a half century ago:

Off the arterial roads are hundreds of small villages where
the tempo of life is in keeping with the general stores, white
frame churches, and schoolhouses; where a good corn crop is
more interesting news than the murder of a Manhattan artist's
model, and where the county's chief horse trader is more representative of the community culture than the automobile
dealer. People in these villages are independent of cities. They
are as firmly rooted to their homesteads as the stone walls and
rail fences that mark their lands.

It goes without saying that much of this has changed. It
may not be impossible in today's technological and mass-
cultural world to be utterly independent of cities, but it's
hard. Rural New Jersey is far less isolated now than it was in
1939, when those words were published; you can see this in the
satellite dishes next to farmhouses on Routes 49 and 47, in the
big trucks hauling the consumer goods of the outside world
into communities that not so long ago were far more self-
sufficient, in the cars bringing vacationers from Philadelphia
and Baltimore. But rural New Jersey, especially in the southern end that begins more or less at Atlantic City, is still
essentially bucolic, still heavily agricultural, still lovely,
and—it should count its blessings—still relatively isolated. It
is no more the "real" New Jersey than are Hackensack and
New Brunswick, but it is an important part of the whole and
one that needs to be given its proper place when the overall
character of the state is contemplated.

I had brought *New Jersey: A Guide to Its Present and Past*
along for the train ride so that I could read about these and
other matters. The chapter on Atlantic City was especially
interesting. Clearly it was written by someone—or, because
we rarely know when it comes to the WPA guides, many
someones—with a taste for the raffish. Reading this chapter
as the train clacked eastward, I was filled with nostalgia for
a place I had never seen. Atlantic City a half century ago must
have been a wonderful place, alive with excitement and funky

energy, at once seedy and innocent. In those days people came
to it by the trainload, day-trippers and vacationers alike,
fleeing the great city directly to its west in such numbers that
it was known—both humorously and fondly—as "The Lungs
of Philadelphia."

Atlantic City in 1939 was "a glittering monument to the
national talent for wholesale amusement." It was "many
things to many people"—the "ideal vacation spot" for the
16,250,000 who visited there each year; for others "a carnival
city as characteristic of this country's culture as Brighton or
the Riviera are of Europe's"; to some "it represents the con-
centrated Babbitry of America on parade," while "to those of
the city's 66,198 inhabitants who profit from the pleasure of
the 16,250,000 it is simply a year-round business." It was
"one of the most fascinating man-made shows playing to
capacity audiences anywhere in the world," to wit:

> Here Madame Polanska reads your life like an open book;
> here Ruth Snyder and Judd Gray sit for eternity in horror-
> stricken suspense on an electric chair that fails to function;
> here an assortment of the World's Foremost Astrologers reveal
> the future at so much a glimpse; here hundreds sit and play
> Bingo; here the bright lights of Broadway burn through a sea
> haze; here Somebodies tumble over Somebodies and over No-
> bodies as well.

Approaching Atlantic City from the west, the train rolled
over marshes—Atlantic City is not mainland but an island—
past which could be seen the massive towers of the casino
hotels as well as others built or refurbished in hopes of capital-
izing on the rejuvenation that legalized gambling, authorized
by the state's voters after a long and difficult political fight,
was supposed to bring. It was an eerie sight, as if we'd come
across a moonscape and suddenly found ourselves in Las
Vegas. I hadn't set foot in the place and already I was disori-
ented.

The Amtrak station was bright, antiseptic, new, still further evidence of the hopes the gaming tables and slots had aroused. I'd meant to walk to the Taj, but when I got outside the station I immediately realized that the maps over which I'd pored had been misleading; the station was farther away than I'd thought and in any event there seemed no clear pedestrian route between it and the skyscrapers a few blocks away. So I took a cab, riding down a low, bleak street called Absecon Avenue before turning onto Virginia Avenue—here I was at last, on the biggest Monopoly board in the world— and heading for the main entrance of the Trump Taj Mahal Casino-Resort.

Words fail me. Open, Sesame! Before me was a wet dream by Ali Baba, or Richard Burton, or Rimsky-Korsakov—a grandiose parody, albeit entirely unintentional, of American notions of Middle Eastern opulence and seductiveness. This wasn't *A Thousand and One Nights*, it was a million, or a billion, or even a trillion. What figure could possibly be in- flated enough to do full justice to the astonishing vulgarity and unfathomable self-esteem of Donald Trump, the arche- typal folk hero of post-Reaganite America?

Minarets sprouted this way and that, each more gaudily decorated than its neighbor; the people who had the gold leaf contract at the Taj Mahal must have retired early on the profits. Chromium and brass were everywhere. The canopy under which the taxi passed was lit by a zillion bulbs, though it was only a few minutes past high noon. A doorman came out to greet me. He was clad in a phosphorescent greatcoat into which several mere mortals could have been stuffed; on his shoulders were epaulets that rivaled the wingspan of a Boeing 747.

I stumbled inside, there to find a notice that check-in this day would begin at three o'clock. I had two and a half hours to kill. I checked my bag with another member of the Persian Air Force and wound my way to the hotel's Boardwalk en- trance. I left the hotel, took a few steps toward the Atlantic, and turned to survey the eastern front of the Taj.

Here indeed was sheer majesty. At its front end the imagi-

nation of the casino's architects had been cramped by the
limitations of space, but at oceanside they were free to give it
full rein. Yard after yard the building stretched along the
Boardwalk. The backdrop was its great hotel tower, with
TRUMP TAJ MAHAL TRUMP writ large across its top in some
pinky-ringed fantasist's notion of Arabic lettering. The long,
low facade that graced the boardwalk was painted a bright—
nay, blinding—white, which made the colors of its attendant
minarets and window boxes and stair rails and decorative
trim all the more . . . again, words fail me.

Reeling, I turned to the south and walked into the sharp
winds coming off the Atlantic. The water of the ocean was a
dark, angry blue; the beach that separated it from the man-
made pandemonium of the Boardwalk was flat and bare. I
had barely recovered from the aesthetic overload of the Taj
when I was confronted by pop-cultural overload. Now I was
standing before Resorts International. It had been the first of
the Atlantic City casinos to open—on May 26, 1978—and its
glory days already looked behind it. Something called the
"Players Club" could be seen through its glass facade, its
name clearly intended to lure strollers inside under the utterly
unwarranted illusion that they are "players," but it was
empty. I stepped back and looked at Resorts; it was dingy,
uninviting, and—by contrast to the riotous rainbow right
next door—colorless.

But Resorts International has a proud history, and this too
it presents to the passerby. At its Boardwalk entrance I was
again struck dumb. There it was: THE ENTRANCE OF THE
STARS. Over the years the most celebrated ladies and gentlemen of twentieth-century American artistic life had come to
Resorts. By way of marking the occasion each had been invited to press his or her hands into wet concrete and to add
a signature, perhaps even a word or two of wisdom. There
they all were: Johnny Carson, Dom DeLuise, Diana Ross,
Kenny Rogers, Joan Rivers ("Are you sure this is cake
mix?"), Perry Como, Shecky Greene, Dean Martin ("It has
been a pleasure"), Engelbert Humperdinck, Cher . . . not since

my last trip to the Baseball Hall of Fame had I felt myself so
surrounded by immortality.

Then the drums rolled and the Holy Trinity presented itself. To one side was Liberace. To the other was Wayne New-
ton. In the middle, all by Himself as always He must be, doing
it His way, the Chairman of the Board. Under His plaque had
been affixed a smaller one:

> THE ENTRANCE OF THE STARS
> DEDICATED ON THIS SITE BY
> FRANK SINATRA
> MAY 22, 1981

It was more elegance—more sheer, unvarnished *class*—
than I could cope with. I shook myself out of my reverie and
turned back to the Boardwalk. "Along its four-mile length,"
I'd read that morning, "the city side is lined with huge hotels,
broken by blocks of shops, restaurants, exhibit rooms, booths,
auction houses, an occasional bank and even a private park.
Architecturally the motifs are mixed, but functionally they
unite in presenting a glittering, luxurious front." But that was
a half century ago. These were the 1990s. Except for the Taj
and a few of its competitors, the glitter and the luxury were
gone.

The tacky little Boardwalk shops soon became a blur.
Irene's Gifts, touted in one brochure I'd read as *the* place to
find that Atlantic City souvenir, selling T-shirts warning,
"Shit Happens," playing cards with pornographic pictures to
suit your persuasion, boxes of cheap saltwater taffy. Dan's
Deli, peddling custard and yogurt and jumbo hot dogs. Mme.
Edith's Temple of Knowledge: "Phrenologist, Reader & Advi-
sor, Special Reading $2.00, Also Tarot Cards, Crystal Ball,
Palm Reading," her price list running from $2 to $50. The
Lucky Horseshoe, boarded up, battered, for sale through
Longo Associates. Tepee Town: "Moccasins, Jewelry, Knives,
Gifts." A nameless store a few paces away: "99¢. Everything
in Store One Price. 99¢." The Hotel New Belmont, a folk

mural plastered across its boarded-up facade: it was for sale,
too. Boardwalk Roger's "Famous Ice Cream, Hot Dogs, Ice-
Cold Beer, Tacos," an ornate and oddly appealing old building
that might well have been—who knows?—a bank in better
days.

I wasn't alone in my stroll past these establishments, but
on the other hand I didn't have much company. Most of those
poking their way through the wind were of a certain age: "To
benefit from the mild climate and healthful sea air come elderly folk, who find respite from cold winters on the warm
Boardwalk and in the chatty living rooms of scores of rooming
and boarding houses." There wasn't much respite to be had
today in those bitter breezes knifing in from the southeast,
but the senior set was out for a stroll anyway. I was just as
glad it was winter; I'd rather see them all wrapped up than
stripped down to the skin for the hot breezes of July and
August.

I passed another monument of the new Atlantic City,
Bally's, its oceanfront side decked out in a montage apparently intended to celebrate the resort's many charms, chief
among them slot machines. A bit farther down I came to a
sudden halt, once again taken aback. There before me was a
massive statue of Julius Caesar, his right arm raised toward
the sea—not to hold it back but to beckon the stroller in, to
his very own Caesars (no apostrophe for *this* emperor) Atlantic City Hotel Casino. I wandered in. On either side of an
escalator stood more ersatz statuary, *sans* fig leaves; the brass
escalator glittered as it wended its way upward, to the Circus
Maximus.

I bid farewell to these noble Romans and returned to the
Boardwalk. Across the way, jutting into the ocean, was Ocean
One Pier, described in the AAA tourbook as the "centerpiece"
of the Boardwalk's alleged commercial revival, "a mall built
on the site of the legendary Million Dollar Pier." Some centerpiece. Some revival. Inside were more tacky shops, marginally
less so perhaps than those outside but utterly devoid of allure.

I am a fool easily parted from his money, but none left my wallet here.

Walking back to the hotel, I took the inland route, up Pacific Avenue. It didn't look exactly bombed out, and probably in summer it perks up a bit, but it was lifeless and empty. There was nothing new about that: "Backstage of the Boardwalk, there is a gradual falling from the splendor of Atlantic City's front. Narrow side streets leading from the beach are crowded with phalanxes of small hotels, boarding houses, restaurants, and saloons. The majority are frame buildings and, unlike the Boardwalk, recall that Atlantic City was founded in mid-Victorian times."

I knew at once where I was: in the seedy, tatterdemalion streets of Louis Malle's splendid film *Atlantic City,* one of the few movies for adults produced in the United States during the 1980s. My immediate reaction to the film had been that it was presenting us with reality and truth; now I knew that I was right.

I got back to the Taj at quarter of three, assuming that I could step right up and get my room key. Instead I found a long line, roped off into a tight multiple-S pattern. I took my place at the end of it; forty-five minutes later, plus ten minutes for the clerk to track down my reservation, and I had my room. Meantime I chatted with my fellow customers. The retiree in front of me had come with his wife from Toledo; the trip was a present from their children, except that they'd had to pay their own airfare and bring their own gambling money. Behind me was a younger man, from upstate New York, brusque but friendly, one of many building materials dealers in town for a convention; business, he said, was "dead."

I'd been looking for high rollers. I found Middle Americans. What the old petty crook played by Burt Lancaster in *Atlantic City* said about the casinos was exactly right: "They're too *wholesome.*" This may have been a den of thieves but it wasn't a den of iniquity; the people patiently waiting in line for their rooms were the same people you meet at Disney World and

Busch Gardens, ordinary Americans out for a safe, tame,
sterile toot.

The old fellow from Ohio was idly rubbing his foot back and
forth across the glossy marble floor. He looked up at me.
"Must've spent a lot of money," he said.

"Oh, no," I said, "not yet. I haven't bet a nickel, yet."

"Not you," he said, pointing to the floor. "Him. Trump.
Must've spent a lot of money to build something as beautiful
as this."

Up in my room, I quickly realized that I was deep into fanta-
syland. On the cover of my "guest directory" were words
designed to seduce and enchant:

> Welcome to the magnificent Trump Taj Mahal, a world of
> magic, mystery and minarets. Experience the excitement and
> enchantment . . . indulge in the exotic . . . feel the merriment
> . . . and taste the spectacular! Sensations will abound at the
> Trump Taj Mahal!
>
> This guest directory is a guide to the myriad wonders the Taj
> Mahal has to offer. Our entire staff looks forward to serving
> your every whim and desire. We have only one goal, and that
> is to make your every wish a dream come true.

The room, in fact, wasn't bad: considerably larger than the
average motel room, a comfortable king-size bed, a functioning television set in one of those hulking bureau-cabinets that
have become standard in the best and the worst of American
hostelries. Except for the bed and the television, nothing in
the room had been designed to make me want to stay there—
there wasn't a comfortable place to read and the lighting was
dim—but then roombound customers aren't exactly in the
best interests of a hotel with a casino downstairs.

I headed out of the room. Hanging on the doorknob was a
sign that could only have been the inspiration of Herself, La
Ivana, the erstwhile Mrs. Trump, during her brief tour as the
Taj Mahal's duenna. On one side it read, "My Wish Is Not To

Be Disturbed." On the other: "My Wish Is To Have My Room Made Up."

If wishes were horses beggars would ride, and quarters would come tumbling from the machines. 'Twas not to be. I am a creature of many vices both small and large, but gambling, mercifully, is not among them. I have no skill at cards, indeed have forgotten the rules of all card games since abandoning bridge in the early 1970s. The notion of flinging away my perfectly good money into the insatiable maw of an insensate machine strikes me as, on the whole, insane. If, as one adage has it, a lottery is a tax on imbeciles, then what pray tell are slot machines?

Not only that, but when it comes to gambling I am utterly without either sense or luck, neither of which reared its head during the couple of hours I spent playing the slots. The tables were another country; afflicted as I am by an ignorance about these games that is far beyond the redemptive powers of education, I stayed away. Instead I lined my pockets with nickels, quarters, and half-dollars, to all of which I said in time a permanent farewell.

The casino at the Taj must be as big as a football field and as brightly lit as Times Square on New Year's Eve. It wasn't unduly crowded that afternoon, but the clangs and rattles of the slots filled the air. Dollar machines were easy to come by, nickel ones almost impossible to find. According to John Alcamo, the author of a book called *Atlantic City Behind the Tables*, the "slot players' market" consists of "Mr. and Mrs. Average America, the blue-collar worker, the family man." Certainly those were the people at the slots that day: nickel players, quarter players. The lowest rollers around.

They guarded their territory ferociously. I saw what looked like a free nickel machine, slid onto the stool in front of it, and slipped in a coin. "Hey! That's my machine!" shouted the old woman who was jerking the arm on the next machine; she was running two at once—double the money, double the fun.

Except that *fun* wasn't the word for it. The floor of the casino at the Taj was about as joyless as any place I'd ever seen. Slouched in front of their slots, plunking in coin after coin, from time to time reaching down to haul in a small bonanza, the polyestered multitudes weren't on holiday, weren't having a lark, weren't blowing their cares away. If anything their cares seemed to have deepened. Scarcely a smile was to be seen.

I was out $25. I'd decided that I'd play a total of $50 over the day and evening—hey, big spender!—and go wherever it took me, flush or busted, though I knew perfectly well where *that* would be. In any event $25 seemed enough for one round. I went to my room, poured a glass of wine, and sat down to watch the news. After a couple of drinks I braved the cold rains that suddenly had blown in and walked down the Board-walk to New York Avenue, where I found Mama Mott's, a restaurant of local ancestry that long predated the era of casinos and was reputed to have good food. It did. Of course Yardley's Law was observed: In a room of perhaps twenty tables, two of them occupied, I was given the worst, next to the station where the waiters and maitre d' occupied them-selves by banging the silver around. But the Fettucini Mama Mott was delicious; I wouldn't have done half so well, at twice the price, Chez Trump.

At ten o'clock I went back to the casino for more punish-ment. For a while, playing the half-dollar machines, I got a few dollars ahead, but that was just bait for the sucker. It took less than an hour for the balance of my $50, plus an extra $5 for good measure, to take flight. I was wiped out.

I was also filthy. Playing the slots is like smoking, at which I was once something of an expert: You get dirty all over. Spend fifteen minutes fooling around with nickels that untold others have fooled around with before you, and your hands look like a coal miner's. I am not unduly fastidious, but I made as many trips to the washrooms as to the change ma-chines. So what it came down to was that I paid $55 for a few grams of dirt. Somehow I think Trump got the better of the deal.

Yes, the slots do have their hypnotic side, as I'd learned

that night nearly thirty-five years before at the roadhouse on
U.S. 301. The notion that if you keep plugging away at something it will eventually pay off is not unappealing. Perhaps it
has something to do with why I like pinball machines. But
they at least require some element of skill. The longer you
play them, the better you're likely to get. The more you play
the slots, on the other hand, the more you're likely to lose.

I drifted off to sleep to the accompaniment of the late news
and slept, amazingly, until nearly nine the next morning, later
than I had in years. I ate an ordinary breakfast at one of
Trump's sultanates downstairs, then visited the gift shop,
where I purchased a postcard on which it was claimed that
"the Taj Mahal is the most elegant and spectacular casino in
the world."

I went back to the Boardwalk; with my train not due out
until 2:05 P.M., I had time to kill. I walked inland and wandered around the side streets. If Atlantic City had enjoyed a
renaissance as a result of the casinos, there was not a scintilla
of evidence of it. To the contrary, the buildings were shabby
and battered. The people on the sidewalks, most of them
black, looked idle and listless. It was the same old story, as
told in this WPA guide:

> North of Atlantic Avenue the city deteriorates into a dingy
> section somewhat improved by recent slum clearance and
> street repairing. This is the Northside, home of Atlantic City's
> Negro inhabitants—23 per cent of the total population and,
> next to that of Newark, the most important Negro population
> of the state. They form a reservoir of cheap labor for the hotels,
> amusement piers, restaurants, riding academies, and private
> homes. . . . They have three elementary schools, and hold
> positions in the city and county governments. By tacit under-
> standing the Negroes frequent certain portions of the beach at
> certain hours.

The black community of Atlantic City was supposed to be
given a lift by legalized gambling. That was the deal, but

somebody reneged. These streets and the people who walked them were drained, tired, sad. A couple of hours later, in line to check out at the Taj, I heard one of my fellow customers say to another, "Did you look down the side streets? It's really a slum down there. You wouldn't get me there for anything." Those are the two worlds of Atlantic City: in one the natives and residents, poor and lower-middle-class; in the other the comfortable tourists, high rollers and low, separated from the real world by the safe fortresses in which they play.

At noon I checked out. I wanted nothing more to do with the Taj. I picked up my small bag and wandered west on Virginia Avenue. Barely a block away from the casino, I found a little bar and restaurant called Stolfo's. It wasn't crowded and it looked friendly. I took a seat at the bar. In a minute the bartender appeared. She was pert and cute—*she* would have looked good on the Boardwalk in July—and when I asked if she could do a martini, she immediately asked what kind of gin I'd like. At first, city boy that I am, I thought she was steering me toward a premium brand and a premium price; then I realized she just wanted to give me what I wanted.

The martini was delicious, close to perfect. So too was my club sandwich, which I polished off forthwith.

"How was the sandwich?" the bartender asked as she took my plate away.

"It was wonderful," I said. "I eat a lot of club sandwiches and this was as good as I've ever had."

"Well, it's a specialty of the house," she said. "We cook our own turkey and take a lot of pride in it." She paused, then looked me over. "Are you from around here?"

"No. I'm from Baltimore. I just came up overnight. Tell me. Has the Taj Mahal helped your business much?"

"Not hardly," she said. "It was great while they were building it, because for four years the construction guys came in every day. But the tourists never come. They're scared."

"What about you?" I said. "Are you from around here?"

"I come from Brigantine. That's where most of the casino workers come from. That and Margate. Places like that."

"What about from Atlantic City?"

"No," she said, "not many of the jobs go to people from Atlantic City."

She went to the other end of the bar to serve another customer, then came back. "So," she said. "You've seen Atlantic City. What do you think?"

I thought for a moment. "I think it's a pretty strange place," I said.

She laughed. "It's strange, all right," she said.

8

THE ROAD
OF THE FUTURE

I found what I wanted in the Maryland Collection of the
Enoch Pratt Free Library. It stands on Cathedral Street just
north of downtown Baltimore, where construction on the
white (now gray) marble structure was undertaken in 1881 at
the instigation of Enoch Pratt, an emigrant from Massachusetts who, like many others, had made his fortune selling
supplies to the Union army. For years the Pratt was not
merely the city's chief library but the state's as well. Now it
had been grievously undermined by budgetary difficulties and
the disappearance of middle-class readers into the suburbs,
but even in a diminished condition it remained a primary
resource for anyone interested in the history of the city and
the state.

I wanted to know what the Maryland highway system
looked like in the years I rode over it in the back seat of my
parents' car: say, in 1951 and 1955, the latter being just before
I got my driver's license and began relieving my mother and
father at the wheel. But finding old road maps turned out to
be a lot easier said than done. As one who'd rather read a map
than a novel I find it astonishing, but almost no one saves
them. The Baltimore office of the American Automobile Association had none and hadn't a clue as to where I should look.

None of the used-book dealers had any and there wasn't a single used-maps store listed in the Yellow Pages.

Finally I went where I should have gone in the first place. The Maryland Collection at the Pratt turned out to have a collection of official state road maps in near-mint condition. The woman at its reference desk—where a sign warned that in these parlous times, the library was understaffed and service might be slow—found the maps I wanted and permitted me to photocopy them.

They told me exactly what I had suspected. In 1951, a traveler from Virginia to New England came up from Richmond on U.S. 1, drove through the heart of Baltimore, and picked up U.S. 40 there; in Delaware that merged with U.S. 13, which went on to Wilmington, Philadelphia, and points north. By 1955 there were two major changes and another in the making. The Baltimore Harbor Tunnel was still under construction (it opened in 1957), so it remained necessary to negotiate Baltimore; but the Baltimore-Washington Parkway, the Delaware Memorial Bridge, and the New Jersey Turnpike were now open, which meant that the passage from Washington to Baltimore was greatly facilitated and that Wilmington and Philadelphia could be bypassed.

Say whatever you will about the automobile culture and the slabs of asphalt it has pasted across the landscape, this cannot be gainsaid: The arrival of these first great bridges, tunnels, and toll roads was greeted with near-universal applause. Nobody could see into the future; people still thought that Robert Moses was truly worthy of his surname and that his works were to be emulated in all corners of the nation. It's easy enough now to criticize the interstates and the highway lobby; I've done my full share of it, and then some. But it is rather harder to put oneself back in time and recall just how it was back then. That was what I proposed to do.

As closely as possible, I wanted to retrace my parents' steps on an early-fifties journey from the southern approach to Baltimore to an evening's stopover just west of New Castle, Delaware. So a few days after coming back from Atlantic

City, I headed back up the line from Baltimore to Philadelphia. I got onto U.S. 1 south of Baltimore via State Road 175, barely visible on the 1951 map but now a wide concrete slab serving the "new town" of Columbia, which the Rouse Company opened in 1966. If much of what I now saw along the roadside was here in 1951, I'd be amazed: a Luskin's discount house, an office park, Hubcap City, Sonny's Surplus, the Speed Shop—this was the detritus of a later time. A battered old service station surrounded by a steel fence and sporting a No Trespassing sign doubtless was a relic of my childhood, but little else along the first several miles appeared to be.

The road was four lanes, undivided, curvy and hilly, riddled with stoplights. To my surprise a bucolic stretch suddenly opened up, giving me a brief glimpse of the green expanse that in the early fifties occupied the middle of what is now the Washington-Baltimore megalopolis. I went through an intersection with something called the Old Baltimore–Washington Boulevard, but my 1951 map offered no clue as to what it had been—presumably, in its day, a major thoroughfare. Soon thereafter I passed a sign for the Harbor Thruway, which certainly is a dreadful road, as anyone who has driven it can testify, but when it opened it seemed entirely miraculous to those on the route along which I now passed.

I had the road almost to myself. This was mid-afternoon on a Saturday in February that held the possibility of snow showers. Thus it was not a time when traffic would be likely to be heavy, and such of it as there was presumably was on I-95 and the Balto-Wash Parkway; in 1951 all of it would have been right here, and on a Saturday in late spring—we usually left for New England in the first or second week of June—it would have been ungodly.

On my right Amtrak's main tracks came into view. All at once I realized that I was seeing from a motorist's vantage point the sights that had become stupefyingly familiar to me from the train: the long blue edifice that, I now learned, was the Southwestern Professional Building; the overpass that also serves as the tiny Halethorpe commuter station; the

shopping center with a Super Fresh grocery store. I'd wondered for years what the road was that ran parallel to the
tracks; now I knew that it was U.S. 1 and that it, too, had
been part of my life.

Traffic was still light but bound to intensify, as the Baltimore skyline could now be seen. For a split second none of the
skyscrapers of more recent vintage was in view; what I saw in
that instant must have been quite similar to what I'd seen
forty years before. By now the road was called Wilkens Avenue and I was in southwest Baltimore. I passed St. Agnes
Hospital, Cardinal Gibbons High School; I drove down a long
line of classic Baltimore red-brick row houses with their white
steps, tidy and sturdy. Then the cityscape started to change,
to become more battered and desperate. Union Square was on
my right and, a few steps away on Hollins Street, the residence of the Sage of Baltimore; with a jolt I realized that
Henry Mencken himself almost certainly would have been at
home the first several times we passed by, as he was largely
housebound from the time of his stroke in 1948 until his death
in 1956. Now his beloved neighborhood was bravely trying to
return from the dead, but a bombed-out house at the corner
of Gilmore and West Baltimore streets gave grim proof of how
far it had to go.

Just like that I was lost. The intersection with U.S. 40 so
clearly depicted on my 1951 map no longer existed; it had
been eliminated by new streets and one-way streets and public
housing. I worked my way over to Lexington Street, and
pulled to the curb near its intersection with Stricker (pronounced "Striker") Street to check my maps. Here's another
literary tidbit: During the years before World War I when he
worked as a Pinkerton operative, Dashiell Hammett lived on
Stricker Street.

I realized that an absolutely faithful recreation of our old
route was now impossible; I'd better get to Route 40 the best
way I could. I maneuvered over to Mulberry Street, turned
right on it, and a few blocks later, following a sign that said
40 KEEP LEFT, found myself where I wanted to be: on the

Orleans Street Viaduct and then on Orleans Street itself, heading east-northeast, home free.

En route I'd gone right past the Pratt Library; past the Basilica of the Assumption of the Blessed Virgin Mary, one of the most important Catholic churches in the United States, designed in the early nineteenth century by Benjamin Henry Latrobe; past the shuttered storefront of Fallon & Hellen, once the furniture store of choice for Baltimore's elite but now a victim of suburban competition; past the Johns Hopkins Hospital, towering over its East Baltimore surroundings.

Approaching the hospital I'd been in the midst of public housing, some of it badly deteriorated. Now I was amid row houses, most of them occupied but forlorn. The decline of this part of Baltimore over four decades is heartbreaking. It hadn't been anything beautiful when I first saw it, but it was alive and in various ways productive. Now it was moribund, wasted urban infrastructure that housed, I fear, too many wasted lives. Just ahead of me stood, incongruously, a billboard for Bass Ale; I couldn't imagine that many living here could have pockets deep enough for that costly British brew. More within their reach was the ancient White Tower ahead of me, or the glossy Hardee's across from it on North Highland Street.

Leaving the city at last, Route 40—Pulaski Highway, now—turned industrial and automotive. It looked to me as if the Marylander Motel, right in the midst of all the smokestacks, could be a survivor from the fifties; so could Duke's Motel, the Colonial Motel, the Star Motel. I was so intent on the motels that I almost drove right by the Price Club, the wholesale outlet at which I am in regular attendance. I pulled into its huge lot and went inside, but turned right around when I saw the mob; Saturday afternoon is *not* the best time for the Price Club.

There was more strip development farther on up the road, but within a few miles it had settled into a mixture of countryside and occasional commercial or residential patches. The road was four lanes, separated by a modern, collision-preventive concrete divider; the speed limit was fifty-five, but most of the traffic was five or ten miles over it. Apart from the divider, this must have been just about what the road looked like in 1951, and in all honesty it didn't look bad.

Twenty-five miles out of Baltimore I passed over the Bush River. Later, reading *U.S. 40: Cross Section of the United States of America,* by George R. Stewart, published in 1953, I learned that "U.S. 40 at this point makes its earliest contact with recorded history":

> On July 23, 1608, Captain John Smith set out on his second voyage of exploration on Chesapeake Bay. A few days later he entered an estuary which he called "Willowbyes river," and which can be positively identified with the present Bush River. . . . Thirteen men were packed into [Smith's boat], but eight of them were down and out with a sickness, probably dysentery. In Bush River the Englishmen encountered several canoes full of Massawomeck Indians, who seemed to be advancing with hostile intent. Smith propped up the sick men's hats on sticks along the gunwale, and the Indians drew off and contented themselves with staring amazedly at the spectacle of a sailing vessel. Smith steered boldly down upon them, and by this firm front won their respect and friendship.

I was moving along at a steady pace; I-95, a couple of miles to the left, couldn't have been a great deal faster. From time to time there were reminders of what 40 had been like when it was the only divided highway between Baltimore and Delaware. I stopped at a grade intersection while a train passed; I hadn't had to do so in years, but train delays used to be a commonplace of interstate travel. So too was the dreadful mixture of local and long-distance motorists that these highways carried—the locals setting the pace with their stoplights and poky speeds, the travelers chafing angrily at each delay.

I was almost out of Maryland. A mile from the state line I went past Elkton, now receded into obscurity but once famous, or notorious, as, in the words of *Maryland: A New*

Guide to the Old Line State, "the Gretna Green of the East." Until 1938, when Maryland at last imposed a forty-eight-hour waiting period for marriage licenses, "the town made a lucrative business of marrying couples unwilling to wait the time required in other states to receive a marriage license."

> Taxicab drivers met the trains and, for a set fee, took couples to the courthouse for the license and then to a parson for the ceremony. Legal marriages could only be performed by a minister, so signs advertising "marrying parsons" lined Main Street.

Now Elkton is just another road sign on I-95, unremarked by all but a handful of the speeding millions; but my parents always laughed about it as they drove through, and I was delighted to find my memories of what they'd said confirmed in print.

Here was Delaware. FIRST TO RATIFY THE U.S. CONSTITUTION, read the sign that greeted me. I was also greeted by a flurry of the snow that had been threatening all day; none of it stuck, but it did obscure the view, such as there was of it. Nor was there much time to look, for in what seemed an instant 40 hooked up with 13, which had merged with 301 to the south. Now I was on the highway that I remembered, with not a whiff of pleasure, from my childhood.

It isn't really true that the entire Mid-Atlantic squeezes into this bottleneck; it just seems that way. Forty years ago George R. Stewart thought this stretch of road was pretty amazing. It had been constructed between 1911 and 1924 in the expectation, according to a member of the Du Pont family who had been instrumental in building it, that it would be "the road of the future." Stewart wrote: "Except for strictly urban development this is the only part of U.S. 40 that at present attains six-lane width, and it is the section that carries the heaviest traffic. According to the latest official count the average day's traffic at this point totaled 22,688 vehicles."

This astonishing traffic volume "is borne out," Stewart

added, by the photograph immediately above the text. Today's reader can only look at it and laugh, or weep. The picture shows a near-rural stretch of six-lane highway divided by a grassy median amply planted with trees, "in which ten cars and two trucks appear, even though only a short stretch of highway is visible." By today's standards, that road is deserted. Today the median has just about vanished, gobbled up by the eight or ten lanes that now throb with a steady, thunderous flow of traffic; the scenery has been gobbled up, too, by Penn Mart Plaza and Airport Plaza and other adornments of the age.

The "road of the future" was out of date within a quarter century of its construction. Two miles away, on I-95, some twenty-one million vehicles pass through the tollbooths each year, an average of 57,692 a day. Add to that all the local traffic that doesn't go through the toll gates and the traffic that still uses 40-13, and somewhere close to two hundred thousand vehicles must pass over the route of the combined Delaware highways every day. If there is another place in the Mid-Atlantic that comes closer than this to being Auto Hell, I am entirely—and blissfully—unaware of it.

I checked into my motel, changed clothes, and decided to have a look at New Castle. I knew absolutely nothing about it, but I was curious. A few weeks earlier my neighbor, Tim Sellers, had given me a reproduction of a map of Pennsylvania that had been drawn in 1687 by Thomas Holme and is now in the collection of the Library Company of Philadelphia. Tim gave it to me because it shows the "lotts" along the Delaware River then owned by his distant ancestor, Sam Sellers, and mine, William Yardley. But I had also noted that in what is now the state of Delaware the map showed only one settlement. It was not Wilmington but New Castle, and by the looks of it, it was a substantial place.

So I got on State Road 141 and headed there. I passed Penn Mart Plaza, anchored by an Ames department store. Tract houses of 1960s vintage lined the road. On my right was the

William Penn High School, a low orange-brick structure so
vast as to have housed the entire populace of Delaware;
beyond it was the First Baptist Church, almost as big and
considerably uglier. On State Road 9 I turned left, drove past
the Mother Hubbard Child Care Center and Domino's Pizza,
then bore right at a three-pronged intersection toward the
little town.

My first glimpse of it wasn't promising: For Your Nails
Only, specializing in "Sculptured Nails and Sculptured Nail
School." But then I was on Delaware Street and quickly
realized that I wanted to stop. I parked in front of Oak Knoll
Books and went in. I was startled to see that in this out-of-
the-way location there was an antiquarian bookseller dealing
not merely in books about Delaware—no surprise, that, and
not many books, either—but also in "books about books."
Any bibliophile such as my father had been would have found
something of interest in the shelves.

I walked a block east on Delaware Street and stopped in my
tracks. I was struck dumb. Before me stood the most beautiful
town I had ever seen. In Williamsburg not long before I had
been surrounded by the artificial, the "restored." Here I was
right in the middle of the real thing, a small town of Colonial
and Revolutionary buildings that seemed to have emerged
intact from the past. I'd scarcely taken a glimpse before dark-
ness closed in, so I decided to come back in the morning. But
before leaving I went to the Newcastle Inn and asked if they'd
be willing to take a reservation for a party of one for dinner;
they were happy to oblige.

Back at the motel I read about New Castle in *Delaware: A
Guide to the First State.* Its history turned out to be illustrious.
The construction of its first structure of defense, Fort Casimir,
was directed in 1651 by Peter Stuyvesant; in 1682 possession
of "the land of the twelve-mile circle about New Castle" was
given to William Penn; in 1776 New Castle served as first
capital of "The Delaware State," though the forbidding presence nearby of British troops soon caused the seat of government to be moved to Dover. As the *Guide* put it:

> New Castle . . . the oldest town in the Delaware River
> Valley, lies in a curve of the shore, once a fine harbor for large
> vessels, with a commanding position and view. Along the first
> street, the Strand, parallel with the river, the houses face not
> the street, but each other. The streets and the broad Green
> preserve unspoiled the work of seventeenth, eighteenth and
> early nineteenth century builders. History, adventure and ro-
> mance are written in the doorways and roof lines, in the broad
> chimneys, and in glimpses of spacious rear-gardens.

At seven I was at the Newcastle Inn. Yardley's Law was
flagrantly violated; I was given a choice corner table with a
commanding view of the entire room and a waitress eager to
serve me. The inn, on the town green, was built in 1809 as an
arsenal, and subsequently had a checkered history, functioning variously over the years as fort, garrison, schoolhouse, and
offices of the Unemployment Commission of Delaware. It was
turned into a restaurant in 1980 and remodeled accordingly;
its two main dining rooms were elegant and spare, fitted with
substantial tables and chairs.

I read the menu slowly. "What," I asked the waitress, "is
'Delaware Crab Cake'? Is it somehow different from a Maryland crab cake?"

She thought a moment. "Well, for one thing it's baked
instead of fried or broiled." She thought a bit longer and
added: "The chef is from Maryland anyway, so there probably
isn't any difference."

This struck me as mildly disappointing. For a moment I'd
nurtured the hope that hidden away in Delaware was a delicacy of the Mid-Atlantic that, unlike its cousin in Maryland,
had to date gone undiscovered. But I decided that I'd just as
well try it anyway, in the ecumenical spirit, and ordered it.

The Delaware crab cake was in fact delicious. By baking
rather than broiling, charring the outside meat was avoided;
the meat itself was tender and tasty. As a self-taught crab
cake manufacturer of moderate accomplishments, I had to
bow to a far superior craftsmanship. Indeed the entire meal

was a success, devoid of radicchio-and-raspberry cuteness or ye-olde quaintness. If only the wine selection had been more comprehensive, my dinner would have been in all respects up to the surroundings in which it was served.

The surroundings of my next meal were considerably more bizarre. For Sunday brunch I went to the Air Transport Command, hard by the airfield, the description of which in the AAA guide had aroused my curiosity: "Authentic World War II atmosphere inside & out." AAA wasn't kidding. The restaurant was modeled after American air headquarters in Prestwick, Scotland, complete with jeeps, ambulances, airplanes, and a sign reading, MINE FIELD—KEEP OUT. Inside, the bathrooms were "latrines"; framed wartime newspapers decorated the walls; vintage songs were playing over the Muzak system, Glenn Miller and Vera Lynn and Tommy Dorsey.

If New Castle itself wasn't a theme park, the Air Transport Command most certainly was. It struck me as not entirely tasteful to turn the most destructive war in human history into a dining "experience," but it also struck me as priggish to complain. All the local families out for a Sunday treat clearly were enjoying themselves, including the table of fourteen right next door, and there seemed no reason why I shouldn't, too. So I did.

I'd come to the restaurant after an hour's walk around New Castle. I'd have stayed much longer except that it was twenty-four degrees and windy. But I managed to walk out on the wharf, not far from the ferry slip where motorists departed for New Jersey until the Delaware Memorial Bridge was built; I could see that magnificent suspension span just a mile away, dominating the view to the north as the Delaware River worked its way toward Philadelphia. A historic marker placed near the wharf read:

LANDING PLACE OF WILLIAM PENN

Near here October 27, 1682, William Penn first stepped on American soil. He proceeded to the fort and performed livery of seisin. "He took the key, thereof, . . . We did deliver unto him 1 turf with a twig upon it. A porringer with river water and soil, in part of all."

I walked along Second Street and the Strand, along Delaware and Third streets, across the green. There I saw yet another indication of New Castle's remarkable if little-known history:

THE GREEN OR MARKET PLAINE

Laid out by Petrus Stuyvesant, Dutch governor, 1655. On this green stood the old jail and gallows. Here were held the great fairs and weekly markets from early times.

The residences and businesses were row houses. No doubt the town had been so tightly built because of its exposed position on the river; like the colonists of Jamestown and Flowerdew Hundred, those of New Castle huddled together in defense. I wondered as well if they might have built their town in the expectation that one day it would be a great city, and that land should therefore be used frugally. This hope was disappointed as Wilmington assumed domination of the state, with the result that New Castle was left a perfect miniature, a town of less than five thousand souls, every one of whom should count his lucky stars for the privilege of living there.

For years I'd thought that Cooperstown, New York, with its spectacular location on Lake Otsego, its leafy streets, and its majestic white frame houses, was the prettiest town in the United States. New Castle made me think again. In style the two are very different, Cooperstown tending to the Victorian and New Castle to both the Colonial and the Federal. Neither of them precisely fits the Norman Rockwell vision of the archetypal American small town, but then that vision was

always as much hokum as actuality; you can get close to it in
New England, when you find a town with white steeples and
autumnal leaves turning red and yellow, but out in the rest of
the country there is more variety than stereotype.

I'd never seen a town quite like New Castle—I liked it so
much that a few months later, when the temperatures were up
and the foliage out, I came back for another look—but in one
respect it struck me as typical of Mid-Atlantic small towns:
Its principal construction material is brick. The Norman
Rockwell vision calls for white clapboard, but drive around
the Mid-Atlantic as much as I did over all these months and
the chief impression you're left with is a jumble of red-brick
courthouses, red-brick churches, red-brick houses, red-brick
storefronts.

It's not hard to figure why. Take a look at the ground,
especially in the region's southern states. What you see there
is red dirt, or, if it has recently rained, red mud. In New
England the settlers found trees and built frame houses; in the
Mid-Atlantic they found red clay and built brick houses.
Never did they do so with more exquisite or loving artistry
than in New Castle, the perfect little town on the banks of the
great river.

9

THE WASP CATSKILLS

"I think I ought to check out the Greenbrier and the Homestead."

This was said during an autumnal lunch in Washington with Jim Conaway, oenologist and bon vivant, who knows just about everything about just about anything. His reaction was immediate and emphatic. "Absolutely," he said. "You've got to do it." He thought for a moment, then added: "What I hear is that these days the Greenbrier has the edge."

So that evening I said to Sue, "I'm thinking that as part of my travels I'll spend a few days at the Greenbrier and the Homestead. Would you like to take a couple of days off and come with me?" She was reading the evening newspaper, which usually occupies her full attention in the early minutes of the cocktail hour, and she'd just come home from another ten-hour day at the office. For five years she'd been absorbed by the tribulations and triumphs of starting her own business, and she was exhausted. Small wonder that she brightened up immediately. "I certainly would," she said.

So whereas up to now I'd been riding solo, this time I'd have company in the shotgun seat; the allure of the region's two most famous resorts was more than Sue could resist, so she arranged to let her staff run the office for a couple of days.

Meantime I got on the phone with the clerks at the hotels—it took three separate calls to hook up with a reservations person at the Homestead, not exactly an auspicious sign—and arranged to commit sums of money approximately equal to the annual budget of the state of Rhode Island in return for the privilege of spending two nights at each in March 1991.

A few days later confirmation slips arrived in the mail along with fat packages of literature, a perusal of which helped me identify the hidden urge that drew me to these historic inns in the Allegheny Mountains of West Virginia (the Greenbrier) and Virginia (the Homestead). Going to these places, I realized, is just the same as going to prep school, which I had done for six interminable years of my youth: You apply, you are accepted, you make a down payment, you are sent catalogues and lists of regulations, and finally you matriculate.

The catalogues came in the form of elaborate lists of the services offered by the resorts, most if not all of them sold *a la carte*. The sum of $294 a night at the Greenbrier and $290 at the Homestead would buy us a place to sleep as well as breakfast and dinner, under the Modified American Plan, but not much else. A walk through the grounds, a swim in the pool, a movie in the evening, a seat in the lobby: Any of these was ours for the asking, no extra charge. But a frame or two in the bowling lanes (*lanes,* mind you, not *alleys*), a round of golf, a spot of skiing or ice-skating, a set of tennis, a horse ride along the trails, a massage and mineral bath, a quick spin on a bicycle: for these and other pleasures of the mountain life there will indeed, dear sir, be an additional tariff.

Ah yes, life in the mountains. It may conjure up images of the quaint folk to be found in novels by Erskine Caldwell and John Ehle and Lee Smith, but those aren't crackers at White Sulphur Springs and Hot Springs, those are slickers. It did not take me long to realize that the $1,200 plus change I had budgeted for this little excursion would barely scratch the surface. "For your convenience," the Homestead unctuously advised us, "the hotel will add to each individual bill a charge of $11.00 per person daily," but went on to note: "No arrangements have been made for bellmen, doormen, locker attendants, bath attendants or room service waiters who should be rewarded at the guest's discretion when service is rendered." The Greenbrier put it more bluntly: "Service Charge—$11.75 per person, per day." It also added, somewhat mysteriously: "ABC Club Membership Fee—$4.75 per person for entire visit."

That wasn't the half of it. Quite apart from the various surcharges—"student fees," they called them in my prep school days—there were the regulations. The Homestead was brief and direct: "Daytime: Casual recommended. Walking shorts are permitted in the Dining Room for breakfast. Bathing suits and aerobic attire are restricted to spa area and guests are required to wear robes over suits when passing through the hotel. Evening: Men are required to wear coat and tie for dinner and in all public areas after 7 P.M. Jeans are not permitted."

The Greenbrier, by contrast, was in its requirements for "dressing to fit the occasion and the weather" at once officious, oleaginous, and encyclopedic. Where the Homestead contented itself with a paragraph, the Greenbrier went on for an entire sheet about "our dress code, established as a complement to the standards for which we are noted." Sounding for all the world like a corporate Uriah Heep, the Greenbrier offered "guidelines as to what our guests consider appropriate to wear when visiting us," as though the "guests" had formed the adult equivalent of Student Council and adopted a dress code to be "strictly enforced for the greater enjoyment of all guests." In essence the "code" was no different from the Homestead's, but in detail it was as baroque as anything inflicted upon me during three years at Woodberry Forest and three more at Groton. All that was missing was an admonition to have name tags sewn in my clothes.

The cumulative effect of these warnings about fees and codes was to put me in a dour and defensive frame of mind as Sue and I climbed into the SHO and motored through the Shenandoah Valley to White Sulphur Springs. As is my wont,

I spent the trip imagining and nurturing all the grievances sure to befall me at these rustic clip joints. We'd pull up to the Greenbrier and it would cost me $50 in tips just to get through the front door, then they'd take the SHO and valet-park it and throw the keys away; the modified bikini suit in which I swam my daily laps would be rejected by the indoor-pool apparatchiks as insufficiently modest and I'd have to spend $75 on a pair of madras boxers at the Swim Shop; the bottle of R. H. Phillips Chardonnay California I'd snuck into my exercise bag would be ferreted out by the doorman and I'd be hit with a $25 corkage fee, not to mention a $10 tip for the room service fellow who'd deliver the ice; I'd be thrown out of the dining room at breakfast for failing to wear a jacket over my sweater, and expelled from dinner for wearing a tweed jacket instead of a business suit or black tie.

By the time we rolled into the Greenbrier's driveway and caught our first glimpse of its immense white Georgian exterior, I was positively smoldering. I pulled up to the front entrance and leaped out of the SHO; I met the doorman's greeting with one of my own, but what I was thinking was, *"Wanna fight?"* He took our bags from the car, and I steeled myself for the bad news.

"Sir," he said, "the spaces in front of the hotel are taken, but if you'd like you can park your car in that guest lot off to the right."

I was dumfounded. "Do you mean," I stammered, "that I can park the car myself?"

"Of course, sir," he said.

I drove off in a daze, one that scarcely ended when the bellman took us to our room. This involved an excursion of approximately three miles, from the main lobby through a succession of corridors ending at an elevator in the bowels of something called the West Virginia Wing. We were taken to the sixth floor, then escorted to an immense room—subsequently I paced it off as approximately twenty-two feet square—to which were attached a similarly immense dressing room and bathroom. In a corner stood the obligatory minibar, atop which was perched an ice bucket.

"Uh, I assume I call room service for ice," I said.

"If you wish," the bellman replied, "but complimentary ice is delivered each afternoon by five."

You could have knocked me over with a modified bikini bathing suit, to which not a soul objected when I showed up at the indoor pool half an hour later. I was directed to the men's locker room, which seemed to have been transplanted intact from the New York Athletic Club, complete with complimentary combs and shoehorns and disposable razors, as well as dispensers for skin lotion, deodorant, and shaving cream. The pool turned out to be a swimmer's dream: a hundred feet in length, tiled throughout, with a lane set aside for lap swimmers. For an hour I had it to myself, swimming two of the happiest miles of my life. I was in heaven.

So was Sue. By the time I returned she had made an appointment for the next morning with the Greenbrier Spa Salon: "For the ultimate experience of total relaxation, you begin with a sulphur soak, then a stimulating swiss shower and scotch spray followed by special hydromassage to gently relieve muscle tensions and promote deep, inner release of stressful feelings. Next a steam session prepares you for a luxurious massage. Perfect Relaxation is completed with a soothing herbal body wrap to leave you feeling completely renewed. This is a 90-minute treatment. $85." She couldn't wait. As we strolled along the row of shops a few minutes later she said, "I could get used to this very easily," to which I replied, "Yes, and I could get used to someone else paying for it."

Over a glass of wine we watched the news and browsed through the thick stack of literature on the desk. There was a schedule of the day's activities; mercifully we were too late for the Greenbrier historian's presentation of "The Greenbrier, Past and Present," but should we prove sufficiently desperate we could watch Sally Field in *Not Without My*

Daughter at 8:45 P.M. in "the Theatre." There was also clarification of a small mystery: "Under West Virginia state law, an individual partaking of alcoholic beverages has to be a club member. The Greenbrier adds a nominal charge of $4.75 per person for the entire visit for such a club membership." That struck me as stealing from the blind, but what the hell: I raised my glass in a toast to West By-God Virginia.

In the dining room they let my tweed jacket pass without a word of complaint and the maitre d' showed us to our table without making a single move toward my wallet. Each of us was given the day's menu—"Dinner at the Greenbrier," printed on a single sheet of heavy stock—by a waiter who, like everyone else we'd encountered in the past five hours, had mastered the art of friendliness unencumbered by either servility or pomposity. The glasses of wine we ordered fetched a handsome price of $6.25 apiece, for which we could have bought a whole bottle of Phillips Chardonnay, but by now "What the hell?" had become my personal anthem. We dined on crab cakes and salmon tartare and romaine lettuce with garlic croutons and Seafood Medley Virginia and beef tenderloin and chocolate parfait, and at the end we staggered off to an early bedtime.

But sleep came slowly, so we turned on the television set and found our way to a local Public Television station. It was inflicting a fund-raising campaign upon its viewers and, for reasons known only to the geniuses in its programming department, was showing these residents of what may well be the country's most stubbornly Protestant state a ninety-minute special on Jewish-American humor. "Try it, you'll like it," the hosts kept saying, or words to that effect, while I amused myself with the thought of rockbound Clampitts staring at Lenny Bruce and Jackie Mason and Alan King and trying to figure out what planet they came from. But the show proved unintentionally edifying, for when we were reminded that for generations the Catskills have been known as the Jewish Alps, it came to me in a flash that here in the Alleghenies, we were in the heart of the Wasp Catskills. Small wonder

I felt so at home; the sleep into which I drifted was a blissful one indeed.

So it went for another thirty-six hours. I returned from my swim the next morning to find Sue in a state of utter euphoria thanks to the ministrations of the masseuse and other agents of Perfect Relaxation. We had lunch at Draper's Café adjacent to the Shop Arcade and then strolled around the premises; a tournament of sorts was under way at the indoor tennis courts and several golfers were out and about on the resort's three courses. I took another swim; we read for a while in the room, then had tea and cookies (complimentary!) in one of the innumerable public rooms; we ate another elaborate dinner, and another excessive breakfast the next morning. When, at checkout time, I was presented with a bill for $898.28, I even managed to contain myself, an act so uncharacteristic that Sue was rendered speechless.

The fifty-mile drive to the Homestead wasn't as advertised on my Triple-A map; what looked to be a nice straight shoot up U.S. 220 in the Virginia mountains turned out to be an exercise in hairpin twists and turns, fun for the SHO if not its driver. But my sense of imminent disaster quickly lifted when the famous red-brick tower of the Homestead hove into view, dominating the little hollow in the Warm Valley to which seekers of mineral-water cures have traveled for more than two centuries. I wasn't in the market for a cure, but I was eager to get into our room and discover how, if at all, the Homestead differed from its neighbor and competitor to the southwest.

It differed in a hurry, and a lot. The doorman who took our bags also took the SHO, though God knows where; I didn't see it again for two days. We were escorted to the front desk, off in a corner of the Great Hall, a cavernous room that nonetheless managed to achieve a striking degree of old-shoe intimacy; unlike the public rooms of the Greenbrier, which had a certain stiff convention-hotel quality to them, this room and the many others branching away from it seemed to have been transplanted from a wood-frame Victorian resort in New En-

gland, complete with sagging wing chairs and backgammon
sets and drafty windows and . . .

Everything except people. By contrast with the Greenbrier,
which was about half full at this slow hour in the calendar, the
Homestead never yielded more than a couple of dozen fellow
customers. I had asked that we be put in a room near the pool,
which indeed we were, but we seemed to be the only occupants
of the immense West Wing in which we were quartered. Our
room was large and had a loggia with a lovely view of the
lawn, the Homestead Golf Course, and the mountains, but the
furniture had an exhausted look and an excess of chilled air
managed to work its way through the windowpanes. Yes,
there was a minibar and free ice delivery and a pile of literature, but the carpet in the hall gave off that musty seaside
odor I'd smelled at the motel in Williamsburg and throughout
there was an air of the shabby genteel.

Oh, well, I thought, if any phrase fits me to a T it's "shabby
genteel," so go with the flow and enjoy. I put on my bathing
suit and the robe supplied by the hotel and set out for the
pool. This involved a descent in a creaky elevator, a trek
through a corridor even draftier than our room, and a complicated passage through the labyrinthine rooms of The Spa, all
of which were shrouded in a deathly silence. I peeked into the
men's locker room—no disposable razors, no deodorant, only
a battered scale—and at last found myself in the indoor pool,
accompanied by no one save two lifeguards who watched idly
as I did my swim. This was not an especially pleasant task,
inasmuch as the design of the seventy-five-foot pool was inhospitable to lap swimmers and the water was thick with
what appeared to be dirt, or tiny bits of fern leaves, or in any
event something of an alien and disagreeable nature.

I asked what it was, and was told that it was merely sedi-
ment from the two mineral springs—no wonder the white
cord on my bathing suit had turned brown—that feed directly
into the pool. They clean it twice a week, the lifeguards said,
leaving me to wonder silently why, for $290 a night, they
couldn't clean it once a day. But that was better than the next

morning, when, after a night of rain, I found the pool closed. Someone poked his head out of the recreation director's office and explained that heavy rains cause the mineral waters to cloud over, "which guests don't like," so the pool was being emptied, cleaned, and refilled. This time I was left to wonder silently why, in the age of high technology and $290 hotel rooms, some device couldn't be invented for shutting off the flow into the pool when rain began to fall.

Well. I got back to the room to find Sue similarly out of sorts. To test the Homestead's services she'd had in mind a trip to the Hair Salon and Barber Shop, where she proposed to treat herself to a manicure and—the first she'd ever had— pedicure. "All hair-styling services," the brochure promised; "facials, manicures, pedicures, available for men and women by appointment. Hair accessories available. Hair pieces serviced. Located on mezzanine." The only problem was that its phone didn't answer that afternoon, or the next day either; like almost everything else at the Homestead, it was shut tight.

That included the Dining Room, which we could only glimpse through closed doors; it looked handsome and inviting, though its great windows probably were letting in more chilly March air than they kept out. Instead we and the handful of other "guests" were directed to the Commonwealth Room, a mahogany-paneled place with a dance floor in its center. At seven that evening we were the only diners there, which may explain why the maitre d' greeted us with an excess of familiarity that doubtless would have been even warmer had a gratuity been forthcoming; but tipping maitre d's has never been part of my repertoire—I've never seen one *earn* a tip—which in turn may explain why our subsequent visits produced nothing chummier than a wintry smile.

The food? The food was all right, especially the crab cake appetizer and the baked salmon, but on the other hand the raspberry vinegar poppy seed salad dressing struck me as a silly *nouvelle cuisine* conceit and the chocolate cake—*Gateau au Chocolat Supreme*—was dry. The waiter was friendly and eager, but nothing he did could blind us to the spectacle unfolding before us. About half an hour after we arrived, by which time we'd been joined by perhaps a dozen others, the Dance Band from Hell limped onto the stage: a woman who played violin and gourds, though not simultaneously; a man, evidently the leader, who shifted from clarinet to baritone saxophone to tenor; a guitarist who contented himself with phlegmatic plunks; and a pianist who bore a startling, not to mention disconcerting, resemblance to the late General George Catlett Marshall, himself of course a Virginian of great distinction. This odd quartet attacked the stalest popular music of the past half century with immense determination, with surprisingly great noise considering its number, and with almost total lack of musical effect. It was impossible not to feel sorry for these feckless balladeers, emitting their noises into the vast and uncaring silence; it was also impossible not to wish that they would shut up and go away.

Our sleep was reasonably pleasant and restful, if broken from time to time by the hisses and clanks of the radiators, but the following day was cold and bleak; the rains that had closed the swimming pool had not cleared the skies. This to be sure was not the Homestead's fault, but on the other hand the "resort" offered nothing to help us through what proved an interminable day. The shops featured the usual run of over-priced boutique merchandise, none of which you'd buy were you at home and in your right mind, and in any event we'd seen all the same stuff in the shops at the Greenbrier; the rooms at The Spa may have been antique, but that is not an inviting quality in a health resort; our room was dank and so were the public rooms, save for the Great Hall, where two fireplaces worked against near-insuperable odds. I huddled in a chair near one of these and escaped into the amusing world of a novel by Christopher Buckley, while Sue retreated to the room and napped under a blanket. Dinner offered scant re-lief—yes, the band played "Feelings"—and when bedtime came I fled into sleep sure in the knowledge that it brought me ever closer to departure.

I rose with hopes of a swim—the recreation director had promised that the pool would be full by seven—but they were dashed. After racing through the early morning cold in bathing suit and robe, I found the pool still closed; perhaps two feet of water languished in the deep end, while the rest remained empty. No one was on hand to offer either explanation or apology. I went to breakfast in a foul humor, snarled at the maitre d', ate in a hurry. At the front desk, the bill—the damage—came to $708.01. I paid it silently, as Sue is properly embarrassed when I succumb to the temptation of public scenes upon such occasions, but as I did so I resolved that the Homestead had lost this customer for all eternity.

That's too bad. The place has a genuine period charm and in warmer weather the deficiencies of its insulation doubtless are of no moment; into the bargain no innkeeper should be held responsible for bad weather in a slow season. But a case can be made that precisely such conditions are the toughest and fairest test of a resort; if it can keep the customers happy when business is slow and the climate is inhospitable, it is doing its job. By such a test the Greenbrier proved itself admirably worthy; the Homestead flunked, just the way I did in prep school calculus.

Possibly it's all beside the point. A friend who knows about such things tells me that even with the punitive rates it charges, the Greenbrier loses money; it's kept afloat as a matter of pride by its owner, the CSX Corporation, he says, and if CSX is ever bought out that could mean the Greenbrier's end, or at least the end of the Greenbrier as we know it. Ditto, he says, for the Homestead, which evidently lacks either the money or the will—or both—to undertake the modernization of services and accommodations it so desperately needs. Perhaps both of these old places, one grand and one shabby, are just dinosaurs, lurching down the last steps of the path to extinction. If so, then I'm glad I caught a glimpse of them, warts and all.

10

SMOKY CITY

Thanks to the good offices of Sylvia Sachs, the book editor of the *Pittsburgh Press*, I had an invitation to speak in that city at a book-and-author dinner. I seized it gratefully and enthusiastically, not because I expected to reap any sales for the notably unimportant book I'd just published but because it provided an excuse to visit Pittsburgh for the first time since the summer of 1959. It is a city about which I knew almost nothing but for which I had uncommonly warm feelings: It was there, on October 27, 1939, that I was born.

This momentous event occurred in Pittsburgh because two months previous my parents had moved into an apartment at Shady Side Academy, across the Allegheny River from the city, where my father had accepted a position on the faculty. We were there for just under four years. This was at the time when Pittsburgh was celebrated, or notorious, as "The Smoky City," due largely to the steel mills that spewed out pollutants by the ton, giving Pittsburgh an air-quality index to rival that of any begrimed late-twentieth-century East European city.

My parents hated the soot and the bad air, and thus were eager to move on to another place, but Pittsburgh probably was never anything more than a stopover in their plans. Both

of them were East Coasters, a bias I have inherited notwithstanding my fondness for much of the interior American landscape. Thus my birth in the city was more accidental than
planned; had my father's career gone a bit differently, I could
just as easily have been born in Bedford, New York, where
presumably I was conceived, or Tuxedo Park, New York, to
which we moved in 1943.

So I was too young to have acquired anything in the way
of a native Pittsburgher's manner, tastes, and style. The city
hadn't made a dent on me, yet I retained a certain interest in
it. The same girlfriend whose parents had a summer place
outside Baltimore was a Pittsburgher, and I visited her there
in the summer of 1958; my chief memory is of beautiful old
Forbes Field and the first National League baseball game I'd
ever seen, in particular the massive biceps of the Pirates'
famous but over-the-hill first baseman, Ted Kluszewski. The
next summer I worked on a small railroad in the Alleghenies
and developed a deep admiration for the Pirates, who were at
last beginning a return to respectability after years of inferior-
ity, and when they won the 1960 World Series I was ecstatic.
But that, in sum, was all I knew of Pittsburgh.

I left home on a bright spring morning; flowers were bloom-
ing and the trees were beginning to sprout their leaves. Less
than a mile from our house, Roland Avenue was jammed with
cars and buses, bringing children to school. Most of the passengers in the buses were black kids, exercising their freedom
of choice in order to attend Roland Park Middle and Elemen-
tary School, one of the city's best public institutions. Most of
the cars—a disproportionate percentage of them Volvo wagons—were taking white kids to Gilman and Roland Park
Country, two of the most noted of Baltimore's numerous
private academies; the private school clientele in Baltimore
may well be proportionately larger than in any other city
outside New York, with an attendant and devastating lack of
support for public education among the city's most affluent
and influential residents—white *and* black.

I turned left on Northern Parkway, the six-lane road that

cuts across the top of the city from east to west, and rolled down the steep hill to its dangerous, congested intersection with Falls Road, at rush hour one of the worst spots in town. It took a few minutes to get through; I continued due west a couple of miles to the intersection of Northern Parkway and Park Heights Avenue. The latter was once the main thoroughfare for the city's Jewish community, but Park Heights Middle School, right there at the intersection, is now almost entirely black. The suburban scenes in Barry Levinson's wonderful film *Diner* and his far less successful *Avalon* are meant to take place in Park Heights, but the community they depicted has long since moved outside the city limits and Levinson had to do his filming elsewhere.

I followed that migration to the northwest: out Reisterstown Road to Pikesville, wealthy and predominantly Jewish, then beyond to the new walled developments springing up outside the beltway. Almost none of these existed when I moved to Baltimore in 1978; as recently as then, this was still farming and horse country and the preserve of the Garrison Forest School for Girls, behind its own walls off to my right. Now a few pristine fields gave testimony to the area's past, but you could almost see them shrinking as the shopping centers and "town homes" raced to grab up any available unspoiled land.

By the time I reached Reisterstown I was in old Maryland. It is a pretty little town, nine miles from the beltway, with unpretentious houses lining the road—red brick, painted brick, wood, some with modest columns—and a few antique stores. It had the look of a place that's just on the verge of being discovered by all the wrong people, who will open up their boutiques and their restaurants and their Saab dealership and who will ruin it faster than you can say "Laura Ashley."

Evidence of the impending invasion was on a sign right outside of town: COMING SOON, HUNT MILL ESTATES. This was on a piece of land surrounded by the handsome white fencing of the horse country, soon to become "estate" country. Here

the road was four lanes, far more than present traffic really
needed but clearly built in anticipation of commuters speeding from their quasi-rural nests to the offices of Baltimore.
Past Finksburg and I was in real country. That trailer park
on the left may have been a blot on the landscape, but it
looked a lot better to me than a "tract mansion" thrown up
to suit the vanity of a self-regarding, overprivileged stockbro-
ker and the hard-charging lawyer to whom he's married. The
next substantial town was Westminster, but I'd been there
before and I stuck with the bypass. It's an uncommonly
pretty town in which is located Western Maryland College,
one of the many little-known but very good private colleges
with which the states of the Mid-Atlantic are blessed: Hood,
Guilford, Franklin and Marshall, Bennett, Muhlenberg, Mary
Baldwin, Sweet Briar, Belmont Abbey, Wesley, Elon, Hamp-
ton . . . the list is long and distinguished.

I turned onto State Road 97. The map made it look like the
back route to Gettysburg, but it scarcely was a secret; traffic
was heavy and the truck in front kept me well under the speed
limit. Thirty-two miles out of Baltimore, I crossed into Pennsylvania and the hamlet of Littlestown: old houses with por-
ches and small columns, hugging the sides of the road—it was
a bit down-at-the-heels but didn't seem impoverished. The old
theater in the center of town now advertised "Auto Parts,
Washer Solvent"; a café nearby had been christened Heart-
break Hotel.

Five miles south of Gettysburg, looking off to the left I
could see the mountains for the first time; I'd be there soon
enough. Suddenly Route 97 widened from two lanes to four
and turned into Route 15, with not a single sign to announce
the event. Pennsylvania highway markings are incredible. A
decade before, Sue and I had run up into the state with friends
and, thinking to explore the byways south of Pennsylvania
Dutch country, went off on a side road. Within minutes we
were utterly, incredibly, and for a long time it seemed hope-
lessly lost. Scarcely a sign guided our way and when we did
find one it was either of no help or unintelligible. Some years

later I mentioned this in a talk to a group in Harrisburg; all
I got was a knowing laugh.

The approach to Gettysburg—Ike, its most famous
adopted citizen, called it "Jettysburg"—was surprisingly
pleasant considering all I'd read about the commercialization
of the battlefield. An observation tower beckoned me to that
hallowed ground but, with all due respect to those who fought
and died there, no thanks; nothing puts me to sleep faster
than a battlefield, unless it's a work of military history. I
passed Fields of Glory: Civil War Memorabilia and Gettysburg Toy Soldiers, now out of business. Right next to Robert
E. Lee's headquarters of July 1, 1863, stood General Lee's
Family Restaurant, featuring "Spirits & Salad Bar." Lincoln
Estates turned out to be a trailer park—nice touch, that, after
the "estates" of suburban Baltimore—and a rug shop was
called Carpetbraggers. A billboard for WFKI promised EX-
PLOSIVE CHRISTIAN RADIO, a fetching prospect indeed.

At last I reached my first important destination: U.S. 30,
the Lincoln Highway, the road that provided, until the opening of the Pennsylvania Turnpike in 1940, the principal connection between Pittsburgh and the East. For a few miles I
entertained myself with the thought that at some point my
parents must have taken me along this route to see my grandmother in Philadelphia, but I quickly realized that I almost
certainly was wrong. Even before the war came along and
gasoline rationing was imposed, most long-distance travel was
done by train, surely the means preferred by my sensible,
frugal parents.

After a few miles I couldn't imagine why anyone in possession of his faculties, given any reasonable alternative, would
choose to drive the Lincoln Highway. It was one of those
infuriating three-lane roads on which passing is even more
dangerous than on two-lane roads because the temptation is
so much greater. The speed limit was fifty-five but I was
stuck, as I would be for much of the day, behind a line of cars
and trucks going closer to forty-five.

At least I had time to look at the passing show. A barn with

CHEW MAIL POUCH TOBACCO painted on its side: How many years since I'd last seen *that* bit of Americana? Mr. Ed's Elephant Museum, with a plaster elephant outside: I drove on. A trailer by the side of the road: RSVP HEALTH SPA & MASSEUSE. What do you suppose goes on *there*?

On the outskirts of Chambersburg, twenty-four miles west of Gettysburg, I got to wondering: What about "inskirts"? Don't cities have them, too, the urban equivalent of petticoats? I looked in Webster's when I got back home, but found that no such word existed. Be that as it may, the outskirts and the inskirts of Chambersburg were indistinguishable, though I pulled up short at the sign outside Cressler's Market, which read, THE FUTURE IS NOT SOMETHING WE ENTER, THE FUTURE IS SOMETHING WE MAKE—roadside philosophizing of the most dubious validity.

The difference in the weather was striking. Baltimore had been heading for a day in the sixties as I left a few hours before. Here the air was raw, the temperature hung in the forties, and evidence of spring was far more difficult to come by. Save an occasional weeping willow, there was little green; the mountains off to my right were as bleak and forbidding as could be.

In those mountains the road suddenly turned curvy and narrow. At the top was the Tuscarora Summit Inn, elevation 2,123 feet, with a breathtaking view. I admired it, but couldn't help wondering what it had been like up here when U.S. 30 was the only road between Pittsburgh and Philadelphia.

An entrance to the turnpike loomed ahead. The thought of jumping aboard was just about irresistible, but reluctantly I decided to stick with the game plan. This was at Breezewood, famous among truck drivers throughout the East for the diners and motels clustered near the intersection of Route 30 and the turnpike. Sixteen miles farther west was the intersection with U.S. 220, a road I knew well during my years in Greensboro. These federal highways cover a lot more distance than we often realize; it had never in those days occurred to me that 220 went any farther north than Martinsville, Virginia.

A sign: NEW PARIS, 6 MILES. I wondered what grandiose hopes had inspired the founders of this remote settlement to name it thus, but got no help from the WPA guide to Pennsylvania, which listed New Bethlehem and New Philadelphia, but not New Paris. Nor did it list New Baltimore, which cropped up a few miles later.

Back in the mountains, I hit the day's high spot: Bald Knob Summit, elevation 2,906 feet. This was God's Country. The Indian Lake Christian Center advertised: "Jesus Is Lord." Soon I passed Camp Allegheny, of the United Methodist church. There was a lot of religiosity along this stretch of the road, far more than I'd ever have imagined. There's plenty of it, too, in the mountains of western North Carolina; maybe it has something to do with the air, or the proximity to the firmament.

The chilly air, the snow that still clung to the ground in patches, and the impressive altitude reminded me of the role these mountains play in the weather of Mid-Atlantic states to the east. Far too often for the good of Maryland and Delaware and southern New Jersey, all of which were troubled by low rainfall in the late eighties and early nineties, storms heading in from the northwest slam into the Alleghenies and spend themselves right there; Pittsburgh gets soaked and we get drizzled, if that. On the other hand it must be acknowledged that in the winter, while western Pennsylvania struggles under snow, we in Baltimore escape it; a typical January or February evening news weather report shows the Alleghenies dividing the nasty weather from the tolerable.

TRUCK ALERT: AVOID U.S. 30 WEST. STEEP HILL, SHARP CURVES. I didn't like a single word of that, but plunged ahead, past a public golf course with the ominous name of Sliding Rock. I slid along very nicely; for once in the course of this drive, Route 30 turned out to be far from as bad as I'd feared, and I came to the end of the danger zone unscathed.

On flat road, I got an unsolicited test of the SHO's antilock brake system. Going along at fifty or fifty-five, I simply didn't see a stoplight perhaps a hundred and fifty feet ahead. It turned red and I had to slam on the brakes. They responded as prettily as you please, bringing the car to an undramatic stop well short of the light. But then the SHO was doing everything I could ask or expect. I'd run it long enough now to have a feel for it, and I liked everything I felt except the Goodyear Eagle tires especially designed for it, which seemed to me to have poor traction on wet roads. In every other respect, though, the SHO—like Mother Taurus herself—proved that Americans really can make a world-class car, even if they do put a Japanese engine inside and license crooks to sell it.

Outskirts again, this time of Latrobe. I pulled into a fast-food place adjacent to a shopping center and got a hamburger. As I ate it, I gazed across the highway at Arnold Palmer Motors, an Oldsmobile-Pontiac dealer, and briefly contemplated the career of this son of the Mid-Atlantic: native of Labrobe, graduate of Wake Forest in North Carolina, winner of golf tournaments in, I suppose, every state of the region. He and his army were reaching full strength in the early 1960s, as my own modest career got under way. I'm no golfer—God forbid—but he is an admirable man. Latrobe's pride in him is understandable and just.

The rest of the drive was without incident or interest. The landscape grew steadily more urban and steadily uglier as I drew closer to Pittsburgh. Just east of the Smoky City, I picked up I-376, but was on it only briefly. I got off at the exit for the University of Pittsburgh and drove up Forbes Avenue. This wasn't just wandering, this was a mission. I'd seen something utterly unexpected on television a few days earlier, and I badly wanted to see it in person.

The area around the university reminded me a little of Waverley, the neighborhood in Baltimore between Johns Hopkins University's Homewood campus and Memorial Stadium—a little funky, pleasant, racially mixed, busy. I made a right on Schenley Drive, just across from the mildly preposterous, forty-two-story Cathedral of Learning that is the university's chief landmark, and miraculously found a parking space in a lot near my destination.

This was Forbes Quadrangle, a large, modern classroom building. I walked down a long corridor, looking intently at the floor. It didn't take me long to find it, embedded in the floor under a transparent cover. The plaque told all:

HOME PLATE—FORBES FIELD
FINAL GAME
Pittsburgh Pirates vs. Chicago Cubs
June 28, 1970

O lost, and by the wind grieved! I had seen the old park only once, but it had fixed itself irrevocably in my memory. Here were its grounds and its remains, of which the rest stood immediately outside: the old brick left-field wall, ivy climbing over it, the foul line and power alley measurements still standing out in large, bold numbers.

It would have been easy enough to feel sorrow or anger at the demolition of the handsome, historic park, but I felt neither. Like other buildings and like people themselves, ballparks come and go, often leaving nothing but memories, and fading ones at that. But someone at the University of Pittsburgh had had the good grace to preserve these two mementos, and thus to allow an old sentimentalist such as I to stand there, knowing exactly where I was.

I checked in at the Hyatt Regency Pittsburgh at Chatham Center. In the course of my wanderings I'd begun to accumulate a pretty impressive inventory of unsatisfactory lodgings; price considered, this took the prize to date. The women at the desk were friendly, but in the room, nothing worked. Furniture either had already fallen apart or was well along the way. The indoor pool was all right, though, and I got in a couple of restorative miles. By now it was almost dark; I had all the next day to walk around. So I had a drink, read the Pittsburgh papers, watched the evening news.

Then I got out my map and walked a few blocks to dinner. Sylvia Sachs had suggested several places to eat; I chose Klein's Restaurant & Seafood House, in business under one family's ownership since 1900, a much-beloved local institution, as eventually I learned. It was a splendid choice. I was put in a room dominated by several tables of women holding a farewell dinner for a colleague who was retiring from the staff at Kauffmann's, the department store that is to Pittsburgh what Strawbridge & Clothier is to Philadelphia; they were a mixture of ages and races, in high humor, chatting animatedly—all in all, excellent company. The swordfish— three hundred fifty miles from the ocean, *swordfish?*—won hands down the competition against the Old Original Bookbinder's that I'd set up in my mind; so too did the service and the ambience. Klein's was old-shoe, unpretentious, friendly— and delicious.

In the morning I took my walk. The heart of Pittsburgh— the Golden Triangle, as it's known in its post–Smoky City incarnation—was crowded with office workers. Banners hanging along the streets celebrated the city's sporting life: The Penguins, of the National Hockey League, were only a few weeks from winning their first Stanley Cup championship trophy, and the Pirates, who had won the National League East the year before, were set to open the baseball season in a matter of days. The mood was cheerful but the air was cold and the wind sharp.

The business district was dignified and prosperous, as befits a city that houses the corporate headquarters of more Fortune 500 companies than any other. One of the most famous of these is Pittsburgh Plate Glass, now occupying its glassy new buildings designed by Philip Johnson. Like the Allegheny County Courthouse and Jail a few blocks away, to which they allegedly pay homage, they are Romanesque and crenellated and massive. Pittsburghers take great pride in them, though whether because of their alleged architectural virtues or the mere celebrity of their architect is far from clear. I hated them. They seemed to me all too typical of Johnson's ventures

into postmodernism: self-conscious and self-satisfied, condescending to their surroundings, calculatedly fey rather than
witty.

But that was just about all I found to complain about in the
Golden Triangle. I walked out to Point State Park, where the
Allegheny and Monongahela rivers join to form the Ohio. Not
long before I had met a historian of landscape architecture
with whom, in the course of idle conversation, I discovered a
common bond: a capacity to be moved far more deeply by
landscape than by buildings or other human edifices. This one
moved me powerfully. This was the place where the West
began. I found it surprisingly easy to imagine away the
human clutter that littered the rivers' banks and to see my
surroundings fresh and unspoiled, as George Washington,
twenty-one years old and in the service of Virginia, saw them
in 1753: "I spent some time viewing the rivers, and the land
in the fork, which I think extremely well situated for a fort,
as it has the absolute command of both rivers."

That night I went to Kauffmann's for the book-and-author
dinner. I was startled to discover that in this age of suburban
department stores, several hundred Pittsburghers regularly
show up at Kauffmann's downtown store—tickets, in fact, are
at a premium—for the dubious privilege of listening to authors plug their wares. It was as friendly a group as I have
ever addressed, but by then I had concluded that Pittsburgh
was the friendliest of cities, hiding its financial and industrial
might behind the good manners and modest style of ordinary
America at its best.

My remarks that evening were of small consequence, but I
listened with the utmost sympathy and admiration to those
made by Michael Chabon, a gifted young writer of fiction. He
had made his reputation with a first novel bearing the lovely
title *The Mysteries of Pittsburgh*, in the process becoming
something of a local hero in the city where, at the University
of Pittsburgh, he had attended college.

He talked about his deep fondness for Pittsburgh and then
about the difficulty he had now, as one who had moved away,

in coming back. So much of the Pittsburgh he had known only a few years before, he said, already had disappeared. He thought of it as "lost Pittsburgh," and he spoke of it in terms and tones that clearly touched his listeners.

It occurred to me, thinking about Chabon's remarks as I drove away the next morning, that in talking about "lost Pittsburgh" he had touched on the commonality of experience that is so much a part of city life. The places whose names he had mentioned were things he shared with the people in that room, tiny yet essential elements in a conglomeration that, taken as a whole, is a place called Pittsburgh. I was glad to have had this small taste of it.

Day was just breaking as I entered I-376, heading east, but commuter traffic bound for Pittsburgh was already backed up to a near standstill. Within minutes I was on the Pennsylvania Turnpike, which I followed for thirty-four quick and uneventful miles before exiting at Donegal on State Road 381 South.

I was in the Laurel Mountains, popular for years among vacationers in Pittsburgh and environs. They had left their mark. Trailers and recreational vehicles were all about, though summer was still many weeks away. Roadside shops peddled the usual assortment of lawn decorations and other junk. Ramshackle houses with debilitated cars parked beside them lined the road. The area may have been popular but it certainly wasn't rich.

I'd left Pittsburgh with the idea of having a good country breakfast somewhere hereabouts, but it was a hope born of ignorance. Fool that I was, I'd passed up a McDonald's on the turnpike in the expectation that I'd find real food soon after making my exit, but no restaurant—good, bad, or indifferent—was in sight. I drove for miles. By this point a Coca-Cola and a Moon Pie would have suited me fine, but there wasn't even a gas station. I saw *two* signs for tanning salons, one called the Bear Run Tanning Salon, but none for food of any variety.

At last, several miles past my destination, the Falls Market Restaurant came into view. It offered everything from overnight rooms to "Ice Cream, Slush Puppies, Sandwiches, Pizza, Video Machines, Live Bait, Pure Mountain Honey, Gallicker's Fresh Hand-Dipped Ice Cream and Topographical Maps." It even offered coffee, orange juice, and toast—which in the circumstances tasted almost as good as that swordfish dinner I'd had at Klein's.

I got back in my car and drove along the Youghiogheny River. Its name—which is pronounced "Yock-a-ga-ny"—comes from the Shawnee Indians, who called it "the river that flows in a roundabout course," which certainly was accurate, but the locals have their own mythology, as described in *Pennsylvania: A Guide to the Keystone State*:

> Local residents, tongue in cheek, tell the following story concerning the name Youghiogheny. A white hunter and an Indian crossed trails in the woods. Both took cover, but the white, resorting to an old ruse, placed his hat on his rifle barrel and poked it above the embankment. The Indian fired, saw the hat fall, and approached incautiously. Leaning over his "victim" to take the scalp he uttered a grunting sound something like "yuck." The white man grabbed him, cried, "Yuck again," and inflicted a fatal wound. The fact is that the suffix "heny" is a corruption of the Indian *hanna*, river.

There was no mention in the *Guide* of the place where I was headed, indeed there was no mention of Mill Run, where it is situated. I was on a mission dating back to my teenaged years, when for a time I had been greatly interested in architecture. I belonged to one of the many book clubs from which, in those days, I acquired books without ever getting around to paying for them. As a bonus for joining this one—I think it was called the Reader's Subscription—I had received copies of a couple of retrospectives of the work of Frank Lloyd Wright, through which I pored, rapt, for hours; my Uncle Harry had once served as one of Wright's slave laborers at Taliesin, which gave me a wholly unfounded sense of familial connection with the great architect. But nothing I learned in those two books seems to have adhered permanently except a deep fondness for Fallingwater, the house Wright designed over a waterfall on a stream called Bear Run.

No doubt as a result of the obtuseness with which I am often afflicted, it had never registered with me that Fallingwater was in Pennsylvania, a four-hour drive from Baltimore. Wright was a Midwesterner; most of his greatest buildings were either in cities or in the West, and I assumed that this was true of the greatest of them all, Fallingwater. So I was genuinely surprised to read a newspaper story about day trips in the Baltimore-Washington area and to discover Fallingwater therein. Immediately I called and made a reservation for the $20 "in-depth" tour en route home from Pittsburgh.

On a breezy early-spring morning only five of us showed up at the appointed hour of eight. The others were a retired couple from Connecticut, passing by on their way home from Florida, and a young couple from Pennsylvania; it later developed that the husband in this pair was in construction and came to the tour with a professional's interest. We were met at the Visitors' Pavilion by our guide, a cheerful and irreverent man in his sixties who, when he learned that I would be writing about the day, asked that his name be kept out of it; too bad, because I liked him and would be pleased to give him full credit.

Even with the leaves still off the trees, Fallingwater could not be seen from the pavilion. We had a walk of several minutes through neatly tended grounds and then along Bear Run itself, which was coursing rapidly and quite noisily. Frequently, our guide told us, would-be visitors call and ask, "What time do you turn the waterfall on?" He also said that just yesterday a member of his tour had come to its end and chirped, "Why, this is just a theme park, isn't it?"

We left Bear Run and walked along a path. Without warning, there it was. I suppose that somewhere, sometime, I had seen a building more beautiful than this; as Ike once said in

another context, give me a week and I'll think of one. But
here before me was indisputable proof that a building could
indeed move me as deeply as a landscape.

No doubt much of what stirred in me had to do with the
sheer pleasure and astonishment of being at last in a place
about which I had thought and speculated for decades. But
after all that anticipation, Fallingwater could easily have
disappointed me, could have been, as so often happens, less
than I had imagined. Instead it was even more.

We started at the waterfall itself, first viewing it from the
bridge over Bear Run. Then we scrambled down some slip-
pery steps and stood on the rocks below, the cold water rush-
ing past the bottoms of our shoes as we looked up in
amazement. "I've been here thousands of times," our guide
said, "and this never ceases to astonish me. Each time I look,
I see something new." Looking for the first time, I saw that
Wright had done exactly what he set out to do: He had
brought about a perfect marriage of nature and man, a building so much a part of the landscape that it *became* the landscape. The great cantilevered decks leaning over the water,
the thick stone walls rising from the rock as though they had
evolved from it, the windows with their dark red frames—this
was as close to the architectural ideal as I had ever seen.

Inside there was more of the same. To be sure none of
Wright's houses is especially comfortable and his furniture, as
he himself admitted, is aggressively hostile to human wants
and needs. Never mind. The living room, its glass walls seeming to embrace the trees outside and bring them in—I could
have stayed in that room forever. Beside the massive stone
fireplace Wright had suspended a large metal ball. The guide
explained that if the owners wanted mulled wine, they simply
filled the ball and swung it directly over the fire. Mulled wine,
the sun slipping slowly through the trees, the water bubbling
below—some people have all the luck.

These people were named Kauffmann, Edgar Jonas and
Lillian Sarah. They were first cousins, the son and daughter
of, respectively, Morris and Isaac Kauffmann, who with two

other brothers, Henry and Jacob, established a haberdashery in Pittsburgh in 1871. They called it Kauffmann's, and in 1885 moved it to the corner of Fifth Avenue and Smithfield Street. It was in their store that I had spoken the night before. I had not made the connection until now.

In all the tour took about three hours. I dislike tours—as when driving, I prefer to set my own pace, usually faster than most people prefer—but I wanted this one to go on forever. We went through the small, antiquated kitchen—who in his right mind would want to "modernize" it?—and the compact but adequate bedrooms, all of them carved right into the woods. We walked through a striking passageway guarded by a Buddha perched on a throne of rocks, up a short rise, and into the guesthouse that both mirrored Fallingwater in miniature and provided a somewhat more humane and comfortable alternative to it.

I say more humane because Fallingwater is less a house than a work of art. If the Western Pennsylvania Conservancy, which now owns Fallingwater, should in its wisdom after seeing these words decide to present the house to me, I would accept with pleasure, but with no sense that living in it would be easy. It cries out for many of the comforts to which the modern age has accustomed us—easy chairs! queen-size beds! microwaves!—but to install a single one of them would be to corrupt Wright's vision. Beyond that, I suspect that living in a work of art—a *masterpiece*; no other word will suffice— would be in its way exhausting, not merely because of the sense of stewardship that would descend upon the owner but because all that greatness could become, in time, simply too much.

These thoughts were in my mind as I thanked the guide for his witty, informative tour and then stopped at the pavilion, where the shop was now open. I took out a modest membership in the conservancy by way of thanks for its good works. I bought Sue a pair of earrings sporting a Wright motif and, for myself, a copy of *Fallingwater,* a stunning coffee table book with text by the late Edgar Kauffmann, Jr., the original owners' only son, a bachelor who devoted much of his life to the preservation and maintenance of the house. It was a life well spent.

Now I was on my way home. A dozen miles through rolling country on 381 South and I hooked up with U.S. 40. Half an hour later I was in Maryland, headed east on the merged U.S. 40 and 48, just about to be redesignated as an interstate highway. It was the first time I'd been on the road since its reconstruction; the results were spectacular. The road was straight and fast, the views of mountains and fields bordered on the histrionic. At an elevation of 2,980 feet, I passed over Negro Mountain. *Maryland: A New Guide to the Old Line State* enlightened me:

> Negro Mountain . . . is in the northern portion of the Savage River State Forest. It was named to honor Nemesis, a black member of an expedition headed by Capt. Michael Cresap, one of Maryland's leading pioneers. The expedition was attacked on the mountain by a party of Indians, avenging the Ohio massacre of the family of their chief, Logan, an act that had been erroneously attributed to Cresap. The massacre led to a general border uprising in 1774, known as Lord Dunmore's War, after the governor of Virginia at the time. Nemesis, a giant of a man, was killed during the attack and is buried on the mountain.

The Crispus Attucks of Maryland, known now only to those lucky enough to chance upon his name in a book. But his monument is there, a mountain for a giant.

I was in Maryland's western panhandle, a slender piece of land between West Virginia and Pennsylvania, in one place no more than a couple of miles deep. I noticed that most of the cars on the road had West Virginia or Pennsylvania tags, evidence that this part of Maryland really has more in common with those states than with the rest of its own. Politically and otherwise, western Maryland is and has always been a stepchild, courted at voting time and then left to fight life's battles for itself.

I was just west of Cumberland. Hardly anyone was on the road with me; it was wonderful. Except for an occasional house or church, the countryside was empty of everything except its own natural grandeur. Every once in a while I rolled to the top of a rise or came around a bend and found myself presented with a vista so magnificent that I blurted out, "My God!" I found myself hoping that the people who live in this uncommonly beautiful place have a sense of gratitude for what they have been given.

In time it will be taken away. A sign pointed to an exit for Deep Creek Lake. Heaven knows that lake is lovely, but it is also within convenient driving distance of Baltimore and Washington. Weekend and summer houses are springing up along its shores, and the towns beyond are growing in order to meet the needs of those who own or rent them. The vans are coming, and the RVs, and the Volvos. From the factories of the Midwest, acid rain comes here at an annual rate of thirty-one pounds per acre. Soon we will be saying another farewell.

Now the mountains were behind me and, with them, the chill. I pressed the temperature button on the SHO's dashboard and discovered that it was seventy degrees outside; the turtleneck shirt and V-neck sweater that had seemed almost insufficient at Bear Run now seemed excessive. I slipped off the sweater, cut off the heat, and rolled open the sunroof. Spring was here.

U.S. 40 turned into I-70. I was on the run from Hagerstown to Baltimore, along with everybody else. State troopers were out in force, lending their weight to the fifty-five-mile-an-hour limit that Maryland foolishly insists on maintaining despite federal license to raise it to sixty-five. I stayed in the low sixties and out of harm's way.

At three o'clock I picked up the Baltimore Beltway, drove around the city's western edge, and then headed south on I-83. I took the Northern Parkway exit, turned left, and there I was: smack back in the middle of the same old traffic jam.

11

REUNION

Sue was in the shotgun seat again as I headed south, this time on a route that followed the Baltimore-Washington Parkway to the Washington Beltway to I-95 to I-85 and, at journey's end, Chapel Hill. The sobering occasion of my thirtieth reunion had arrived. It was the second weekend of May, time to go back to my favorite place on earth and to confront, once again, the astonishing changes that have occurred there since I first saw it in the spring of 1957.

Chapel Hill. The two words mean worlds to me. To say that the four years I spent there were the happiest of my life would be untrue, for I have had a fortunate life and have been happy most of the time in most of the places I have lived. It is true, though, that the satisfactions I have enjoyed as an adult almost certainly would not have been possible had I not had those four years at Chapel Hill. In that time, against the considerable odds that had been created by my own late-adolescent foolishness, I made the passage from irresponsibility to the beginnings, however tentative, of maturity.

For this as for much else, I have my father to thank. In the course of a prolonged teenaged rebellion I had compiled a miserable record at preparatory school and, even worse in his eyes, had fixed it in my mind to enter a career in radio or television. For these and other shortcomings I had been rejected not merely by Princeton but by Washington and Lee as well; the latter came as a particular blow to my father, as the *coup de grace* had been administered, reluctantly and apologetically, by an older man of whom he was particularly fond.

He had connections at Chapel Hill and proposed, at the eleventh hour, to use them. He hoped that the existence there of a department of radio, television, and motion pictures would lure me; presumably he further hoped that, once there, I would go on to more serious things. He was right; I was excited by the prospect of that line of study but took only one course in the department, going on to major, if indifferently, in English. But as it turned out, all he really needed to do was take me there and let Chapel Hill work its magic; it was love at first sight.

They call it, half humorously and half seriously, "The Southern Part of Heaven." As is especially clear if you approach it from the east or (as we did in April of 1957) from the north, it indeed sits upon a hill, a green place that seems, on a spring day, to have the softest and warmest air imaginable. When in 1792 the site was acquired by the state for construction of the nation's first state university, it was a crossroads with no name. Thus it became, simultaneously, both a university and a town, and the two have been synonymous ever since.

The university's founders, John V. Allcott writes in *The Campus at Chapel Hill: Two Hundred Years of Architecture*, "envisaged the university at its own special place, the seat of higher learning for the state, requirements for which were set forth in the charter: 'a healthy and convenient Situation which Shall not be situate within five miles of the permanent Seat of Government or any of the places of holding Courts of Law or Equity.' " Allcott further writes:

> The location of what would become Chapel Hill fulfilled these requirements. In the central part of North Carolina,

between established towns along the coast and later settlements among the mountains, Chapel Hill was a "Convenient
location." As the intended home for youths in training to
become good citizens, learned men, and statesmen, Chapel Hill
was a mentally "healthy" spot, well out of sight and sound of
squabbling lawyers and politicians in "the Courts of Law or
Equity" at Raleigh and the Orange County seat at Hills-
borough.

It was a school primarily for North Carolinians, out-of-
state enrollment being limited to 15 per cent, though admission for outsiders was not so difficult in my day as it is now.
In the mid-fifties the university was trying to enhance its
national reputation by using its many charms to bewitch
students from the preparatory schools of the Northeast—
students who would otherwise have followed predictable
paths to Harvard and Princeton. That I was not of this caliber
is self-evident, but I did have both the unenthusiastic im-
primatur of a leading prep school and, more important, convenient connections through my father with men of influence at
Chapel Hill. Somehow—I have absolutely no idea how—a
place was found for me.

The Chapel Hill at which I matriculated in August of 1957
had a student body of about six thousand; the town itself was
approximately twice that size. All the dormitories were within
easy walking distance of the historic central campus and its
four emblematic Colonial structures: Old East and Old West,
South Building, and the Old Well. Freshmen were expected to
live in dormitories, which were crowded; mine had three boys
in a space no larger than twelve feet by fifteen, which helps
explain why I joined a fraternity as soon as possible and
moved into a room there at once. Coeds were second-class
citizens; girls were not allowed to enter until their junior year
and were confined to their own dormitories or sororities.

It may have been "the seat of higher learning for the
state," but my seat for the first month or so was at the Tempo
Room, a subterranean dive off Franklin Street in the heart of

town that sold beer by the pitcher and played recordings by
the musicians who were and are at the very heart of my life:
Duke Ellington, Gerry Mulligan, Miles Davis, John Lewis,
Milt Jackson, Bob Brookmeyer, Count Basie. . . .

Yes, I was wasting my time; I should have been in class.
But education of another sort was under way. For all of my
eighteen years I had been isolated and protected, first within
my family's loving embrace, then within the suffocating ones
of the two preparatory schools in which I spent six long years.
I needed a taste—more than a taste—of life's racy and rambunctious sides. Chapel Hill was just the place to get that.
Along with its neighbor and rival a couple of hundred miles to
the north, the University of Virginia, it was celebrated in the
journalism of the day as a "party school." In a great gulp of
partying, I made up in a hurry for all that lost time.

Yet there was other, more serious learning too. Not so much
in the classroom—I had always been edgy and impatient in
class, and this Chapel Hill failed to change—but in the offices
of the *Daily Tar Heel*. The only gift of note that anyone had
as yet detected in me was an ability to put words together; it
occurred to me that the student newspaper might be the right
place to put that gift to work. I wrote a letter to the editor.
It was published and in time led to an offer to write regularly;
I accepted it, and in so doing began the work of my lifetime.

The *Daily Tar Heel* became my real university. Its offices
were in four small rooms on the second floor of Graham Memorial, the student union. The staff was tiny; journalism had
yet to become a fashionable career so most of the time the
editor was out begging for help. During my four years on the
paper the basic editorial work was done by a core staff of not
much more than a dozen, most of whom were unpaid for their
labors.

The unsurprising result was that we were a close, clannish
group. We started drifting over to the offices in late morning
and stayed there until early evening, when one or more of us
drove to the printing plant owned by the *Chapel Hill Weekly*
and supervised the makeup of the next day's four, six, or eight

broadsheet pages. Then, around ten, we gathered at a couple of tables in Harry's, an indescribably seedy place on Franklin Street, to eat bad sandwiches and drink pitchers of beer.

It was a lousy life; I loved every single minute of it. My colleagues were the best friends I'd ever had. I was changing from a boy whose notions of his own life were hazy at best into one who knew exactly what he wanted to do and couldn't wait to start doing it.

But if the *Daily Tar Heel* was the center of my little world, there was much else in it. I loved the football games in Kenan Stadium, a large bowl crowned by a ring of majestic pines. Making my way across campus I might be accosted by Otelia Connor, a tiny old woman who made a career of upbraiding students on the niceties of manners. At Y Court, between South Building and Garrard Hall, I drank Cokes and swapped gossip. I actually became friends with a few teachers, notably David Henderson in the classics department, David Orr in English, and Peter Walker in history. I developed previously undetected social skills—it was in my junior year that I met the girl who became my first wife—and even became president of something called the Germans Club, which presented dances and concerts. I bought records at Kemp's, books at the Intimate, magazines at Jeff's, pizzas at the Rathskeller, clothes from Milton's, Sunday breakfast at Sutton's Drugstore. I never had a car; it never occurred to me that I was entitled to one. If I got rock-bottom broke, as often I did, I'd hitchhike over to Durham with John Colescott; we'd take the tour of the R. J. Reynolds tobacco plant and walk away with complimentary packs of cigarettes, enough to tide us over until morning. I watched basketball games in Woollen Gymnasium; the foldaway wooden stands were so close to the court that players and students were what they're supposed to be, one and the same.

It was a tight, intimate, self-contained place, one more attuned then to its Southern roots than to those in the Mid-Atlantic. There was only one black undergraduate; he was isolated from the rest of the campus in his own separate quarters. The civil rights movement began to make itself felt during my tenure—it was in Memorial Hall that I first heard Martin Luther King, Jr., speak, an event that shivered many of the local timbers—but not until my senior year did it start to seem really, genuinely possible that Chapel Hill would be able to alter the ingrained racial habits of the past.

But candor, rather than nostalgia or sentimentality, compels me to say that discrimination and prejudice were the only flaws in my Chapel Hill. The lens through which I view it may be misty, but what I see was real: the glow of pure happiness.

I left Chapel Hill in the spring of 1961, but hardly for good. From 1964 to 1974, while living an hour away in Greensboro, I was a frequent visitor: for football and basketball games, for journalistic meetings and seminars, for weekends with Peter and Daryl Walker—for any excuse I could invent. Then in the 1980s both of my sons were enrolled there, so I visited as often as permitted by the greater distance between Baltimore and Chapel Hill.

These visits pleased me enormously, but they also troubled me. Chapel Hill in those years grew not merely at an alarming rate but with little evidence of any controlling intelligence, on campus or off. In order to accommodate an enrollment that rose rapidly to twenty-four thousand, the campus threw up new buildings, some of surpassing ugliness, willy-nilly. The integrity of the old main campus remained essentially untainted, but all around it were high rises of undistinguished modernity and lower buildings of Williamsburgish neo-Colonialism. In order to get from the new campus to the old, students disinclined toward long walks had to ride jitneys. Parking, never easy even in my day, became insane. A second deck was added to Kenan Stadium, compromising its unique beauty, and one new basketball arena was quickly replaced by another so grandiose as to make a mockery of the proper relationship between athletics and academics.

Off-campus, matters were no better. Franklin Street, once a place of considerable small-town charm, was appropriated

by the vendors of souvenirs and tie-dyed clothing. Like Raleigh twenty-five miles away and Durham just down the road,
Chapel Hill fled to the suburbs and the shopping centers. By
1990 its population was just under forty thousand, many of
them retirees lured by such college town atmosphere as remained and by a climate where spring had always seemed to
arrive two weeks before it reached anyplace else. Traffic was
a nightmare; the Route 54 Bypass made a mockery of its
name, reduced as it was to gridlock during what seemed a
perpetual rush hour. Condos and "town homes" sprang up so
fast it was impossible to keep track. A new leg of I-40 passed
within a couple of miles of the campus, enhancing both the
accessibility of the university to the wayfarer and the auto
population of the entire area.

The result of this was that my feelings about Chapel Hill
became somewhat unpleasantly complicated. On the one
hand my love for the place I had known as a young man was
undiminished. But on the other hand I became convinced that
my generation was the last to have known what I thought of
as the "real" Chapel Hill—the "academical village" where
everyone knew everyone else and all was writ small. I came to
see Chapel Hill as yet another of my favorite places that had
been destroyed by an excess of popularity and the unreined
forces of what passes for progress.

Thus it was that I made this most recent trip in what had
come to be my standard state of apprehension. It was com-
pounded by the edginess that occasions such as reunions bring
out in me. Until my twenty-fifth, in 1986, I resisted all invita-
tions to rejoin my class; the excuse I offered was that I'd had
more friends in other classes than my own, but the real reason
was shyness in crowds. In 1986, though, I had no choice, for
my reunion coincided with the graduation of my elder son,
Jim, an occasion that I could not imagine missing.

So I joined the reunion, and of course I had a wonderful
time. In great measure this was because, inexperienced as I
was at reunions, I had not known that one of their great
virtues is their capacity for surprise. I learned that one at-

tends a reunion in dread that too few of one's real friends will be there, but that in fact this makes no difference. If old friends aren't to be had, you simply make new ones. The shared experience of being in the same class at the same place is enough to get people talking, and the gradual unfolding of mutual interests does the rest. That had happened to me at Chapel Hill in 1986—Sue and I had come away from the twenty-fifth reunion with several new friends—and I looked forward to it happening again.

There was yet another inducement. My *Daily Tar Heel* associate editor, Mary Stewart Baker, decided to come over from her adopted home of Israel with her husband, Herb Krosney. I hadn't seen the Krosneys for a quarter century; Sue had never met them. If they could come all the way from Israel, certainly we could find a way to drive three hundred miles from Baltimore.

We were in Chapel Hill by mid-afternoon, but we weren't in Chapel Hill at all. We could find accommodations no closer than the glossy new Sheraton Imperial Hotel & Towers, a dozen miles away just off I-40. It was a high-rise business hotel, its real market being not Chapel Hill or the university but the think tanks of the Research Triangle nearby; at the risk of seeming a dewy-eyed old grad, the word *imperial* somehow doesn't seem to me to have much to do with Chapel Hill.

Oh, well. In late afternoon we drove to the university, somehow found a parking place, and walked to Carmichael Field, adjacent to Carmichael Auditorium, the arena that had been built after my graduation but had been discarded as outmoded in the late eighties. We were there for what the Alumni Association insists on calling "Friday Frolic":

> Outdoor social and supper for the Classes of 1934, 1935, 1936, 1937, 1941, 1946, 1951, 1956, 1961, 1966 and members of the Old Students Club. Beer provided with the compliments of Reunion Class Presidents and Reunion Committees. Each Reunion class will have a designated tent at which class members

will gather. Live music by the Shady Grove Band. Degree
candidates and their parents, all Carolina alumni, faculty and
friends also are invited. Tickets at $12.00 each are required and
may be secured from any Reunion Registrar or at Carmichael
Field. In case of rain, events will be held on the concourse of
Carmichael Auditorium.

It was more fun than that description would lead one to
expect. Of course there were the usual strained efforts at
conversation with people I hadn't seen for five years, few of
whom I'd known well, if at all, while I was in college. It
seemed to me appalling that out of a class of about fifteen
hundred, only thirty-five actually showed up. Perhaps because they're dulled into complacency by the regular bestowal
of state appropriations, public universities don't do the energetic job of alumni stroking that private ones do, with the
result that all too few are inspired to show up for reunions or
to contribute to fund-raising campaigns.

Gradually, though, our tiny band of loyalists got back into
sync, a process helped not merely by the beer but by the
barbecue that was being ladled out along with the necessary
accompaniments—slaw, hush puppies, sweetened iced tea. It
was authentic Piedmont barbecue, greasier than the pigs who
gave birth to it and tastier than anything on the menu at the
Four Seasons. I came close to taking a fatal dose.

The next morning we met Herb and Mary Stewart Krosney. Except for a few becoming streaks of gray in her hair,
Mary Stewart hadn't changed a bit; she was still the tall,
pretty, inquisitive, gentle person whom all the boys on the
Tar Heel had loved. We caught up on a quarter century's
worth of news, then drove to the campus. Mary Stewart
hadn't seen it for thirty years. I'd warned her at breakfast
that she was in for a shock, but feared that there scarcely
could be warning enough.

We started to walk. It was just another beautiful day in
Chapel Hill. As the local saying has it, "If God isn't a Tar
Heel, why is the sky Carolina blue?" The trees had reached

their full, mature green. Wilson Library, facing South Building across the grassy rectangle lined on both of its long sides with red-brick academic buildings, loomed as imposingly as ever it had, its great stone walls and columns bearing the full gravity of higher education. To its right was a cluster of buildings Mary Stewart had never seen: the undergraduate library, the student stores, the student union—squat, modern edifices surrounding a concrete "pit" that has replaced good old Y-Court as the center of undergraduate socializing.

"See how hideous it is?" I all but snarled, but Mary Stewart was having none of that. Instead she marveled at the wide selection of titles in the bookstore, at the services offered by the student union, at the newness and the vastness of it all.

"Talk about ugly!" I muttered as we passed the new Davis Library, a red-brick high rise, but she wasn't having any of that, either. Instead she was amused by the peculiar metal sculptures—they purported to represent typical students—right outside its main door.

We walked past Carr, a Romanesque dormitory dating to the turn of the century, and the Playmakers Theater, built in 1852 though much remodeled since. I had to admit, however grumpily, that they looked pretty much as they had thirty years ago, though I made a point of remarking on the excessive amount of space in the immediate area given over to parking. Mary Stewart said everything looked wonderful.

On and on we went. I groused and Mary Stewart exclaimed. Passing Spencer, the vaguely Colonial dormitory where she lived during her junior year, she waxed almost literally rhapsodic, caught up as she was in a web of memory. It was the same at Graham Memorial; the old offices of the *Tar Heel* were locked—along with everything else, the *DTH* had moved into the new student union years before—but she clearly was delighted to be able to show Herb the place in which she had spent so many happy, productive hours.

By now it was beginning to dawn on me: If I let myself see Chapel Hill through Mary Stewart's eyes, I could see it more clearly and accurately than through my own. I had allowed myself to be blinded, by the changes in Chapel Hill, to the unaltered essence at its core. Chapel Hill was a different place—it wasn't "my" Chapel Hill anymore—but it was still Chapel Hill. However saddened I might be by the growth and the gridlock and the bad architecture and the decline of Franklin Street, not to mention the insidious presence within the humanities departments of deconstructionists and other nihilists—despite all of these things, the place was at its heart still the same. Mary Stewart had seen it for three decades only in her mind's eye, yet was neither shocked nor offended by the changes she saw; she was able to understand that what had happened to it was necessary if imperfect accommodation to the new realities of a more populous world, while I was the prisoner of what, I fear, looked very much like mere nostalgia.

As we walked I thought about this, which led in turn to the realization that to my sons, Jim, of the Class of 1986, and Bill, of the Class of 1989, Chapel Hill meant every bit as much as ever it had to me. Didn't it stand to reason, therefore, that it had given them the same things, if in somewhat altered form, that it had given me? Yes, the place was bigger and less intimate and more crowded, but it still taught the same lessons and still inspired the same loyalties.

I was in debt to Mary Stewart for that little lesson of my own, though I'm only now getting around to thanking her for it. At the moment I was more preoccupied with what we saw as we left the campus and walked along Franklin Street. Kemp's was gone, a fast-food shop in its place. Harry's was gone, replaced by a characterless restaurant called the Four Corners, in honor of a basketball strategy popular hereabout in the 1970s. The Tempo Room was gone; the sign over its dingy door said, FRANKLIN ST. BAR & GRILL. Town & Campus, a prosperous clothier of my day, was out of business, its storefront vacant. Milton's, which once thought of itself as Brooks Brothers South, was one step removed from a discount house. Tacky souvenir shops were everywhere, peddling T-shirts ("DOOK Is Still a Four-Letter Word") and clothing ("Buy a pair of champion shorts and get a FREE T-shirt!")

and auto tags ("UNC-USA") and even plain old Carolina sweatshirts.

It was all too much for me. I nudged my companions into the Carolina Coffee Shop for lunch. Nothing in it had changed except that in the front room there was now a bar, liquor-by-the-drink having at last been approved by the people of North Carolina; not every change in Chapel Hill had been for the worse.

There was one last stop to be made on Mary Stewart's tour. It was a first for me, too: the Dean E. Smith Student Activities Center. This vast edifice, built at a cost of about $25 million, all of it forked up by alumni and others known collectively as athletic supporters, sat at the far end of the new South Campus, surrounded by tennis courts and parking lots and high-rise dormitories. Immediately next door was the swimming pool, or natatorium, a mere glimpse of which left me thunderstruck; its indoor pool seemed to go on forever, the blue water reflecting the Carolina blue decor of its walls.

But the Dean Dome, as it is called, was something else altogether. Though it is used occasionally for concerts and various university activities, its designation as "student activities center" is nothing but a euphemism. It is a basketball arena, pure and simple, named in honor of a basketball coach who not merely became a legend in his own lifetime but had the poor taste—it is described by those who know him as out of character—to permit a building to be named in his honor while he was (and is) still on the job.

The building was tightly guarded; apparently the "activities" undertaken there do not include free and easy entry by students and other mere mortals. But a special exception had been made that afternoon for alumni, who entered with much the same reverence as is inspired, a few miles away, by the immense Gothic chapel at Duke University. In the secular religion of public education, the Dean Dome is a cathedral, a place for the communal worship of hired horseflesh masquerading as "student-athletes." A disproportionately large number of the parishioners are not students at all but the aforementioned athletic supporters: overpadded middle-aged men, all got up in blue-and-white Carolina apparatus, who made their fortunes in textiles and real estate and development and who now choose to spend some of their money by acting like superannuated adolescents. Sitting in one of the padded blue seats, looking down a mile or so to the parquet floor below, I imagined that I could hear them all, howling and baying in the night.

That evening we gathered in circumstances far more to my liking. A couple of years earlier my classmate Bettie Ann Everett had moved to Chapel Hill with her husband, Spencer. They had bought an old house in the country some miles out of town, fixed it up handsomely, and settled down. Now they were playing host to our thirtieth-reunion dinner—an incalculable improvement over our twenty-fifth, which had been held in the icily institutional quarters where, when school is in session, the "student-athletes" are served their high-octane fuel. It was a perfect spring evening, warm enough for a light dress, cool enough for a jacket. All told there were about seventy of us, spouses included; I had known only a handful of them during our mutual schooldays. But slightness of acquaintance was no barrier to easy, friendly familiarity. After all, we'd spent four years together at the same place.

No doubt this is true of any group of people who attended any college at the same time—or served in the same army unit, or played in the same band, or sailed on the same cruise ship. But the place where I had this shared experience was Chapel Hill, and thus I tend to think that the feelings it arouses in me are peculiar to Chapel Hill. It is hard for me to imagine that seventy people gathered under similar circumstances in Charlottesville or College Park could have the same feelings, though of course they can and do. It is simply that in my mind to have spent four years at Chapel Hill marks a person both indelibly and uniquely, and affords to him or her a bond with anyone else who was at that same place in that same time—a bond that transcends all differences of character, personality, and occupation. We had a good time that

night because we liked each other and found things to talk
about, but mainly we had a good time because we were back
in Chapel Hill.

At the dinner's end some continued on into the night at an
occasion with the egregious name of "Hallelujah on the Hill,"
a "special 'homecoming,' graduation, and reunion live-music
dance featuring the Bill Bolen Band," held in the cafeteria of
an especially grotesque off-campus student residence called
Granville Towers. Sue and I hated to say a relatively early
good-night, but we had an early wake-up call, and in any
event, as in such circumstances Sue invariably acknowledges
with a resigned sigh, I won't dance.

Nor did we go to the commencement exercises, which began
at ten the next morning in Kenan Stadium. I had attended
my own thirty years before, and with Sue had attended both
Jim's and Bill's. I knew exactly what would happen and could
see it in my mind: the west stands filled with parents and
friends; the soon-to-be graduates pouring across the green
field in a riotous parade, pausing in mid-passage to toss foot-
balls or form pyramids or throw each other in the air; the
interminable procession of individual candidates for advanced
degrees, followed by the mass conferral of bachelor's degrees,
in turn followed by a stadiumwide launch of bright blue mor-
tarboards; the heat building up as the ceremony drags on, and
at its end the merciful escape into the cool trees beyond, and
the snapshots, and the hugs, and the hurrahs.

I knew as well that the best part of the new Chapel Hill
would be on display. Among the parading degree recipients, as
well as among those watching them from the stands, there
would be not just a sprinkling of black faces but a representa-
tion far more than merely token. Nothing that my old school
has done in the three decades since I left it has given me
anywhere nearly so much pleasure as the progress it has made
toward making itself open to all not merely in name but in
fact. I do not minimize either the difficulties it has encountered or the accomplishments that remain as yet incomplete,
but on balance I am satisfied that it has made a good-faith

effort not merely to meet the letter of the law but to do so with spirit and commitment.

The next morning we were up at six and on the road by seven. I left in high spirits. I had had a happy time with old and dear friends in a place that I love, and thanks to one of those friends my feelings for the place had been renewed and replenished. What I learned through her about the inevitability of change and the wisdom of accommodation to it was as valuable a lesson as any Chapel Hill itself had taught me.

12

BY THE BEAUTIFUL SEA

The road was flat and empty. We were east of Raleigh now, on the same stretch of U.S. 64 I'd traveled as I began my slow trip home after election night. We'd left the Sheraton before its restaurant opened and were starting to get hungry. For a few minutes I had visions of a repeat performance of my search south of Pittsburgh for a real country breakfast, but I should have had more confidence in eastern North Carolina. We found just what we wanted in an unprepossessing place where half of Nash County seemed to have gathered for fried eggs, sausage, and grits; we packed away enough cholesterol to last the rest of the new week and kept heading east, toward the sea.

A third of the way, at Princeville, the road shed two of its four lanes; for the rest of the way we were on straight, fast coastal road. Too fast. I thought to pass a kid in front of me. I did, then a moment later glanced in the rearview mirror and noticed a car peel out from the middle of a line of cars that had just gone by in the opposite direction. Foiled again. Sixty-nine miles an hour, the officer said. He chatted amiably about my fellow Carolina alumnus Michael Jordan, the eminent basketball player, but he wrote my ticket all the same: $51 for the greater glory of Tyrrell County.

It was going to take more than a traffic citation to wipe the
glow off my day. A few miles ahead, just north of Frying Pan
Landing, we crossed the Alligator River. The first time I'd
seen it, nearly a quarter century before, a storm was blowing
in off the ocean so hard that the water was washing over the
bridge; I turned around smartly, found a room in a gruesome
motel, and made the passage the next day. This time the
water was calm. We raced over the bridge—"What's the big
hurry, sir?" the officer had asked—and into Dare County.

Here's the big hurry: A year after our previous visit, we
were returning to what in recent years had become our Mid-
Atlantic home away from home. We took U.S. 158, the fast
route up the shore from Nags Head to Kitty Hawk, made a
quick stop at the Food Lion to stock the refrigerator, and ten
miles later checked into our regular room at the Sanderling
Inn: second-floor corner, oceanfront.

They don't call it Mid-*Atlantic* for nothing. It's tempting to
think of the region in terms of Virginia's rolling hills and
Pennsylvania's mountains, but the fact is that five of its seven
states have their eastern borders on the Atlantic Ocean. From
Ocean Isle at the region's southern end to Highlands Beach at
the north, it contains many of the best beaches on the East
Coast. Their water is neither as steamy as that of the Florida
beaches nor as icy as those of New England; like almost
everything else about the Mid-Atlantic, it's moderate.

Over the years I've visited many of these beaches, prefer-
ring as I do the seaside to the mountains as a source of rest and
recreation. Oddly enough I never joined the annual spring-
time migration from Chapel Hill to Wrightsville, Topsail, and
Carolina Beach—or, just over the border in South Carolina,
Myrtle Beach. During my Greensboro years I tried Atlantic
Beach, Ocean Isle, Wrightsville, and Nags Head; Sue and I
stayed briefly in Nags Head at the famous old Carolinian
oceanfront hotel, then well along the way to decrepitude; as
mentioned earlier, we like the New Jersey town of Stone
Harbor, both for its quiet and for ocean water that remains
pleasant well into September.

But more often during the 1980s we drove to Cape Cod for seaside vacations, though each year I complained noisily about the ghastly drive through the Northeast. Then, in 1988, I chanced upon the place that quickly became our own, in mind if not in fact. I was in the final stages of a book and needed a week of solitude to wrestle with a couple of problems it was giving me. I looked in the AAA guide to North Carolina and found a highly flattering listing for a place I'd never heard of, the Sanderling Inn, in a town about which I knew almost nothing, Duck. I made a reservation and drove there in early March.

The minute I entered my quarters, I knew I'd found just what I was looking for. The huge square room—each wall was nearly twenty-five feet long—was lined with windows on its eastern and southern sides: not the hermetically sealed windows you now find in many motels but real windows, the kind you raise and lower, with wooden shutters. I had my own balcony looking over the dunes directly onto the Atlantic, a dining table in one corner and a miniature kitchen in another, a beach towel and robe in the bathroom, and a huge, comfortable bed. There was a vivid reminder that I was in North Carolina: The room had six ashtrays. In the bright, vaulted second-floor lobby, just a few paces from my room, were dozens of magazines, hundreds of books, numerous games, and easy chairs.

At this moment in the off-season I had the place almost entirely to myself. Mornings and afternoons I worked, the sound of the sea providing a soothing rhythm in the background. At lunchtime I ate in the inn's exceptionally good restaurant, then took long walks on the deserted beach. I went to bed early, slept well, and returned home fully rested, eager to finish the job at hand.

I also went home with the receipt for a deposit I'd made on a return visit, with Sue, whom I'd telephoned and told, in an interminable hymn of praise, about the inn's glories. When we made that visit, in the fall, she was every bit as taken with the inn as I. We quickly came to think of it as "our place," returning for stays of as long as ten days in May or September, enjoying not merely all the pleasures of the inn but also those of a substantial off-season discount. If it wasn't quite the same as renting a house, it offered to two working people the not-inconsiderable relief of letting someone else make the bed and clean up; if having only a single room seemed cramped, it *was* a large room and in any event one of us could always escape to an easy chair in the lobby if the other wanted to nap or watch television.

So here we were, back again. We turned onto State Road 12, heading north. Twenty-five years earlier, when I'd first seen the Outer Banks, this was a trip that almost nobody took. North of Kitty Hawk the Outer Banks scarcely existed then; paved road ran a few miles, through an old-shoe development called Southern Shores, but petered out soon thereafter, somewhere around the minuscule fishing village of Duck. If you wanted to go any farther—to a dot on the map called Corolla—you needed four-wheel drive and a fair amount of luck; I still remember spinning my wheels in the sand before managing to beat a fortunate retreat.

The eighties changed all that. Though the state of North Carolina watches growth on the Outer Banks with a close and wary eye, it permitted not merely the development of the northern end of the banks but, in a few spots, something perilously close to urbanization. Driving to the Sanderling Inn for the first time, I had been astonished at what I saw. Duck, which now called itself "The Village of Duck," had been transformed from a few shacks into Yuppie Shopping Heaven, complete with a shingled shopping center called Scarborough Faire, another called Osprey Landing, and yet another called Loblolly Pines; Laura's Kitchen Emporium was open for business, as were Smash Hit Tennis & Golf, Osprey Gourmet, and Lady Victorian.

Just north of the village, still within Duck's borders, was the community called Sanderling. It had been developed during the 1980s, at the height of the Reaganite real estate boom, and it had been developed well. If we must have developers, and it seems that we must, then let them be those who did Sanderling. Its houses were mostly shingled, with clapboards here and there. The dominant architectural style was seaside-comfortable; though lot prices ran as high as $375,000 by 1991, there was little ostentation or pretense to most of the boxy, spacious houses. The closest to the ocean were still well back from the beach, construction on the dunes now being prohibited on the Outer Banks. The Sanderling Inn, itself long, low, and shingled, was at the community's northern end, across the road from a communal recreation center called, unfortunately, the Sanderling Racquet and Swimming Club.

Driving up State Road 12 to the inn in May of 1991, I made my ritual check on progress, or regress, along the northern Outer Banks. It's easy: Count the stoplights. The first time I went to Duck there was only one light between Sanderling and the junction of Routes 12 and 158, and it wasn't working. The next year there were two. Now, to my dismay, I counted four. It was mid-afternoon on a Sunday in mid-May—high season on the Outer Banks doesn't start until late June—but traffic along 12 was surprisingly heavy, with at least as many cars from Virginia as from North Carolina; on the northern Outer Banks, the big city isn't Raleigh but Norfolk. A friend who'd visited Duck the previous July had reported that traffic in the village approached a state of near-catastrophic grid-lock; in 1991 it clearly was making an early start in that direction.

It's not going to get any better in the future. The long arm of development has stretched well north of Duck. At the Sanderling Inn the two dominant noises come from the surf in the Atlantic and the construction trucks thundering up Route 12 to Ocean Sands and Whalehead Beach and Corolla and Swan Beach and Carova Beach, delivering their loads of con-crete and lumber to Coneflower Lane and Driftwood Way and Mackerel Street and Ocean Pearl Road. All of these places are in Currituck County; the county line is a few hundred feet

north of the Sanderling Inn. Only a decade ago, in *Islands,
Capes and Storms: The North Carolina Coast*, Thomas J. Schoenbaum wrote of this area:

> Beach cottages, mobile homes, and a grid pattern of roads
> have already appeared in many sections of the banks. Hun-
> dreds of four-wheel-drive vehicles run over the beaches and
> dunes. Finger canals have been dredged through the marshes
> on the sound side of parts of the banks. Many people question
> the wisdom of this scale of development. The sandy soil is not
> suitable for individual septic tanks, yet only one developer has
> put in a sewage treatment plant—and it has not functioned
> adequately. The widespread use of septic tanks could endanger
> the purity of the water of the sound and pollute the small
> supply of groundwater under the banks. Other forces have to
> be reckoned with as well. The huge moving sand dunes can
> completely bury houses in their paths. Storm surges from hur-
> ricanes are capable of inundating the entire banks or cutting
> new inlets. . . . A major hurricane has not hit since the 1930s,
> but this has been very unusual. The big storms will surely
> return.

These are not the words of an environmental fanatic;
Thomas Schoenbaum, who participated in the formulation of
North Carolina's Coastal Area Management Act, believes that
"the *human* coast is as important as the natural one," and
makes a powerful argument for the peaceful coexistence of the
two. But what is happening on the northern banks isn't coexistence; it's destruction, and Sanderling, I fear, is part of the
problem.

At no place in the Mid-Atlantic do I feel more a hypocrite.
I'm no fanatic either, but I'd like to leave my sons and their
children something better than slabs of concrete and overrun-
ning septic tanks; that I have a responsibility to the air, land,
and sea seems to me a given of human existence. Yet I love
Duck and Sanderling not merely because of their natural
beauty but also because of what humans have made of them.
I love to sit on my balcony at the inn, drinking my coffee and

watching the sun come up from behind the ocean; I love to
swim my laps in the pool across the road, the sun warming my
shoulder blades as I go back and forth; I love to eat a hamburger at the Blue Point Bar & Grill while Sunfish ply up and
down Currituck Sound. I know that even as I deplore the
problem, I am also part of it; I know too that life is short, that
its exquisite pleasures are too few, and that for me Duck is one
of these. So I slip on my hair shirt and take a walk on the
beach.

It is a rough beach, and by Mid-Atlantic standards the water
is cold. Bathers accustomed to the soft strands of Miami
or Myrtle Beach have to make an adjustment here; somehow
the sand seems thicker and heavier, and the shoreline itself is
not smooth but rutted and pitted by the ever-shifting tides.
Seventy-five miles to the south, where the Outer Banks take
a westward turn at Hatteras and head back to the mainland,
the Gulf Stream caresses the coast and moderates its waters;
but here on the upper banks the Gulf Stream has long since
turned out to sea, and the water will not be warm enough for
swimming—not, at least, for me—for yet another month. For
that matter even the pool water is chilly, though in the course
of a week's stay it becomes steadily more comfortable.
    None of that really matters. The cold water in the pool
invigorates me and the iciness of the ocean is excuse enough
to stay away from surf and undertow that can be dangerously
rough; if you bring your children to the Outer Banks, you go
onto Red Alert whenever they hit the beach. When we come
to Duck, what most interests us is rest, and you don't need the
summer heat to get that.
    Our routine rarely varies. Sue would have it otherwise, but
to my way of thinking, routine is the spice of life. We eat
breakfast in the room; read or exercise or sit in the sun; go out
for a substantial lunch at one of the nearby restaurants; read
or nap or take a drive; have wine and a light dinner; watch
television—the inn's cable system picks up the Baltimore
Orioles' subscription channel—and fall asleep early, to the

sound of that eternal sea. Presumably the homeowners and renters in the cottages nearby do much the same; in human if not ecological terms, it's why the Outer Banks exist.

They also exist for prowling, or recreational shopping, or whatever you want to call it. My comments on Atlantic City to the contrary notwithstanding, I like the funky, seedy side of the seashore. To the south of Duck, in Kitty Hawk and Kill Devil Hills and Nags Head, there's more than enough of that.

Not that there's all that much this committed recreational shopper really wants to buy. To be sure I treasure my coffee mug with its cartoon duck, and Sue is fond of her pink T-shirt across which waddle four baby ducks, but otherwise the pickings are pretty slim, especially in the shops a dozen or so miles to the south, where coastal kitsch reigns supreme.

Shopping at the beach is compulsive, as the existence of so many otherwise inexplicable stores attests. You hang around your cottage or room for a day or two and sooner or later you get bored; no matter how beautiful the beach may be or how swimmable the water, give yourself enough time and you'll get cabin fever. Your urge to shop rises and your sales resistance wanes, as is proved by any number of polo shirts in my bureau drawers and pairs of sandals on my closet floor. Suddenly, against all your better instincts, you find yourself prowling the likes of the Cotton Gin, where you roam in a daze through "room after room of handmade quilts, teddy bears, collectible dolls, wicker baskets and more." At the Seaside Art Gallery, where "art is never an extravagance," you find yourself staring at paintings of a provenance you'd perhaps not really want to know. You check out T&A, "The Outer Banks' Only Gourmet T-Shirt Shop," and then you "get lost in the luxury of 'Royal Velvet' by Fieldcrest" at the Warehouse Towel Outlet.

On and on you go, searching for a chimera. Fool that you are, you enter the Christmas Mouse, "an enchanting place where the magic of Christmas abounds year 'round," offering a "traditional and contemporary selection of Christmas collectibles and favorites, sure to bring a twinkle to eyes of all ages!" In desperate need of a break, you drive through Brew Thru, the "Outer Banks' ORIGINAL Drive-Thru Beverage Store!" You try Kitty Hawk Sports and Kitty Hawk Kites, T-Shirt Whirl and Souvenir City, Rack Room Shoes and Mom's Sweet Shoppe. Exhausted, you contemplate another beer-on-the-go at Cooler Cruz or The Keg Drive-Thru Beverage, but decide instead to eat a real meal.

The place to go is on Beach Road at the six-mile post in Kill Devil Hills. If you live in the Mid-Atlantic and go to its beaches or its baseball games, you've seen its T-shirts and hats—Awful Arthur's Oyster Bar, a legend wherever college students gather to drink beer and eat fish. Actually it serves just about anything in the line of bar food and thus qualifies, like Stolfo's in Atlantic City, as my kind of place, but its seafood is, on a good day, the real thing. From time to time it even has barbecue, no competition for Allen & Son or Bill's, but a lot better than the stuff we once drove halfway to Hatteras to eat at a restaurant the name of which I have fortunately forgotten.

The food of the Outer Banks is eclectic. Much though I like the Blue Point Bar & Grill, there's no getting around its essentially yuppie character—mixed seasonal salad with red grape vinaigrette, grilled chicken breast sandwich with smoked mozzarella—but then Elizabeth's Café & Winery across the street in Scarborough Faire is worse, or, if that's your cup of tea, even better: grilled tuna steak marinated in canola oil, balsamic vinegar, and herbs; Chicken Tahachape; fresh tuna salad with grapes, pecans, herbs, and spices in a honey wheat pita with romaine leaves. That stuff is all right in its place, but its place is Georgetown or Harborplace, not Duck, North Carolina.

To my taste the best eating on the Outer Banks is at the Fisherman's Wharf Restaurant in Wanchese, a fishing village about twenty-five miles south of Duck that's gone almost entirely untouched by the explosive growth with which the area has been afflicted. The village is at the southern end of Roanoke Island at the Wanchese harbor, of which the restau-

rant claims to offer "an expansive view." But the chief object
in its windows' line of sight is a rusty hulk that's been half-
sunk in the harbor for as long as I've been going there.

Scenic beauty is not, in any case, the *raison d'être* of the
Fisherman's Wharf. It is instead a classic North Carolina
seafood restaurant, one to rival what many consider the epit-
ome of the breed, the Sanitary Fish Market & Restaurant at
Morehead City, midway between Wanchese and Wilmington.
No alcoholic beverages are served—as Walt Rand once said of
barbecue proprietors, these people are God-fearing Chris-
tians—and the diner who fails to order iced tea betrays his
ignorance of things North Carolinian. If you must have hamburger or chicken you are free to do so, but you must then
suffer the ignominy of ordering from the "Landlubber's Din-
ners" section of the menu; if you are a child your only choice
in this department is called, with clear intent to embarrass,
"Never Did Like Fish."

No, the reason to drive the twenty-five miles to Wanchese
is fish. Fried or broiled are your choices; you won't find any
canola oil or balsamic vinegar. My own preference is for fried
shrimp, which I first ate more than a quarter century ago at
Calabash, a spot in the road just to God's side of the South
Carolina line that consists of nothing except about a dozen
seafood restaurants, all of which compete to serve the tastiest
fried shrimp. When it comes to shrimp I pay no heed to the
urgings of surgeons general past or present; I like my grease.
I also like my hush puppies and my cole slaw; I even take a
stab at the French fries, which by seafood restaurant law are
thick, gummy, and tasteless—as redolent of the freezer as the
shrimp are of the sea.

We got down to Fisherman's Wharf only once during this
trip to Duck; the food is a powerful lure but the drive down
Route 158 is an equally powerful deterrent, crammed as it is
with stoplights, cars darting in and out of parking lots, and
policemen on patrol. Once having suffered that trip, though,
we made a point of stopping at Manteo, a couple of miles
north of Wanchese, to see the Fort Raleigh National Historic

Site. This is the location of the "Lost Colony," the English settlement that vanished sometime between 1587 and 1590, leaving only a single mysterious trace, the word *croatoan* carved on the trunk of a tree. It was the first English colony in the New World and the birthplace of its first English child, Virginia Dare. As at Jamestown, the site is maintained by the National Park Service with characteristic good taste and fidelity to historical authenticity; the tiny original fort was destroyed, but it has been restored and the visitor can stroll through it—amazed, as at Jamestown and Flowerdew Hundred, by the fragility of the defenses the early settlers erected against man and nature.

There's so much commerce on the Outer Banks now that it's easy to forget how much of our history is there. Driving up from Manteo to Duck we passed, on Route 158, children flying big, colorful kites atop an immense sand dune; a few hundred yards away, drawing only a handful of visitors, was the place where flight began, the Wright Brothers Memorial. Somehow it seems incongruous, a couple of slightly cranky brothers from Ohio coming all the way to this distant and desolate spot to propel the world into a new age, but then amid the clutter of today's Kitty Hawk it's hard to imagine the place as distant and desolate. For all its unique qualities, it's become just another way station of Leisureland, U.S.A., its past swept away in the headlong rush to dig and build.

There was plenty of both going on to the north. One afternoon we decided to get in the car and have a look. We started a quarter mile away at the Sanderling Sales Center, and we started with a jolt. The least expensive building site it offered was a soundside—but not soundfront—lot for $95,000. The most expensive was just north of the Sanderling Inn at the Palmer Island Club, "a private enclave of large beach homes established on rare, unspoiled coastland"; it was a hundred-fifty-foot oceanfront lot at a cool $850,000. The sales center also offered, at Palmer Island, one five-bedroom house at $1.15 million and another at $1.5 million. The cheapest house it listed anywhere was a soundside in Sanderling for $265,000.

But whatever might be said about its prices, at least the houses were relatively subdued, architecturally more or less in keeping with their sand dunes and saw grass setting; to be sure they emitted their fair share of sewage, but it was *tasteful* sewage.

That was scarcely the case as we drove north. With only the rarest of exceptions, the developments north of Duck were vast agglomerations of architectural horrors. At many of them the sales pitch was the same: a hypocritical nod in the direction of the history and ecology of the Outer Banks followed by a hard-sell pitch for glossy real estate developments and ludicrous creature comforts. Invariably a lavish brochure was handed out, its Technicolor illustrations accompanied by indigestible prose: "You must see Corolla Light, feel its presence, and experience the true life of leisure and pleasure. If seeing is believing, believing is but a visit, and returning will be your desire and choice. A select few will be privileged to grasp the concept—Come own a part of the dream."

"A select few." "Grasp the concept." It sounded for all the world like the "estate" country north of Baltimore, which is exactly what it looked like. A promotional piece for something called Monteray Shores featured photographs of houses that defied both description and architectural categorization. One looked like a giant spider, another like a Spanish nightmare. Shingle and clapboard were only occasionally in evidence; the principal building materials seemed to be concrete and other poured substances, often covered with stucco. The impressions given off had nothing to do with the sea, indeed seemed openly hostile to it. Except for the great unopenable plate glass windows they presented to the ocean, these houses turned their backs to it; they retreated into the defenses set up by their central air conditioners and wall-to-wall carpets and built-in microwaves.

Driving along Route 12 south of Corolla I noticed a sign, HURRICANE EVACUATION ROUTE, with an arrow pointing to the south. Pointing, that is, to the Wright Memorial Bridge, which connects the upper banks to the mainland. That bridge is twenty-four miles of crowded two-lane road from Corolla. The only other ways to get from Corolla to the mainland are by ferry, by boat, or by air. You can, if you wish, swim, although Currituck Sound at that point is several miles wide. It is true, as Thomas Schoenbaum says, that there hasn't been a major hurricane on the Outer Banks since the 1930s; it is also true, as he says, that sooner or later a big, mean one will stalk in off the Atlantic. What then for Corolla?

I shudder to think. So too do many who live there. But quite apart from hurricanes, what they really dislike is the inconvenience. If their principal residences are in mainland Currituck County or in Virginia, they have to drive twenty-four miles south to the bridge before they can begin driving west or north to get home. With increasing persistence, they are demanding that a second bridge be built, connecting Corolla or another settlement to the north with Aydlett or Waterlily or some other town on the western shore of Currituck Sound. Their argument is impeccable: A second bridge would improve evacuation routes and ease congestion at the lower end of the upper banks.

What they neglect to say is that they built or bought in full knowledge of transportation realities on the upper banks; they knew that there was only one bridge and that it was a long way down the road, though it's not hard to imagine a real estate agent saying to them, "Once enough people buy houses up here, the state will *have* to build a second bridge." They also neglect to say that a second bridge would merely make the upper banks accessible to still more people, with their automobiles and sewage and power lines and trash.

That a second bridge would spell the death of the upper banks seems a certainty; it might be a slow death, unlike the quick one a great hurricane would bring, but death by any name and at any speed is still death. There seems this certainty as well: By the end of the century a second bridge will be built. Traffic on the Wright Bridge and Route 12 will get worse and worse, and it will do so in a hurry. Not merely will the people of Corolla and Carova lobby for another bridge; so too will those of Duck and Southern Shores, as it becomes impossible to cross the road during much of the day and a trip to the supermarket becomes a strategic exercise. If I were a betting man I'd bet on the bridge, and if I had spare cash to invest I'd put it into Currituck Sound bridge bonds.

Gloomy thoughts, all of them; sunny and lovely though the day was, it was impossible not to think them as we drove past mile after mile of elephantine structures squatting on their tiny lots. One development hadn't progressed much beyond its entrance, but that alone set the tone: A tiny kiosk of a guardhouse blocked the way in, putting all who passed by on notice that this was strictly for the "select few." Another development was reached by a low, heavy bridge that deposited the traveler between two great lumps that lacked only minarets to rival the Taj Mahal; that people could actually live in them, much less live in them by the sea, struck me as beyond imagination.

But the best rule by which to abide, on the upper Outer Banks or anyplace else, is *de gustibus.* After driving around for a couple of hours we decided to see one of these places on the inside. A show house was open right by the side of the road. It was three stories tall, reached by short flights of stone steps that quickly established a mood of incongruity. The windows were tall and eerily church-like. The exterior walls seemed to be stucco; they had been painted off-white, with purplish brown trim. The front door was immense and heavy; it would have been right at home as the entrance to one of those dark, mannish restaurants that serve outsize martinis and surf-'n'-turf.

Inside we were greeted, or assaulted, by the real estate agent who was showing the house. She was trim and taut, wiry and edgy. She had one of those Southern double names; we'll call her Maribeth. She was ready with brochures and the full pitch, but when it quickly developed that we were there strictly to look, she turned to ice. She pointed to the stairs that wound upward to the living quarters, and sent us on our way.

What we saw seemed to us entirely astonishing. The kitchen had enough electronic equipment to levitate the house and fly it to Los Angeles. The windows looked as though nothing short of an atomic blast could force them open; the air conditioner silently worked away, though the temperature outside was barely eighty. The living room furniture was contemporary overstuffed, guaranteed to retain any sand that hadn't already worked its way into the shag carpet below. The room was spacious and the windows made it seem airy, but it was sterile, lifeless, joyless; I couldn't imagine a child running through it dragging a towel and a pail, or a game of Scrabble being played on the fierce glass top of its monumental coffee table.

Upstairs there was more of the same. Wall-to-wall carpet was everywhere except on the bathroom floors, which were showily tiled. The beds were huge and covered with quilts that would have kept an Eskimo snug: perfect for the Outer Banks in August. The fixtures in one bathroom were Las Vegas gold; in another, Rodeo Drive brass. Mirrors were everywhere. From the master bedroom ceiling a fan was suspended; by its size I judged that it had been taken from a DC-3, then bronzed and lacquered.

Punch-drunk from all this excess, we staggered to the stairs. Halfway down I looked out the window and saw that a car had parked next to ours. Its doors opened and three retired couples poured out. By the time we reached the bottom of the stairs, one of these visitors had opened the front door. He stood there, transfixed, looking at the hallway and up the stairs. A great smile crossed his face.

"Gorgeous!" he said.

The others crowded in behind him. A chorus rang out: "Gorgeous! Gorgeous! *Gorgeous!*"

The man who had first spoken looked at Maribeth. He gave her a little wink. "There's six of us," he said. "You got one for each of us?"

I had to hand it to Maribeth. She didn't miss a beat. "Oh, no, *sir!*" she said, and gave him the cutest little artificial smile. "We couldn't do *that*! No two of *our* houses are alike!"

13

COMMENCEMENT DAY

The invitation was printed on heavy, cream-colored paper in a graceful italic type. It read:

The Rector, The Faculty
and Senior Class
of
Chatham Hall
invite you to attend
the
Ninety-seventh Commencement
Saturday, May twenty-fifth
Nineteen hundred ninety-one
Chatham, Virginia

Inside was enclosed a small card on which was printed the name of my niece, Emily Jane Page, the daughter of my sister Jane and her late husband, Rob Page. It was an occasion I could not imagine missing, not merely for Emily's sake but because it provided a too-rare opportunity to revisit Chatham, the town in which my real life in the Mid-Atlantic had begun.

I drove to Washington on I-95, then went west on the

Beltway until its junction in northern Virginia with I-66. A dozen years before, when Sue and I began making irregular trips between Baltimore and Charlottesville, I-66 was just coming into being and seemed to us a small miracle: a high-speed, limited-access alternative to U.S. 29, a road that could cut as much as half an hour off our drive. But in the intervening years the suburbs of Washington had grown so wildly, had flung themselves so far out into the countryside of northern Virginia, that now I-66 was as crowded as any urban thoroughfare at rush hour—and this was early Friday afternoon, long before the heaviest traffic would start to inch its way out of Washington and the various office parks that now used I-66 as a local artery.

Twenty miles later I took the Gainesville exit. The rest of my way was on U.S. 29. However much I may have complained about that road for more than forty years, it remains the central highway of my life, connecting places of importance to me from Orange and Charlottesville in the north to Chatham and Greensboro in the south. Over the years the road has changed, in most respects for the better, but it still cuts through countryside that I know by heart and that in my mind characterizes, more than any other, the soft beauty of the central Mid-Atlantic.

At Gainesville I passed through an instant of clutter and then was in open country, on what originally had been a two-lane highway but was widened to four many years ago. The job was done with the pay-as-you-go frugality that the political machine of Senator Harry Flood Byrd instilled in Virginian hearts during the 1920s and 1930s. Rather than build a new road, the state simply constructed two additional lanes parallel to the existing ones. It is easy to tell which is which: The new lanes are flat and smooth while the old ones—which I was on now—swoop you up and down on a roller coaster ride.

Byrd was the paradigmatic Virginian of my youth. My parents loathed him, as well they should have: He was parsimonious, narrow-minded, and obdurately racist, in the latter capacity presiding over the doctrine of "massive resistance" by which Virginia held out against desegregation well into the 1960s. But for reasons I cannot hope to explain, I was fascinated by him; it was by Harry Byrd that my interests in politics were first aroused. In the scrapbook that I assiduously kept in the early 1950s I pasted his reelection card ("Your Vote and Influence Appreciated"), and when the great man actually came to Chatham to solicit votes in the early summer of 1952, I attended his rally at the local high school and pasted up the voluminous relics of the event that appeared in the Pittsylvania *Star-Tribune*. These included one photo in which the back of my head is visible and another that, according to its caption, "shows Claude Whitehead, 'Bru' Kendrick, Dr. Haile Fitzgerald chatting with Byrd as he partakes of a sandwich and drink"; ever after, the word *partake* invariably has conjured up in my mind the image of Harry Byrd in his shirtsleeves and straw hat, sandwich and Co-Cola in hand.

Say what you will of the man, he built good roads of which Virginia has been justly proud. This one rolled past New Baltimore—a church, Mayhew's stores, Antique Encounters—and then straightened out. The traffic was the heaviest I'd ever seen on 29; usually it is light, but today there were too many people poking along in the left lane at forty-five miles an hour, too many others passing them too fast on the right.

Just north of Warrenton I picked up the new bypass, one of the most welcome roads in the history of roads. Warrenton may be famous for its rich people and the horse country they inhabit, but until the bypass was constructed it was notorious among motorists for a congested agglomeration of gas stations and fast-food joints that abruptly narrowed from six lanes to two, leaving traffic snarled and bottlenecked.

The Culpeper bypass was welcome as well, though the problems it solved had been scarcely so serious as those of Warrenton. One of the immortal utterances in American history was committed here by Lyndon Baines Johnson during the 1960 presidential campaign. As his train made a brief stop, Johnson went to the platform at the rear and in a ringing voice posed the question of the hour: "What has Richard Nixon ever done for Culpeper?"

Soon I passed a sign for Orange, but declined the invitation. That small and exceptionally pretty town is the location of Woodberry Forest School, at which I was a boarding student from 1951 to 1954. My first two years were happy indeed, as is suggested by my two fat scrapbooks jammed with Woodberry Forest souvenirs and innumerable newspaper accounts of the school's athletic triumphs. But my third was equally unhappy, as I fell victim to several of the psychological maladies that boarding school life induces, and no scrapbook commemorates it; I went north for the last three years of my secondary education, departing the company of the sons of Virginia's First Families and regretting it not at all.

Instead of turning left to Orange, I looked right to the Blue Ridge Mountains and the Appalachians beyond them. It was much the same view that I had been able to see from our house in Chatham, one that never fails to surprise and move me. The Blue Ridge really *is* blue, while the Appalachians behind it seem dark and foreboding, an insuperable barrier between the Piedmont and the West.

Sixteen miles out of Charlottesville the clutter began. In 1979, when I started visiting the city occasionally, the first signs of suburban congestion appeared at the exit for the airport, eight miles out of town, but in that short time another eight miles had been eaten up by auto dealers and mini-shopping centers and all the usual, standard-issue trash. Charlottesville had grown just as Chapel Hill had, hastily and indiscriminately, and with exactly the same results. The closer I got to town the worse it got, the highway crammed with students driving away from the campus in order to stuff themselves with Big Macs and Whoppers and the other delights of roadside cuisine. Picture that: driving *away* from Thomas Jefferson's magnificent Colonnade in order to patronize McDonald's and Burger King!

At last I was on the bypass. The first exit was for Ivy Road, only a few hundred yards from the residence of Sue's father

and stepmother, Julian and Elinor Hartt. They are why Charlottesville has become an important place in my life, but they
were off on one of their frequent journeys.

I drove on, and less than a minute later saw something that
nearly stopped me in my tracks: a group of perhaps a dozen
black men, wearing prison uniforms and working along the
roadside under the guard of a white man carrying a gun. The
yellow bus in which they'd been brought to work was parked
nearby. They were not manacled, but except for that they
were an astonishing anachronism: the contemporary equivalent of a chain gang, commonplace during my youth but, I'd
thought until now, long since abandoned. Perhaps this labor
was no more distasteful, and considerably healthier, than
working in a factory making license plates; but the combination of such clear lines of racial demarcation and the presentation of the prisoners as a public spectacle struck me as
contemptible.

Now I was in hill country. "South of Charlottesville," my
father's copy of *Virginia: A Guide to the Old Dominion* advised
me, "the highway passes through the foothills just east of the
Blue Ridge, and then descends to the flattened south Piedmont. Apple and peach orchards along the route mingle with
farms and vineyards, then give way to lands producing bright
leaf tobacco." Little had changed, at least not yet. The country south of Charlottesville is rapidly becoming fashionable
among motion picture stars and other "celebrities." How long
it will be able to maintain its unvarnished rural character in
the face of this onslaught is at the least problematical.

The road wound down the last of the mountains. Half an
hour out of Charlottesville I was at the edge of Lovingston, "a
one-street community in the center of a large apple-raising
area." As in 1940, so a half century later. The only change I
could detect from the road was the convenience store where I
stopped for gas and a soft drink. Otherwise, Lovingston
looked just as it always had during the forty years in which
I'd known it: a pretty little town nestled at the foot of a
mountain, no doubt remarked upon with pleasure by motor-

ists who pass by, few of whom actually stop there. I suspect that Lovingston likes it just that way.

Twenty more minutes to the south and the entrance to Sweet Briar College was on my right. Its president during the 1950s and 1960s, Anne Pannell, was my father's friend, advisor, and, for a time, Chatham Hall trustee; they were immensely fond of each other, but so far as I know they called each other "Mrs. Pannell" and "Mr. Yardley" to the end of their lives. My sister Jane spent four years there, graduating in 1963; she got a good liberal arts education, made many friends, and remembers the school fondly.

If Sweet Briar is here, Lynchburg cannot be far away. I was there in ten minutes. This small, steeply hilly city is best known now for the Reverend Jerry Falwell and his fundamentalist seat of higher learning, Liberty Baptist University. This is a pity, for it is a pleasant city wherein reside, by my recollection, many intelligent and agreeable people who must be appalled by Falwell's indigestible mixture of religiosity, moralism, and politics. Lynchburg was the big city for us in my youth, more so than Danville, which was closer to Chatham but offered far less in the way of consumer goods and services. My mother used to drive up to Miller & Rhodes to buy furniture—I still have a lamp shade she got there—and in the later years of my father's headmastership, as planes began to replace trains as the favored mode of student transportation, they made frequent runs to the Lynchburg airport.

For me, alas, Lynchburg now means nothing more than what must surely be the oldest—and one of the worst—urban expressways, a narrow, curvy road that lasts for about five miles before 29 pulls away and resumes its southward trek. This time I got off the expressway just before the junction with 29 and checked in at the Lynchburg Hilton, the closest I had been able to find a reservation; Chatham was forty-five miles to the south. I had time for a swim and a few minutes' relaxation, during which I noted with amusement the Hilton's response to the problem of customer souvenir hunting. It was a card that read: "Due to the popularity of our guest room terrycloth items, our Housekeeping Department now offers these items for sale. . . . Should you decide to take these articles from your room, instead of obtaining them from the Executive Housekeeper, we will assume you approve a corresponding charge to your account." *Touché.*

Shortly after six I got back on the road. South of Lynchburg it was littered with establishments selling recreational vehicles and trailers; one was called Mid-Atlantic Mobile Home Supply. I passed a truck sporting bumper stickers that left no doubt as to what part of what state its driver was from. One read: "I'm Proud to Be a Farmer." The other: "I Support Smokers' Rights."

Forty minutes from the motel a familiar landmark appeared: Billy's Restaurant. WOAH! read the sign out front. STOP HERE FOR GOOD OLE HOME COOKING. I often had in the past—it was a place where, as a teenager, I would get a snack on the way home from the drive-in theater—but this time I didn't. I drove on for a few more miles, then bore right onto the exit that put me on Main Street, headed right for the heart of Chatham.

I don't really have a hometown. We left Pittsburgh before I was old enough to have any feeling for it. I wasn't quite ten when we left Tuxedo Park, New York, for Chatham, and I spent only two years there before being shipped off for six years of boarding school and four of college. As an adult I lived in Washington for one year, New York for two, Greensboro for ten, and Miami for five. I've been in Baltimore since 1979 and have more home-like feelings for it than for any other place I've lived; but it's pretty hard to think of a place to which you moved at the age of thirty-nine as your "hometown."

What I have is a hometown of the mind. It is called Chatham. The possibility that it is as much the product of wish and invention as of memory has occurred to me more than once, but I persist in feeling about it as I do. Perhaps this is because Chatham—with its red-brick storefronts, wood-frame houses, and thick, massive trees—looks and feels so much like the ideal American small town that the phrase "hometown" just comes naturally to it.

It had, when the WPA guide was written, a population of 1,143 souls. Nine years later, when the Yardleys got there, it had grown by perhaps a hundred more, so our arrival made a significant dent on local demographics; now its population is 1,390, which is to say that in some respects it's scarcely changed at all. The WPA's anonymous writer called it "a quiet town enlivened by students," this in reference not merely to the girls of Chatham Hall but also to the boys of Hargrave Military Academy—with whom, in my father's day, the girls socialized at peril of dismissal, which leaves me wondering how the town was thus "enlivened."

Be that as it may, Chatham is the seat of Pittsylvania County. As a boy I was excessively and inexplicably proud that, of the state's counties, it is the largest in area. The story of how Chatham got its name, as recorded in the WPA guide, is worth telling:

> When a permanent courthouse was to be built, a long dispute over where it should be rent the community. When in 1807 the legislature settled the matter, the town was designated Competition and so remained until 1874, when it was renamed in honor of William Pitt, Earl of Chatham, for whom the county had been named in 1767. Henry St. George Tucker, clerk of the House of Delegates, wrote on the blotter:
>
> > Immortal Pitt! How great thy fame,
> > When Competition yields to Chatham's name!

The county courthouse at the center of town is indeed, as in the guide's dry appraisal, "nondescript"; my only experience of it was the considerable embarrassment of failing to parallel-park successfully on a street at its rear and thus flunking my first driver's license examination. Today it looked as stolidly red-brick as ever, though the Faulknerian characters sometimes to be found on its front steps and benches were nowhere to be seen. I remembered the kind black man who had dropped me off there nearly thirty-five years before, and was grateful that I had no business to transact therein.

Elsewhere on Main Street, everything looked almost exactly as it had forty years before. For months I had been witness to change, some of it dreadful and traumatic, but Chatham was still Chatham. To be sure Whitehead's and Jones's competing drugstores had vanished, as had the Mick-or-Mack where my mother bought groceries until Kroger came to town, but the Western Auto where I got baseball bats and 3-in-1 oil was at the same old stand, just as were Chatham Jewelers, Chatham Furniture Company, Thompson's Haberdashery, the *Star-Tribune*, Chatham Cleaners, and Tune & Toler Air Conditioning and Heating—though air-conditioning, an unimaginable luxury in my day, was new to this list.

The years had dropped away. Except for the contemporary autos on the street and some of the clothes the pedestrians wore, it could have been Chatham in the mid-1950s. When I made a left turn and headed down Pruden Street toward Chatham Hall, I thought for a moment I'd gone back to the future—though I was quickly disabused of that fantasy when I saw that the Chatham Theater, where I regularly attended Saturday matinees, had metamorphosed into a temple of some mysterious religious cult.

But I knew that in one important regard Chatham had changed dramatically, and that most of this change had taken place since 1971, when my parents retired from Chatham Hall and removed to Rhode Island. I was quite well aware that relations between blacks and whites in Chatham were still far from perfect, but I had learned through various friends still living there that they were markedly different from, not to mention better than, they had been in the little town that I had known.

Until my family moved to Chatham I knew nothing at all of race relations; the question had never crossed my mind. I do not believe that I had ever spoken to a black person until I arrived in Chatham one hot day in the summer of 1949, a couple of months shy of my tenth birthday. My mother seemed at ease with the servants whom the school routinely supplied to the Rectory, as our house was called, so I tried to be at ease with them as well. But I didn't understand them—not just their speech, which was not much stranger to my Northern ears than much of what I heard in Chatham from the lips of whites, but their lives. I didn't understand why they couldn't do things that I could, why some of them treated me with an embarrassing deference, why I was expected to address them by their first names.

I didn't have the experiences common to the white boys of my age in Chatham. I hadn't grown up around black people; I hadn't had a close black friend who suddenly was barred from my house when he was eight or nine; I hadn't been taught to assume as givens all the rituals and assumptions of segregation. I had to learn my own way, and I did it imperfectly. On the one hand I was troubled, if inarticulately, by the inequality of the rights and liberties enjoyed by the two races; my mother, a fair-minded if undemonstrative person, made sure I was aware of that. On the other hand I had no particular difficulty settling into a situation in which, by no virtue of my own, I had the upper hand; because blacks were in all situations treated as inferiors, I came to accept them as such.

Chatham wrote the book for me on race, though it did so quietly and unobtrusively. It was as implacably segregated as any hamlet in the darkest Black Belt. The few members of what passed for its local power structure may have been for the most part ignorant and narrow men, but they held absolute power over all but the most intimate aspects of the lives of the town's black residents. It is an awful measure of how cramped were the opportunities available to them that a job at Chatham Hall—as a maid, a cook, a farmhand—marked a person as a member of the local black elite, well above the washerwomen and sharecroppers and day laborers who made up the far larger part of the black work force.

I knew nothing of their lives, only that they must be hard.

Once the phone rang at the Rectory with news that two grandchildren of one of the women had died in a fire that swept through the tarpaper shack in which they lived. Two days later the woman was back at work, the same as ever, with not a sign of her loss and grief. I was confused: How could a person be so callous? But I was a privileged little white boy. I knew nothing of suffering or fatalism.

Reading through the WPA guide, I was struck by a chapter called simply "The Negro." In ten pages it treated the history of black Virginians quickly but—considering when it was written—fairly, describing the rebellion of Nat Turner with none of the hysteria common at that time and treating the slave trade with dry distaste. It closed with a paragraph that certainly contains its share of happy-darkies patronizing but that also is sympathetic and observant:

> The lure of the crowd is strong among Virginia Negroes; every city and town has a "street" that serves as the social and business center of Negro life. Here Negroes from every walk of life congregate to purchase from Negro merchants, to ply their trades, to discuss the latest developments in Negro America, or simply to see who else is abroad. Here race pride is triumphant; drug stores, cafes, barber shops, pool rooms, grocery stores, theaters, beauty parlors, and garages are operated by and for Negroes. To the uninitiated, the crowd is a group of idlers wasting time in meaningless banter. That banter, however, is the Negro's escape from a day of labor in the white man's world. No matter how carefree the outward appearance of Negroes may be, behind their happy dispositions is the imprint of poverty, disease, and suffering—birthmarks of a people living precariously, but of a people wholly Virginian.

That is a fair portrait of black life in the Chatham that I knew, at least as seen through white eyes. I suspect that it is in some measure true today. When I am greeted warmly now by men and women who worked for my parents at Chatham Hall, I do not know whether it is genuine affection or a manifestation of lingering habits of obsequiousness; I hope it is the former—and am encouraged in that hope by the self-confidence with which they go about their business—yet, as I say, I do not know. But there are black girls at Chatham Hall now, though not many, and in recent years these have included relatives of people who once worked at the school. Doors that were closed to their parents are open to them; their lives include possibilities that their parents cannot have imagined for themselves.

The school looked absolutely, heartbreakingly beautiful. The great trees on the main lawn were a deep green, as was the grass at their feet. The shrubbery had been trimmed, the brick walks were neat, the red-brick Georgian buildings with their white columns were as imposing as ever. A couple of years earlier the school had rented itself out for the filming of what turned out to be a singularly mediocre movie, an unfunny comedy called *Crazy People*. I saw it notwithstanding the reviews, and was astonished that never in the course of the ninety minutes allotted to them did its makers take the slightest advantage of the setting; it was the equivalent of making a film at Charlottesville and leaving out Monticello.

Emily was in the entrance hall of the main building, impossibly pretty in her white dress. She introduced me to some of her classmates. They were nice girls and we chatted for a few minutes, but I was glad when Jane showed up with her husband, John Amos; I quickly realized that I had lost the skill Chatham Hall once had trained me in, that of talking to eighteen-year-old girls.

An informal dinner was served in the school dining room, in a building called Yardley Hall. A quite inadequate portrait of my father hangs in the entrance to Pruden Hall, the school's main building; a considerably better one of my mother is immediately outside the dining room. The impression I have had in recent visits is that the only people to whom these portraits mean anything are those few remaining teachers and staffers who worked under my father; to everyone else they seem to be nothing more than pictures of a couple of old people.

But then Chatham Hall, like the other single-sex private boarding schools that somehow have survived into the 1990s, is a different place now from the one I knew; it looks the same, but it's had to adjust to new realities. It has fewer students—about a hundred and twenty-five, as opposed to a peak of two hundred in my father's day—and it has to work harder to get and keep them; large public rooms that were previously used for teas and other social occasions have been cut up into offices for people who do admissions and development and counseling and other modern things that my father often handled by himself.

By nine it was dark. The Lantern Ceremony began. The girls of the graduating class passed their lanterns on to members of the next senior class, to the accompaniment of school songs and hushed commentary from the adult onlookers. I was aware that these girls knew far more of the world than did their counterparts a few decades ago—not least because the school let them see far more of it—but the essential innocence of the ceremony was unchanged.

The next morning Emily's family contingent increased mightily with the arrival of my sons. Jim had come up from Alabama, Bill down from Washington; their bonds with their cousin were strong and deep, and the day would have been incomplete without them.

It began with the Baccalaureate Service in St. Mary's Chapel. I had last been there almost exactly two years before, when I spoke at a memorial service for my father, who had died two months earlier. Standing in the pulpit from which he had preached thousands of times, I had to hold back my tears as I read a few words of my own and a few words of his. What moved me was not the words but the place, and the knowledge that in the hearts of my family it would always be uniquely sanctified.

This morning I was in one of its two hundred astonishingly

uncomfortable cane-bottomed chairs, listening to words from
the revised prayer book. If they lacked the majesty of those
in the Book of Common Prayer, they nevertheless had their
own ample measure of dignity and grace, as in this "Collect
for Graduating Seniors":

> We commend, O Lord, under your Fatherly care, your ser-
> vants about to go forth from this place, beseeching you that
> your loving kindness and mercy may follow them all the days
> of their life. Succour them in temptation, preserve them in
> danger, assist them in every good work, and keep them ever in
> the right way.

From this place we went, following the procession of faculty
and seniors, outside to the lawn. Chairs had been set up before
a platform. I stood off under a tree with my sons and John
Amos; Jane, as the mother of a graduate, an alumna herself,
and the daughter of a former rector, had been asked to sit on
the stage and present an iris to each girl as she accepted her
diploma.

First the prizes were presented. At the top of the list was
the Catherine Ingram Spurzen Award for Creative Writing. It
was all I could do to keep from letting out an undignified cheer
when the recipient was announced as Emily Jane Page.
Though I scarcely wished upon her a lifetime spent at writing,
with its intermittent rewards and constant disappointments,
I was as proud as I could be that the craft at which I had
spent my own adult life—one for which her grandfather had
an immense if unrecognized talent—was one that she too
practiced and enjoyed.

There were thirty-three girls in the class. Each got her
diploma and her iris; when Emily came up for hers, she got a
kiss from her mother, too. The ceremony ended with the
singing of the school's haunting alma mater, which was immediately followed by much mingling, laughing, and picture
taking. Luncheon was to be served forthwith in the backyard
of the Rectory, but I had an early-evening social engagement

back in Baltimore and was pressed for time. I gave Emily a hug, cautioned her to find a more lucrative line of work than the pen, and headed home.

I did so with an emotion that bordered on grief. I knew that Emily's graduation almost certainly marked the end of any regular connection between our family and Chatham Hall. The only remaining eligible female, my brother Ben's daughter, Hannah, was a year and a half old; that she would ever attend Chatham Hall was singularly uncertain and if she did I would be nearly seventy years old at the time of her graduation, a prospect I was not at the moment prepared to contemplate. I hoped that I might be invited back to the school on some future occasion or other, but it would be as a friendly stranger rather than, as it had been today, a member of the family.

It was thus for me the end of a terribly important part of my life, the precise nature of which apparently would forever be a mystery to me. Chatham was not home, and yet it was. Probably I had spent less time there than I had in Pittsburgh, about which I knew enough to write only part of a chapter in a small book. Yet Chatham had an emotional purchase on me that only Chapel Hill and Baltimore could match. I had been a boy there, even if briefly. It was the last place I had lived, as a resident of their household, with my parents. It was the place where I had learned both a lot about race and even more about how little I knew. Its physical surroundings had trained me in notions about natural beauty against which I measured all other places I saw. It was a town where people still knew me and still said—heaven knows why—that they were glad to see me.

I got in my car. It was parked on an athletic field from which I could see, in the near distance, the school's water tower. It had been built in the early 1950s at the insistence of my father, who worried about the school's protection from fire and wanted a ready supply of water for the sprinkler system he'd had installed. On a clear day you could see the tower from as far as six miles away, as you reached the crest of

White Oak Mountain on Route 29 south of town. When the tower was built the people of the town, who had been slow to take to this rather snobbish and curmudgeonly Yankee, called it "Yardley's Folly." I wondered if anyone still did, but doubted it; the Yardleys and their follies were long gone from Chatham, ancient history. The loss is ours.

14

CENTENNIAL

Shortly after noon on a Saturday late in June, Mayor Kurt L. Schmoke of the city of Baltimore rode down Roland Avenue in a horse-drawn carriage. At the corner of Roland and Oakdale the carriage stopped. A green-and-white reviewing stand had been set up on the front lawn of the DAR chapter house of Roland Park. Schmoke—who was wearing a white boater with a green band—climbed onto the platform, waved to the small crowd clustered under umbrellas in a faint drizzle, and took his seat. The parade was now officially under way.

The ironies of the moment cannot have been lost on Schmoke, who is formidably smart and blessed with a wry sense of humor. Schmoke is young, handsome, and black; the DAR chapter house of Roland Park is old, timeworn, and white, like much of the neighborhood in which it is located, one of several predominantly white enclaves in a city that is now predominantly black. Schmoke, the city's first popularly elected black mayor, is the city's future. Roland Park, though it still flourishes, is the city's past, as was suggested by the occasion for the day's festivities: the centennial celebration of the neighborhood's founding.

Roland Park is my neighborhood; in order to take my place at curbside near the viewing stand I had to walk only two blocks, from our house on Hawthorne Road at its junction with Oakdale. In Baltimore everyone identifies himself by his neighborhood; it has often been called "a city of neighborhoods," because whether a Baltimorean lives in Roland Park or Pigtown, Lauraville or Oakenshaw, Reservoir Hill or Ridgeley's Delight, Pimlico or Govans, Morrell Park or Brooklyn, Irvington or Guilford, Walbrook or Belgravia— wherever a Baltimorean lives, that neighborhood is his *real* Baltimore, the place that defines the city for him and within which much if not all of his life is lived.

Baltimoreans are the most provincial people on earth. Once friends of ours who had lived in numerous cities east of the Mississippi and were now in residence in Baltimore were invited to dinner at the house of a couple whose families had been in Baltimore forever. The subject of our friends' peregrinations came up. The hostess was aghast. How on earth could they have lived in all those places? "Why, I can't imagine living anywhere else except Baltimore!"

These people were prosperous, but their attitude toward the world outside was characteristically Baltimorean. Rich or poor, black or white, row house or mansion, the Baltimorean really does believe his city to be the center of the world and his neighborhood to be the center of the city. His loyalty to the city is intense, his loyalty to his neighborhood even more so. When in the 1970s the city sought to help heal the wounds that had been opened by race rioting after the assassination of Martin Luther King, Jr., it settled upon an annual City Fair as the agent of reconciliation and made neighborhoods its focal point. As many neighborhoods as cared to participate were welcome to do so, and they joined by the scores. Some sold trinkets or T-shirts in their booths, others merely set up photographic or historic displays; in each of their presentations, though, there was at once a bold assertion of individual neighborhood pride and a clear yearning to be accepted as an equal part of the pattern that is the crazy quilt called Baltimore.

Much has been written about Baltimore, some of it very

good. For a long time the best was to be found in the *Days* memoirs of H. L. Mencken, most especially *Happy Days*. Now the world knows the city as filtered through the distinctive, quirky imagination of Anne Tyler, whose novels may seem fanciful and airy but are firmly rooted in the reality of Baltimore. I could show you the street near Johns Hopkins University where resides the Tull family of *Dinner at the Homesick Restaurant*, the house in Roland Park—a block from ours— where Macon Leary of *The Accidental Tourist* lives, the restaurant on York Road where Macon and his estranged wife, Sarah, had their confrontational lunch. Tyler has never drawn a character from life, but the city about which she writes is utterly real and her vision of it is intrinsically bound up with its neighborhoods. The contrast between Macon's leafy surroundings in Roland Park and Muriel Pritchett's on Singleton Street, the "block of row houses that gave a sense of having been skimped on," is at the core of the slow, difficult unfolding of their romance, and Macon's gradual understanding of the humanity of her neighborhood is essential to the novel's own humanity:

> He was beginning to feel easier here. Singleton Street still unnerved him with its poverty and its ugliness, but it no longer seemed so dangerous. He saw that the hoodlums in front of the Cheery Moments Carry-Out were pathetically young and shabby—their lips chapped, their sparse whiskers ineptly shaved, an uncertain, unformed look around their eyes. He saw that once the men had gone off to work, the women emerged full of good intentions and swept their front walks, picked up the beer cans and potato chip bags, even rolled back their coat sleeves and scrubbed their stoops on the coldest days of the year.

Baltimore is a relatively small city by the standards of New York or Philadelphia—its population is about three quarters of a million, triple that in its total metropolitan area—but it has so many neighborhoods that it is impossible for even the most assiduous of journalists or politicians to know them all. From time to time I drive around in parts of the city I have never seen, and invariably I am struck by the distinctiveness of their character, as well as by the suddenness with which one neighborhood ends and another of sharply different personality begins. For example, only a tiny place called Rolden—the name exists in the minds of its residents but not in those of the city's mapmakers—separates the prosperous whites of Roland Park from the working-class whites of Hampden; the two neighborhoods coexist with what has always seemed to me remarkable equanimity in light of the contrasts between them, but then that is par for the course in Baltimore, where coexistence rather than confrontation has usually been the preferred way of life.

That the contrary has sometimes been the case is the central argument of *The Baltimore Book: New Views of Local History*, a collection of rather contentious essays by young historians of "admittedly partisan" viewpoints "nurtured in the dissident politics of the 1960s." Their analyses of conflicts involving labor, race, and economic privilege are useful antidotes to the complacency of the city's ruling classes, but they fail to disprove the fundamental truth that Baltimore, like so much else in the Mid-Atlantic, prefers to take the middle course. Relations between the races are easier than they are in many other old East Coast cities—easier than reality suggests they ought to be, given the desperate conditions in which so many black Baltimoreans live. Although labor relations continue to be a problem at the Port of Baltimore, and an important factor in the decline of that port, by and large compromise rather than acrimony seems to be the rule. Contrasts between rich and poor were exacerbated during the 1980s in Baltimore, as everywhere else, but—for better or worse—the city has never had a strong tradition of home-grown populism.

I am, God knows, neither rich nor a member of one of the

city's ruling classes, but I do live in a neighborhood where some of my fellow residents can be thus described. That this is so is a matter of both preference and accident.

The preference, which Sue shares, is for semiurban rather than *echt*-urban life. I love row houses and could live quite happily in Bolton Hill or Oakenshaw, neighborhoods of narrow streets and dignified buildings, some of them amazingly spacious. But we have dogs and cats, and Sue loves to work in a garden, and I longed for room to install a backyard swimming pool such as we'd had in Miami, from which we moved to Baltimore in 1978. We quite strongly preferred to be in the city as opposed to Baltimore County, even though the tax rate there is half that in the city, and we equally strongly preferred old houses to new.

All of this—no doubt heightened by my radiant Waspishness—clearly rang the bell that said "Roland Park" in the mind of the real estate agent to whom we had been directed. We had little money, but we were in luck. The happy accident was that real estate prices in Baltimore were not exactly depressed, but by contrast with those in Washington and Boston and other cities then enjoying boom times, they were reasonable. By the narrowest of margins, we could afford to live in Roland Park. We were shown a number of houses, the most expensive of which was slightly under $100,000. The one we chose came in well below that, though clearly we would spend the rest of our lives pouring money into it.

The original deed of our house was made on September 25, 1901, "by the Roland Park Company of Baltimore City, a body corporate of the State of Maryland, of the first part and Rosalind Whitmore of Baltimore County party of the second part." She received a piece of land approximately sixty-four feet by one hundred seventy feet, "in consideration of the payment of the sum of six thousand three hundred (6300) dollars," and she further agreed not merely "that no residence or dwelling house shall be erected or kept on said land costing less than three (3) thousand dollars" but also that any house would be "made according to plans which shall have been approved by said first party." Just as the Roland Park Roads and Maintenance Corporation now holds veto over house plans and alterations, so too in the development's early years did the Roland Park Company.

Roland Park *was* a development, so Rosalind Whitmore chose a development house. It was Design No. 327 of Shoppell's Modern Houses, a two-and-a-half-story wood-frame structure of late Victorian or Queen Anne design. A copy of the plan can be found in James F. Waesche's history of the neighborhood, *Crowning the Gravelly Hill*. It shows a porch across the front with the entrance at the right, opening into a hall with a parlor on the left, a dining room beyond at the rear, and, to its right, a kitchen and pantry; upstairs were four bedrooms and a single bath. But Rosalind Whitmore did not stick literally to the design. She switched the front door from right to left and in so doing switched the entire first floor; she wrapped the porch around to include part of the south-facing exterior wall; she added a bay window to one of the upstairs bedrooms; and, as we discovered in the early 1980s while having the house prepared for repainting, she decorated the space above the second-story front windows with pieces of colored glass embedded in stucco. This last was a practice, the painter told us, that had been not-uncommon in her day, but we decided after some deliberation that authenticity has its limits and left the baubles hidden under white paint.

Rosalind Whitmore was not alone either in choosing Design No. 327 or in playing fast and loose with it. On my walks around the neighborhood I have counted about a dozen houses whose original owners chose No. 327 and then put their own stamps on it. These range from the size of the porch to the location of the front door to, most particularly, additions at the rear. Our house expands far beyond the original plans, adding three rooms and a half-bathroom on the first floor, two rooms and a bath on the second. How many, if any, of these additions were original is a mystery. Suffice it to say that like most houses that most people build in most places, those of Roland Park have undergone constant change; this has been especially true in recent years, as the old-house revival has brought younger buyers in and as the high cost of real estate has encouraged people to remodel rather than bear the financial burden of moving "up."

The long, handwritten deed to which Rosalind Whitmore agreed included a number of restrictions and covenants, among them not merely company approval of the design of her house but also a minimum setback distance and the prohibition of many undesirable structures, among them shops, saloons, cesspools, and privies. She did not sign any racial or religious covenants. As James Waesche points out: "Although later . . . deeds did in fact carry racial restrictions until such things were declared unconstitutional, the earliest ones did not. . . . [I]n an age of 'consensus,' such a restriction would not have been considered necessary." People knew their place; Roland Park was a place for well-to-do people who were white, Protestant—no Catholic church was provided for— and primarily Anglo-Saxon, though no doubt members of the city's large, affluent German community, H. L. Mencken being most notable among them, were welcome.

Over the years this has changed, as Roland Park has acquired numerous Jewish residents and fewer black ones, but it is still thought of as a Wasp preserve. A writer for the Baltimore *City Paper*, taking sarcastic note of Roland Park's centennial, suggested that its motto should be: "One Hundred Years of Well-Tended Lawns and Boring White People." The first charge is patently untrue; Roland Park lawns tend, by contrast with the overmanicured ones of the suburbs, to be scruffy. As to the second charge, well, *mea culpa.*

It is true that I live in a neighborhood many of whose residents are people very much like myself; oddly enough, most other neighborhoods in most other places are exactly the same. It may not be an unduly flattering commentary on human nature that we tend to fly in our own flocks, but it is true. In any event there really are two Roland Parks, separated from each other by Roland Avenue and its splendid houses, one of these designed by none other than Stanford

White. The best-known section is on the west, where the houses are larger and more individualistic, the terrain more dramatic, and the typical bank account considerably plumper; our realtor called it the "dollar side." To the east, by contrast, the lots and houses are smaller, the designs were mostly plucked from developers' pattern books, and the householders are more likely to be salaried people who have comparatively little loose change.

Thus our side of Roland Park has been popular for years among faculty members at Johns Hopkins, the main campus of which is a mile and a half away, as well as at Loyola and Goucher colleges and other local institutions of higher education. Writers and editors for the Baltimore *Sunpapers* have long been attracted to Roland Park, though the papers' higher management tends to flee the city for Ruxton and other indisputably affluent communities. We have our share of upper-level city bureaucrats, lawyers and doctors, insurance executives and classical musicians. Because the east side went through something of a slump in the 1960s and 1970s— for a time our house was a communal residence for Hopkins and Goucher students—a number of people whose means were modest were able to afford houses there; some of these, Sue and I probably among them, could not afford to purchase their own houses at the prices they would now command.

It is, I suppose, a fairly privileged place as American city neighborhoods go, but the privilege I feel at living there is purely a matter of physical place. For a few years we had as next-door neighbors a couple who had moved to Baltimore from Cambridge, Massachusetts, which they still missed; having lived there for nearly a year myself, I could understand why. We didn't know them well, but I hoped they were happy in Roland Park and finally asked the woman of the house how she liked it. Her eyes brightened. "Oh," she said, "I absolutely love it. It is the most beautiful neighborhood I can imagine. I feel privileged to live here."

That is exactly how I feel. The sense of privilege to which she referred had nothing to do with wealth or exclusivity, everything to do with a place where, for once, mankind did things exactly right: where natural beauty has been perfectly complemented by human design, where the conveniences and amenities of urban life have been fitted into the serenity and quiet of the countryside.

Roland Park is something of a miracle. It is within the city limits of a metropolis suffering from all the terrible problems of late-twentieth-century urban life, yet it has managed to resist not merely decay but also the intrusions of strip development and uglification. It is ten minutes from Baltimore's business and commercial center, yet it has the feel of a small town; it's a place, Sue likes to say, "where you expect to see Andy Hardy running down the front steps." It is a city community that still cares about country things: bats and squirrels and raccoons, trees and gardens, insects and pets.

Those of us who are lucky enough to live in Roland Park love it for these qualities, and for others that are familiar to all of us: the winding, narrow streets with their canopies of oaks and maples; the long rows of lawns unbroken by driveways; the sharp, dramatic drop—just about the only drama this peaceful place permits itself—from Roland Avenue down to the Jones Falls; the startling display of stylistically multifarious turn-of-the-century architecture to be found on every street; the golden retrievers and Labradors and mutts whose collective presence not merely gives the neighborhood an agreeably canine quality but also causes burglars and housebreakers to think twice before inviting their snarls and barks.

Yes, there is crime in Roland Park, every so often serious crime. I find, in a column I wrote in the early 1980s, the statement that "two weeks ago a man was murdered just a few houses away from us"; that must be true, but I have no memory of it at all. A person out walking alone after dark risks a purse snatching or even a mugging, but considering that this is an old Rust Belt city with a horrifying crime rate, the risk is relatively low. Each week a "Crime Log" is published in the Baltimore *Messenger*, the newspaper for Roland

Park and several contiguous neighborhoods. Here, from a typical week, are a few typical entries: "West Cold Spring Lane. A parking-meter head valued at $386.20 was stolen." "Wickford Road. License plates were removed from a 1988 Volkswagen." "West Cold Spring Lane. A 1991 Honda was stolen and recovered. The suspects were arrested." "Upland Road. A pair of sunglasses was stolen from a car. Entry was gained by breaking a window."

Against the possibility of offenses more serious than these—"Hawthorne Road. Jewelry and electronic equipment valued at $10,000 were stolen"—many residents have installed various protective systems. The prevailing calm is interrupted from time to time by the whooping alarm of a Rollins or Honeywell security system in full bay, more often than not triggered by a cat. But though crime is often a subject of conversation when neighbors gather, the fear of it is not pervasive or stunting. People take sensible precautions but not excessive ones. They act more as though they were living in a small town than in a big city.

To my own tastes, this city-country quality is the most precious of all my neighborhood's charms. On a weekday afternoon, sitting on my front porch, I can read a book or chat with a friend uninterrupted by the noise and distraction of city life; every once in a while a car rolls by, or a mother passes with a baby in a stroller, but it is a small parade, one you'd expect in an archetypal American small town—Cooperstown, perhaps, or New Castle, or Chatham—but not within the borders of a major metropolis. Yet if I leave my porch and take a walk, within ten minutes I can find stores selling almost everything I need or want; I can get several of the country's major newspapers delivered to my front door, I can pick up all the radio and television stations I could possibly desire, and I can see the Orioles play baseball any old time I please.

To have all this country quiet and urban convenience within the confines of one small neighborhood of about three square miles seems to me just about as close to heaven on earth as one could hope to get. Not merely that, but into the bargain it's a natural-fibers place. By this I don't mean the tweeds and cottons at the checkout lines in Eddie's Supermarket or the bar at the Baltimore Country Club, but the natural fibers of wood and stone that are its principal materials of construction. If Roland Park is a man-made place at peace with its natural setting, in large measure that may be because its foundations of stone, its sidings of wood and shingle, are as much a natural presence as its trees and shrubs.

For this reason as well as others, Roland Park is well known and greatly admired among students of American urban planning. Much of its design was done by the firm of Frederick Law Olmsted, the designer of Central Park in New York and other notable urban spaces, though the work at Roland Park was overseen by his son and namesake. He and his colleagues created a place—it was then still outside the city limits—that was calculatedly informal, city convenience married to country beauty with scarcely a nod to the pretentious or grandiose; indeed the one small street that is lined with ostentatious houses, Goodwood Gardens, seems almost aggressively incongruous. As John R. Stilgoe writes in *Borderland: Origins of the American Suburb 1820–1939*, "aside from the one block of stores built in 'picturesque Flemish architecture' like the 'beautified' retail structures in so many other turn-of-the-century commuter villages, Roland Park exhibited no 'official' architectural appearance, only a vital diversity of architectural styles and a population actively gardening." Stilgoe contrasts it with another Olmsted project, Riverside, on the outskirts of Chicago:

Roland Park from the beginning echoed urban rather than rural traditions. Its developers forbade the private stables that the Riverside promoters loved, and lot sizes were far smaller, perhaps because many Roland Park buyers had grown up accustomed to Baltimore row houses and saw Roland Park lots as positively extensive. Not until 1911, when one Roland Park homeowner successfully broke them to build a driveway and a garage, did the general restrictions arouse much opposition. Indeed, the developers understood restrictions as rules not to dictate quality design but to stymie freakish 'anomalies.' By 1910, Roland Park existed as a handsome residential neighborhood within the city limits of Baltimore, a gentle contradiction to designers smitten with European notions of wholly harmonized, wholly static garden cities.

This tolerance for diversity is characteristic of Roland Park specifically and Baltimore generally. Although Roland Park is small and its populace relatively homogeneous, it does not impose rigid standards of behavior or style. Four blocks from our house, across Roland Avenue on the "dollar side," stands the Baltimore Country Club. "Exclusive club in exclusive suburb," reads its description in *The Official Preppy Handbook*, a volume that on several occasions pays reverent attention to Roland Park and environs. At first I took this as a bad sign; I had lived four blocks from a similarly prestigious club in Greensboro, and in various ways had been made to feel inferior for neither wanting nor having the funds to join it. But in Baltimore that turned out to be, as we say locally, "no problem." So far as I am concerned, the Baltimore Country Club could be halfway across the country. I have been in it only twice, the first time for a centennial dinner soon to be described and the second for a wedding reception. I have felt no further longing to pass through its handsome portals, and no one has ever suggested, by word or body language, that I am in some way deficient in lacking this urge. Of the several friends and many acquaintances I have in Roland Park, I have no idea which belong to the club and which do not.

If Roland Park is indeed an "exclusive suburb"—in my view a glib and stereotypical characterization—then this quality of tolerance distinguishes it from most of the rest of its kind. To be sure it does not consider you a real Roland Parker unless your family has lived there for at least three generations, but what is at work therein is less Roland Park than

Baltimore itself, the same innocent and endearing provincialism that our friends encountered in their dinner hosts. Baltimore's neighborhoods like to think of themselves as independent and self-contained, as in many ways they are, but it is the cumulative character of the old city—of all its people, all its neighborhoods—that ultimately shapes them.

One of the ways it does this is through the language they speak. "Linguists and scholars have tried, without success, to pinpoint the derivation of Baltimorese," according to Gordon Beard in a most amusing little book called *Basic Baltimorese II*. "They have suggested various blends of Virginia Southern, Pennsylvania Dutch, Brooklynese, Allegheny Mountain English, Irish and British Cockney." Among the examples culled by Beard from the utterances of those who live in *Balamer* are: *harble*, which is how you feel after you have over-*eht*, which is what you did last night at Obrycki's Crab House; *sore*, which is where goes the stuff you flush down the *zinc*; *Yurp*, which is where preppies from Roland Park go on summer vacations; *jools*, which are what get stolen if you don't have a burglar alarm; *lieberry*, which is where you can find a copy of this book, written by me, the *arthur*.

Not everyone in Baltimore speaks Baltimorese—for a newcomer such as I to do so would be pure affectation—but the natives all have their variants of it. The elderly ladies and gentlemen of Roland Park may speak in softer tones than the working people of other neighborhoods, but they still refer to their city not as *Baltimore* but as *Balamer* or *Balmer* or *Bawlamer* or some variation thereof. Those students of contemporary culture who worry about the decline of singular regional speech and mores in the age of television should take heart from Baltimore, where the banal, oleaginous language of the airwaves has been entirely unsuccessful in its effort to penetrate the local tongue. Thank *Gawd* for that.

The climax of Roland Park's centennial came in June, but it got started back in January. A couple of months earlier we had received this notice:

> You are cordially invited to launch the Centennial Year of the Founding of Roland Park at a Gala Dinner Dance at the Baltimore Country Club on Saturday, the nineteenth of January, nineteen hundred and ninety-one. Cocktail receptions will be held at six o'clock in various Roland Park Homes. Music will be by The Water Street Swing Society.
>
> The ticket price of $119.91 per person includes a drawing for $500. and valet parking.

My immediate reaction had been that this invitation had a good many things wrong with it, chief among them a steep price and an excess of capital letters. But after talking it over with our next-door neighbors, John and Linda Renner, Sue and I decided to make an evening of it. I felt little sentiment about Roland Park's great anniversary, but I was curious to see the insides of the Baltimore Country Club and I wondered how all those people I regularly saw prowling the aisles of Eddie's Supermarket in their worn tweeds and rumpled cottons would look dressed up in black ties and long dresses.

I was, as is my wont, apprehensive in advance, especially about the cocktail party. We had informed the organizers of the affair that we wanted to be invited to the same party as the Renners and two other couples who were joining us, so we would be certain of knowing at least a few people there; but since the organizers had up to that point been primarily disorganized, my hopes were not high, inefficiency apparently being endemic within the Old Roland Park circles where the machinations of the celebration were being conducted.

So what a relief it was not merely to learn that our little group would be allowed to party together but that we had been invited to the house of Barrett and Laura Freedlander. I had known them for years; Laura's family had been my neighbors in Greensboro many years before, and since moving to Baltimore Sue and I had seen her and Barrett often. They lived on the "dollar side" but with a total lack of show; I knew that at their house I would be at ease.

They put on a fine spread for the guests who had been

assigned to them; everyone in our little group had a good time. Thinking about it later, though, I realized that those who had been sent to this party were not merely relatively young but also relatively unattached to the Roland Park in-crowd. Ours, I decided, had been the outsiders' party.

I was confirmed in that suspicion when for the first time I crossed the threshold of the Baltimore Country Club. Two dining areas had been set up. The first, containing the majority of tables, was in the club's grand dining room; the second was on an enclosed porch that ran the length of the club's western wall, looking down through the dark at Baltimore Polytechnic High School and, beyond it, the Jones Falls Expressway, Interstate 83. We had been assigned to Table 30, on the porch.

A jolly, outspoken person of some prominence in local affairs was seated there when we arrived. "Welcome to the land of outcasts!" she said. I gave her a quizzical look. "Look in the main dining room," she said. "All the old fossils have kept it to themselves. The outsiders get the porch."

She was right, but I was vastly more amused than offended. Looking at the old gals in their brocade gowns and the old guys in their moth-eaten tuxedos, I was glad to be out on the fringe where irreverence and youth—or at least Roland Park's idea of youth—held sway. As the night advanced and the wine kept pouring forth, our table bordered on the riotous, with much loud talk and laughter. From where I sat it looked as if we were having a far better time than those in the inner sanctum.

In any event they let us eat the same food. I was startled by the menu, which suggested that the Baltimore Country Club, citadel of old Wasp cookery, had gone giddy and turned Californian. The appetizer was "Jumbo Lump Crab in Endive Cups with Radicchio & Mache in a Cilantro Lemon & Sun-dried Tomato Vinaigrette," a touch-all-the-bases combination far more likely to emerge from the kitchen of Alice Waters or Wolfgang Puck than from the one now serving us. But it atoned for this aberration by subsequently doling out good old roast beef with tomatoes, potatoes and broccoli, and strawberries for dessert. Rule, Britannia!

By the time I'd gotten down the strawberries I was in need of exercise. I turned to Sue and said, "Let's dance." She was dumbfounded. *"Dance? You?"* I insisted, so off we went. The Water Street Swing Society was playing Old Roland Park's kind of music—Glenn Miller, Tommy Dorsey, Glen Gray— and for a while we stumbled around. Eventually we drifted home, in high good humor, just possibly a tad tipsy. But the drive was only four blocks, and we negotiated it like old pros.

That was January. The centennial forces lay low through the rest of the winter and most of the spring, but in late June they came back with a vengeance: a half week of events, ranging from a "Taste of Roland Park" picnic to a lecture on "Early Planned Developments" to a Sunday walking tour to a parade. I wasn't about to take in all of it, but the mere idea of a "Taste of Roland Park" fascinated me—undercooked leg of lamb? Bremner wafers? six-olive martinis? floating island?— and I never turn down the chance to watch a parade. We put both on the schedule.

The "Taste of Roland Park" was presented on a Wednesday evening at what is beyond any doubt an improbable Roland Park institution: St. Mary's Seminary and University, the oldest Roman Catholic seminary—it opened in 1791—in the United States. It now occupies a large tract of land at the southwest corner of University Parkway and Roland Avenue and does its business in a gargantuan building of a quarter-million square feet that it erected in 1929. The building sits far back from the street and thus is easy to overlook, but the passerby who pauses to glance at it can only be struck, or stupefied, by its overbearing stone facade, which unfortunately evokes nothing so much as the monumental architecture of Hitler and Mussolini.

With the exception of this aesthetic affront the priests of the Sulpician order and their students are good but unobtrusive neighbors, so it seemed odd to be having a picnic on a corner of their grounds, though to be sure none of them was in evidence. A large tent had been set up and, inside it, tables were decorated in a predominant scheme of lime green and watermelon pink. This was as it should have been, for these are the unofficial neighborhood colors of Roland Park. Not long after we moved there the *Messenger* reported the results of a Christmas decoration contest in Roland Park; though it struck me as out of character for old Wasps to be holding such a competition, I was relieved to see that the color scheme of the winner was not the traditional red and green of Christmas but the watermelon pink and lime green favored among preppies everywhere.

More than five hundred of them showed up for a "taste." As Jacques Kelly reported the next afternoon in the *Evening Sun*: "The women wore wrap-around shirts, floral shifts and gold circle pins. The men had on seersucker, madras long pants and khaki. . . . There were lots of tortoise-shell glasses." A bit of the old stereotype, that, but all too true, as I in my madras shirt all too cacophonously attested.

The party began at six. We got there shortly thereafter, to find that all the tables had been commandeered by the ever-vigilant codgers of Old Roland Park, the advance scouts for which had turned over chairs and placed themselves in strategic locations calculated to assure that only Their Kind of People got seats. The grass outside turned out to be fine, which was just as well since that was the only choice available to us and our little band of squatters.

The "Taste of Roland Park," it soon developed, was in great measure determined by the taste of the people who run Eddie's Supermarket. This was entirely appropriate. Eddie's, a small, family-owned establishment on Roland Avenue, about a quarter mile south of where we were at the moment, is the center of Roland Park life even though, technically, it is not within the neighborhood's boundaries. Because of restrictive covenants, the only shops permitted in Roland Park proper are those at the aforementioned "picturesque Flemish" shopping center; they include a bank, a savings and loan association, a restaurant, a Baskin-Robbins, and a sandwich shop, but no purveyor of groceries or other staples. For those we must go to Giant Food, a chain store a mile away, or to Eddie's, just to our north.

A neighborhood doesn't deserve the name unless it has a gathering place. In urban communities that used to be the corner market or candy store, perhaps now it's a convenience store; in suburban ones it's a shopping center. In a neighborhood such as ours, part city and part suburb, Eddie's is just right: bigger than a candy store, smaller than a shopping center. It's the place where people see people. As the principal weekday cook at our house, I'm in Eddie's four or five times a week. I've shopped there so long that its employees call me by name—a sure sign of a neighborhood center—and I know where everything in it is displayed except, for some reason, the silver polish. I wouldn't buy Coca-Cola or toilet paper there, but its prices are generally competitive and its clientele is far more diverse, racially and economically, than the populace of Roland Park itself; such red meat as we eat comes from Eddie's, and I wouldn't buy shrimp anywhere else.

This night Eddie's was dishing out roast beef, country ham, and pasta. It was also the principal source of entertainment. For most of the evening the music piped through the sound system had been more of what we'd heard back in January: the Andrews Sisters, Tex Beneke, Vera Lynn. But after dinner the stage lit up and out came the men who stand behind the butchers' counter at Eddie's. Ordinarily they wear white smocks and butchers' caps—the sign behind their work tables reads, OUR BEEF IS AGED, OUR FISH IS FRESH, OUR BUTCHERS ARE BOTH—but tonight they ran onto the stage in bright jackets and boaters. Suddenly loud rock music began to play and the butchers began to dance, lip-syncing as they did. It was a lovely, funny bit, at once an exercise in self-mockery and a gentle tweak at the old parties who looked on in bewilderment, their feet uncertainly tapping to the alien rhythms.

. . .

Three days later we had our parade. At first I was sure it was
going to be strictly a Roland Park sort of parade. Once Grand
Marshal Schmoke had settled into his folding chair, a numb-
ing procession of local folk inched its way past. There were
numerous antique vehicles, several of them occupied by persons considerably more antique than the vehicles. A carriage
with a fringe on top rolled by, its cargo of four old girls waving
merrily to the throngs that lined the parade route one-deep.
A cheerful man from the city sanitation department came
along, pushing a portable garbage can.

There was a long pause—as the afternoon wore on there
were several long pauses—and then we were granted the privilege of applauding Paul Sarbanes, the most inert and least
charismatic person in the entire United States Senate, but our
very own. A truck rolled past bearing students from Roland
Park Country School. An antique station wagon with its own
load of antiques was next, then a long stream of alumnae of
the Bryn Mawr School, then a fire truck of unclear purpose,
then a passel of squawking bagpipers, then a contingent from
Boys' Latin School, then a float promoting "Baltimore—The
City That Reads."

I was just about to fall asleep on my feet; counting snow-
flakes would have been more fun. But then it happened. There
was a great blast of martial music, the American flag burst
into view, and here they came: the Shriners of Boumi Temple.

Talk about anomalies. Compared to the Shriners of Boumi,
the seminarians of St. Mary's are dyed-in-the-wool, pink-and-
green Roland Parkers. Boumi Temple of the Ancient Arabic
Order of Nobles of the Mystic Shrine sits at the neighborhood's eastern edge, a great inscrutable lump of stone facing
North Charles Street, its portals never open to the public, the
affairs of its members an utter mystery to all save themselves.
I regularly pass by Boumi on my walks; I have never seen any
human activity there beyond the occasional surreptitious
movement of a car in the parking lot at its rear. It is as

self-contained as Fort Knox, and probably a lot harder to get into.

But here came the Boumis, in full public view, parading right down Roland Avenue. Their marching band wore white slacks and short-sleeve shirts, gold sashes and red fezzes. A snappy entourage of old gents in pin-striped white suits and betassled fezzes trooped smartly along, smiling benevolently. More tassels. More sashes. More fezzes. The action along Roland Avenue had picked up very nicely.

But that was scarcely a hint of what lay ahead. Here came the "Boumi Temple Camel Wheels," an aggregation of middle-aged men in *silver* fezzes, each steering a little green scooter, zipping this way and that in formations worthy of a squadron of top guns. The children alongside the street were enchanted, though not half so enchanted as the Boumis themselves.

Onward and upward. Here came the "Boumi Temple Motor Corps," a stream of superannuated Wild Ones muscling their gleaming motorcycles down the road. Now there was the "Boumi Flying Patrol," a single aviator piloting a stubby little three-wheeled cartoon plane. The "Boumi Temple Magic Carpet": more little old men, these in *gold* fezzes, perched atop silly little machines designed to resemble flying carpets. At last the highlight of the show: the "Boumi Temple Harem," a great band of old boys in drag, swishing by in capes, pantaloons, and astonishing feathered headgear, waving their arms in choreographed patterns evidently meant to conjure up visions of Arabian seductresses.

They should have swung around to the north and headed for Atlantic City; they would have fit right in at the Taj Mahal. They were ludicrous. It was impossible not to laugh at them, and not kindly. They were middle-aged men and older—if one among them was under forty-five, I didn't see him—but they were acting like grade-schoolers, prancing around in their ridiculous outfits and puttering along in their little cars. It would have been very easy to pass condescending judgment on them; I nudged right up to the verge of doing so. But one thought held me back. These old coots had managed to do what Roland Park itself apparently couldn't: They gave Roland Park a *parade*.

15

CHIPS AND BREW

I'd had a taste of Roland Park; now I wanted a taste of the Mid-Atlantic. Perhaps a nice, cheesy Mid-Atlantic soufflé; or a grilled tenderloin of beef swimming in Mid-Atlantic sauce; or Mid-Atlantic peach ice cream; or—the *pièce de résistance*—a glimmering mixed platter of *Poisson Mid-Atlantique*.

You get the point. There's no such thing as Mid-Atlantic cuisine. You can eat Southern fried chicken or New England boiled dinner or Western omelet, but the Mid-Atlantic has no signature dish. Its best-known culinary achievements—Virginia ham, Maryland crab cakes, Pennsylvania scrapple—are identified not with the region but with the states where they were invented. The Mid-Atlantic has plenty of good cooking, much of it distinctive, but it doesn't have a culinary identity; there are almost as many Southern cookbooks as there are Southern cooks, but if *Mid-Atlantic Cookery* has ever been written, I haven't seen a copy.

Yet there are foods that are both indigenous to the Mid-Atlantic and, in their way, characteristic of it. I decided to go in search of a couple of them. I took I-795 to just north of Reisterstown, then got on Maryland Route 30 and headed north-northwest. I know the first several miles of the road well, because every couple of months I make the half-hour

drive to Hampstead, where the venerable Baltimore clothier
Jos. A. Bank has its warehouse and distribution center. On
weekends an outlet store is open to the public; on a lucky
Saturday or Sunday you can pick up quite a bargain, as on
several occasions I have.

But this was a weekday, so I passed Bank's with barely a
glance and pressed on. It was mid-summer. Soon the day
would be uncomfortably warm, but at shortly before eight in
the morning the air was still fresh and I had the sunroof open.
As is often the case on this pretty two-lane road, traffic was
irritating, a mixture of slow-moving country folk and inter-
city motorists such as I; in such circumstances, in my experience, the country folk always get the upper hand.

I'd allowed for that, though, and pulled into the south-
central Pennsylvania town of Hanover with several minutes
to spare. I drove in on Baltimore Street, which struck me as
appropriate not merely because I'd come from Baltimore but
because it *looked* like Baltimore: red-brick row houses neatly
maintained, marching along in dignified procession.

I drove through town. I was grateful that I'd given myself
a few extra minutes because I briefly got lost. But it's hard to
stay lost for long in Hanover, a town of fifteen thousand, and
harder still when your destination is the factory of Utz Quality Foods, Incorporated. All you have to do is follow your
nose; the smell of potato chips will get you there on time.

The Utz factory is a long, low, tidy building on High Street.
I was met at its reception area by Jack L. Corriere, vice
president and general manager in charge of production. I'd
spoken with him a few days earlier by phone; when, by way
of explaining myself, I mentioned my connection with the
Washington Post, I could sense the phone line freezing up. But
whatever apprehensions he may at first have felt clearly had
been eased. His greeting was friendly. He was about my age,
compact, wiry, intense, enthusiastic, quick-witted, outgoing.
I liked him immediately and immensely.

For half an hour we sat in his office and talked. There were
plenty of things I wanted to learn from him about how Utz

potato chips are manufactured and distributed, but he didn't need to tell me a thing about the chips themselves. Almost everyone in the Mid-Atlantic knows Utz, pronounced "Ootz" at the factory but "Uhtz" everywhere else, including its own television and radio advertising. Go into any supermarket or convenience store and there's likely to be a prominent Utz display featuring chips and pretzels in bags and boxes of various sizes; racks of miniature snack-size bags can be found at sports arena concession stands, corner drugstores, newsstands. Utz is everywhere: Driving into Duck in the spring of 1992 I was amused to find myself making my entrance directly behind a red, white, and brown Utz truck. If any single "food product" can be said to be native to the Mid-Atlantic, the Utz potato chip is it.

But it's more than that. The American marketplace is filled with products that sell well notwithstanding their intrinsic mediocrity; efficient marketing and distribution can paper over a world of mistakes. The real key to Utz potato chips is their quality. I have never eaten a better mass-produced potato chip; except for a chip that came fresh out of the fryer at a now-defunct eatery in Fells Point, Baltimore, I've never eaten a better chip, *period*. By contrast with the heavy, oversalted chips manufactured by Eagle, Frito-Lay, and other colossi of the industry, the Utz chip is light, almost feathery, just salty enough to have a little bite, and it doesn't leave your hand swimming in oil. The "Grandma Utz" chips—"kettle cooked in refined lard"—are crisp and crunchy; the Utz flavored chips, sour-cream-and-onion in particular, sacrifice none of their potato-chippiness in the course of taking on additional taste.

In national terms Utz is a bit player. In the $10-billion-a-year snack industry, Utz measures in the millions. It talks, for public consumption, about "not sacrificing quality for volume and profit," and the evidence suggests that it means what it says. The morning that I visited we were joined in Corriere's office by Mike Rice, president of the company and grandson of its founders, Bill and Salie Utz. He was in his forties, a large, pleasant man who looked as though he enjoyed his own products and spoke about them in rushes of nervous energy. Ordinarily he would not have been at the company's manufacturing plant. He was there that day because workers on one production line had shut it down; they didn't like the way the chips coming off it tasted—they had a smoky quality that suggested too much fat was being used, and Rice was there to check out their findings.

As we all now know, that's the way they do it in Japan: The workers have a substantial voice in how the plant runs, and the supervisors respond readily to their suggestions. While both Rice and Corriere played down comparisons of their production methods with those of the Japanese, they spoke repeatedly of "employee involvement" and "quality control" as virtually synonymous, leaving little doubt that they trust the people closest to the process to keep watch on it. It helps that their labor force is drawn from rural Pennsylvania, where the work ethic is strong. "We have excellent employees," Corriere said. "They're conscientious and hardworking. They do a good job." Of course he wouldn't be so undiplomatic as to say a harsh word about them for publication; but I got no sense that what I was hearing was merely the voice of public relations.

The company's insistence on uncompromised quality is given a considerable boost by its deliberate decision to stay regional; outside the Mid-Atlantic, you'd have to look hard to find a bag of Utz. I mentioned to Corriere and Rice that Cape Cod potato chips, which had been excellent when produced and distributed locally, seemed to me to have turned hard and tasteless since being bought by Anheuser-Busch, which had taken them national. They were too polite to comment unkindly on a competitor's product, but their repeated emphasis on regional distribution left no doubt that they agreed.

You can stay regional and still do very nicely. Since Corriere joined the firm in 1979, he said, its operations had increased sixfold; total sales double approximately every five years. The Hanover plant has a half-million square feet of working space and can turn out potato chips at the rate of twelve thousand pounds an hour. In its core markets of Baltimore and Washington, Utz has 65 and 50 per cent, respectively, of the potato chip business. Its principal distribution center is the Hanover plant, but it added one in Richmond in the early 1980s; all of its distributors are Utz employees. "On a regionalized basis," Corriere said, "we're the toughest competition the big companies face."

It helps to make a fresh chip. Ninety per cent of those distributed in Utz's core markets are sold within a week of manufacture. Inventory at the Hanover plant is no more than a day and a half's worth of chips—which account for 80 per cent of the company's sales—and other snacks. The rest of the industry codes its products for a shelf life of four to ten weeks; Utz codes for three weeks. All of which struck me as impressive, but none of it more so than this: The total time of manufacture from a raw potato in its crate to a cooked chip in its bag is only twenty minutes.

The art of making potato chips isn't exactly complex; what takes technological and organizational skill is making them on a mass scale. As Utz likes to point out, the essence of the chip hasn't changed since it was accidentally discovered by a chef at Saratoga Springs, New York, in the mid-nineteenth century. Utz's promotional literature cites a recipe for "Saratoga Chips" in *The White House Cookbook*, published in 1887. Here is a similar one from Fannie Merritt Farmer's *Original Boston Cooking-School Cookbook*, published a decade later:

SHADOW POTATOES (SARATOGA CHIPS)

Wash and pare potatoes. Slice thinly (using vegetable slicer) into a bowl of cold water. Let stand two hours, changing water twice. Drain, plunge in a kettle of boiling water and boil one minute. Drain again, and cover with cold water. Take from water and dry between towels. Fry in deep fat until light brown, keeping in motion with a skimmer. Drain on brown paper and sprinkle with salt.

It was time to have a look at how that's done at the rate of twelve thousand pounds an hour. Corriere gave me a paper cap to protect my hair from dust, though he conceded there wasn't much to protect, and led me outside to the loading dock. A huge truck was there, just in from the Red River Valley; Utz buys most of its potatoes from the Dakotas, as well as some from Pennsylvania and some, in the spring, from Florida. They were what Corriere called "round white" potatoes, every hundred pounds of which would yield about twenty-eight pounds of chips. Thirteen per cent of total potato production in the United States ends up as potato chips; Utz alone uses ninety million pounds a year.

Most manufacturers store their potatoes in vast piles. Utz stores them in crates that hold a thousand pounds apiece; this reduces the pressure of weight and increases the flow of both air and moisture, thus maintaining freshness. Today's shipment of new potatoes tumbled out of the truck onto a conveyor belt past workers who quickly separated them before they poured into the crates; unacceptable potatoes along with skin shavings and other waste end up as fodder for the cattle of central Pennsylvania.

As potatoes are ready to begin their new lives as chips, they're removed from their crates and put in huge hoppers in which they're washed, or "flumed." From there—at this point Corriere led me upstairs and we began our trip along the assembly line—they undergo a sequence of rapid-fire treatments: peeling, slicing, rinsing, cooking, salting, inspection, flavoring, and packaging. Everything along the way is automated, but everything is closely watched by human eyes. The best way to find a bad potato chip is still to have a human being look at it; this was done by men at the cookers and by women at the conveyor systems along which the chips passed en route to the final steps of flavoring and bagging. Corriere plucked a chip out of a batch hot from the fryer, popped one into his mouth, and smiled. "If we could market them just like this . . ." he said, and shook his head.

I'd assumed that flavoring was done at some point in the

cooking process. I was wrong. The cooked and salted chips are moved into the packaging area and separated. Most go directly into bags without further attention, but those to be flavored—sour-cream-and-onion, barbecue, salt-and-vinegar, crab—are sent into chutes down which are poured flavoring in granular form. I expressed puzzlement about this: Didn't it mean that some of the flavoring merely ended up at the bottom of the bag? Corriere said that I was right, that technology hasn't yet found the perfect way to make the flavor stick to the chip.

But it was the packaging, as would again be the case later in the day, that really opened my eyes. We went to a large, briskly efficient "form and fill" machine through the lower end of which rolled sheets of brightly colored paper; it looked rather like a printing press. From the top, chips trickled down in a steady, unceasing flow into bags that opened and closed with precision so acute that variations were measured in fractions of an ounce; the weight each bag accepted was controlled by a board that looked more like the instrument panel of a jet fighter than what you'd expect to see in a potato chip factory.

That was it. The bags were packed into boxes and stored near the rear loading dock, soon to be picked up by the familiar Utz trucks and distributed throughout the Mid-Atlantic. Corriere and I went back to his office. Earlier in the morning, talking about the not-inconsiderable caloric punch packed by his product, Mike Rice had said that "reasonable consumption" of potato chips "is not going to hurt," but conceded that in a time when the middle class was becoming more sensitive to questions of health, the snack-food industry had to be on its toes. Now Corriere seconded the motion. Popcorn and pretzels, with their lower levels of fat and calories, were on the rise; there was a slight shift toward "health products," he said, but he pointed out that potato chip sales weren't exactly suffering.

Not, at least, at Utz. "Look," Corriere said, "there isn't another company that has the reputation that this one does. We are going to be all right. We have consistent quality and

a reputation people believe in." He thought a moment, then
added: "You know, there's no great secret to this—just a lot
of people doing things right."

I looked at my watch. It was eleven-thirty. I told Corriere
I had an appointment in Latrobe, some two hundred miles to
the west, at four. He knew the drive well, said I'd need every
minute I had, and scoffed at my suggestion that I take U.S.
30, which looked to be the most direct route. "If you've been
on it once," he said, "that's enough. Take the turnpike." He
started to lead me to the door. "Wait a minute," he said, and
vanished. A couple of minutes later he reappeared with a large
plastic bag into which he'd stuffed several smaller bags of Utz
potato chips. "Something for the road," he said, and sent me
on my way.

I followed instructions: north on State Road 94 to Carlisle,
onto I-81 for a minute, then west on the Pennsylvania Turnpike. With the bag of Utz by my side I stood a good chance
of gaining a pound an hour, so it looked like a four-pound
drive. I put Count Basie on the CD player, gave the accelera-
tor a nudge, and pointed myself toward Latrobe, the home of
Arnold Palmer, Mister Rogers, and Rolling Rock beer.

Traffic on the turnpike was light. In recent years I'd read
horror stories about the deterioration of its infrastructure,
and at times the pavement was unpleasantly bumpy, but on
the whole it was in pretty good shape for a highway that had
celebrated its fiftieth birthday the previous autumn. As Dan
Cupper points out in *The Pennsylvania Turnpike: A History*,
it was not merely "America's first superhighway," but it
"sparked a revolution in the way motorists, truckers, engineers and consumers view highway transportation." The
Pennsylvania Turnpike is grandfather of them all:

> The turnpike's pavement does not extend outside Pennsyl-
> vania, yet its influence reaches to every corner of the United
> States in the form of the 43,000-mile interstate highway sys-
> tem. Although the interstate is a tax-supported network while

the turnpike is financed from tolls and revenue bonds, there's no disputing the fact that from an engineering and motoring standpoint, the turnpike was the direct conceptual predecessor of the interstate system. When the turnpike opened on October 1, 1940, a unique curiosity of transportation was born at a junction of circumstances. The need to put people to work during the Great Depression coincided with renewed interest in the existence of a long-abandoned right-of-way left over from a nineteenth-century railroad war.

The story of that war is complicated and not worth telling here. Its pertinence to the Pennsylvania Turnpike is that in his unsuccessful attempt to compete with the Pennsylvania Railroad during the 1880s, William H. Vanderbilt built a sequence of tunnels through the state's mountains. By the 1930s they were in various states of repair and completion, but they provided a base upon which the turnpike could be constructed. It was a massive project for its time, and it engaged the public's interest intensely. At the hour of its opening motorists were lined up by the hundreds for the privilege of being among the first to pay its tolls and drive its four-lane, all-concrete roadway.

They did so at any speed they wished. It had been agreed that the prevailing Pennsylvania limit of fifty miles an hour would not apply to the turnpike; Governor Arthur James changed his mind and ordered that it be enforced, but, according to Cupper, this ruling "was ignored both by motorists and the turnpike detail of troopers." He tells of a truck driver from Ohio, zipping along at seventy or eighty miles an hour, who saw a white patrol car following him and pulled over in the expectation of being ticketed. Instead the officer asked, "How do you like the road?" and then added: "No, we aren't interested in the speed limit. As long as you stay on your own side and watch yourself, we won't bother you."

Now we know: They really *were* the good old days. The posted speed limit this day was a pusillanimous fifty-five, and a sign warned, YOU CAN BEAT A MILE A MINUTE, BUT THERE IS

NO FUTURE IN IT. I had absolutely no idea what ceiling of
tolerance was observed by the Pennsylvania Highway Patrol,
so for a while I inched along at a frustrating sixty miles an
hour. Gradually, as I was passed by a steady succession of cars
with their smarmy "You Have a Friend in Pennsylvania"
license tags, I decided that I could kick it up to seventy and
did so the rest of the way to my exit at New Stanton.

Jack Corriere had been right. I needed every minute I had.
I pulled into the parking lot at the Latrobe Brewing Company
with exactly one minute to spare. I was in a state of high
anticipation. I'd liked Rolling Rock ever since I first tasted it
in the Allegheny Mountains more than three decades before,
and my curiosity had been aroused by the description of its
plant by Michael Jackson—the English beer writer, not the
American pop screecher—as a "small, beautifully equipped
brewery." What, I wondered, does such a place look like?
How does it work?

My appointment was with Albert W. Spinelli, vice president in charge of operations. At Latrobe, as at Utz, I'd been
referred not to a director of public relations but to a ranking
executive, and in both cases I was impressed; the firms were
still small enough to permit the people in charge to maintain
direct contact with the public.

Spinelli was in his late thirties, tall and slightly stooped,
with a mustache and a wary manner; he too clearly had been
put on the alert by the *Post* connection, though I'd tried to
explain that I'm no Woodward or Bernstein. But his guard
came down a bit as he started telling me about Rolling Rock.

These weren't good times for the beer business. Not merely
did it face, as the snack industry did, new public concern
about calories, it also had to cope with a 100 per cent increase
in the federal excise tax and the new prohibitionism that had
been stirred by Mothers Against Drunk Driving and other
groups. "It's getting more and more difficult to sell beer,"
Spinelli told me. "Ale isn't as acceptable as it once was. Beer
is holding on pretty well, but it's just not going to get any

easier. The old lifestyles aren't cool anymore. Business will continue to be flat or to decline slowly over the years."

That's true of the industry generally; at Latrobe it is another story altogether. Since its acquisition in 1987 by Labatt's, the big Canadian brewing, food, and entertainment conglomerate, Rolling Rock has been on a roll. Its annual production had risen from just under a half-million barrels in 1986 to an anticipated eight hundred thousand in 1991. Its annual average increase in sales had been 12 per cent and, according to the 1990 Labatt's annual report that Spinelli gave me, in 1989 Rolling Rock "reported a solid 16 per cent volume increase."

How had this happened? When I had my first Rolling Rock lo those many years ago, it had been what Spinelli called "a local beer," a "working man's beer drunk by people who ordered a shot and a beer." Working people still drank beer, but in an economy headed for a nosedive they didn't look like a growth market. Where was Rolling Rock's new prosperity coming from?

Yuppies. In the argot of marketing and advertising, Rolling Rock had been "repositioned" as a yuppie beer. Instead of aiming its advertising at its traditional market, Rolling Rock changed gears in the late 1980s and pointed itself directly at the young, the affluent, and the self-aware. Spinelli talked about being in a "niche" between Anheuser-Busch on the mass-distribution side and the microbreweries—Anchor Steam, Sam Adams, Old Heurich—on the other. According to a story a few months later in *Adweek*, "The marketing minds behind Rolling Rock . . . saw a window of opportunity in the super-premium segment, where brands like Michelob and Löwenbräu were losing their allure with customers who wanted something unique."

As Spinelli told me: "We sell at premium prices in Rolling Rock's old markets. In our expansion markets, we sell at a superpremium price." The traditional market is Pennsylvania itself, where Rolling Rock gets 30 per cent of its sales; the new

market is the Northeast, which for a decade has been the
beer's fastest-growing area. A beer that by Spinelli's admission had been "undermarketed over the years" was now being
promoted with skill and imagination—and no small knowledge of the self-infatuation and status insecurity of its new
clientele.

Rolling Rock has, as *Adweek* put it, "long history, distinctive packaging and special aura." Its first beer was brewed in
Latrobe in 1893 and named in honor of the mountain rocks
down which poured the springwater that in time found its
way into the brewery's vats. Although it comes in several
different packages, the best known are the long-necked green
twelve-ounce bottle and the seven-ounce "pony," named for
the equine head on its logo. As for the "special aura," much
of that comes from the number 33 on the back of each bottle.
It's really no mystery at all: The number of letters in the
beer's ingredients—water, malt, rice, hops, corn, brewer's
yeast—totals thirty-three, though why on earth anyone
thought to count them really *is* a mystery.

It happens also to be good beer, though among beer drink-
ers taste is more hotly disputed than among potato chip eat-
ers. Michael Jackson calls it "a very clean-tasting beer" and
gives it two stars out of a possible four. I'd give it three. It
doesn't have the body of the heavier beers and ales brewed by
the likes of Anchor Steam and Sierra Nevada, but as a re-
fresher it hardly has any competition. Mow the lawn for an
hour and then reward yourself with a Rolling Rock; you'll
want to mow it all over again, just for an excuse to drink
another. It's lighter than many of the indistinguishable national brands, but its taste is far more distinctive and interesting.

Like Utz, Latrobe makes a fetish of quality. "The ingredients of beer are pretty much standard," Spinelli told me. "The
difference between brands lies in the formulation and in the
consistency with which it's maintained." This is the job of
the brewmaster, whose character has evolved over the years
from that of a man with an instinctive feel for beer to that of

one deeply schooled in chemistry and technology. He wasn't
at his post this day, but as Spinelli began walking me around
the clean, modern plant it became obvious that there was no
particular need for him to be; nothing of the slightest urgency
was taking place.

Except at the packaging end, brewing beer could not possibly be more different from producing potato chips. The latter
is not exactly frantic, but it moves at high speeds and is over
almost before it begins. Brewing, by contrast, takes its time;
from the first cooking of the "cereal" from which beer is made
until the day it is shipped, about a month passes. It is not, on
the whole, a very interesting month.

Spinelli started me at the vats where the aforementioned
thirty-three-letter ingredients are cooked; there was nothing
to see. We then moved on to the two dozen fermenting tanks,
each holding twelve hundred and fifty gallons, in which the
brew stands for eight days; nothing to see there, either,
though the sheer size of the tanks was impressive enough. Our
next stop was the aging cellar, where the mixture sits for three
weeks at a temperature of thirty-three degrees; still more
nothing.

Then we stepped into the bottling room and it was another
story. Capless bottles and topless cans whirled around on a
succession of belts, passing first under faucets from which beer
spurted in precisely controlled twelve-ounce doses, then under
machines that capped the bottles and topped the cans. The
process was incredibly fast and stirred a considerable clatter.
Spinelli told me that Latrobe can polish off eleven hundred
cans a minute, eight hundred tall bottles, and—because they
fill more rapidly—twelve hundred ponies. It happens almost
faster than the eye can comprehend; it astounded me that
there wasn't any breakage with all that glass racing past, but
Spinelli said that it was rare.

Also like Utz, Latrobe works against fairly tight deadlines.
The shelf life of beer is six months, but Spinelli said they start
pulling Rolling Rock at ninety days. Inventory on the floor
covers only a week; figuring out how much to brew, and

keeping its taste exactly consistent with what's been brewed before, is no mean trick. But Latrobe isn't staying put. The plant it now has in place is capable of 1.3 million barrels a year, three hundred thousand more than it produced in 1991; whatever may be happening in the rest of the industry, Latrobe's "niche" just looks to get larger.

Spinelli walked me to my car. I asked if he enjoyed his line of work. "It's a fun business," he said. "It attracts a unique personality, people who have pride in what they do. It's a close-knit fraternity, at least on the production side."

What's more, I thought, you get to test the product.

I spent the night at a Best Western outside the college town of Indiana, Pennsylvania. Not to pick on Best Western, but: Has anyone out there noticed that the American motel is going to hell in a handbasket? I'd stayed overnight at more than a dozen different places in the past nine months, only four of which—the Four Seasons in Philadelphia, the Greenbrier, the Sanderling Inn, and the Hilton outside Lynchburg—had been as pleasant as I'd expected, and all of them were priced well beyond my usual travel budget. The run-of-the-mill motels had been almost uniformly disastrous. Best Western had ranked at the top in ratings published the previous year by *Consumer Reports*, but for the life of me I couldn't see why. The room in this one was dingy, the pool was fenced off and swimming hours were limited, dinner at its restaurant was barely edible; the same had been true at all my other Best Westerns and Quality Inns and Holiday Inns. A few months later I read a story in the *Wall Street Journal* about an increase in crime at inexpensive motels, much of it connected to drugs, and that helped explain some of what I'd encountered; but I was still saddened not merely by the decline in the quality of these establishments but also by the sense that no one was doing anything about it.

I got up early the next morning and got out as fast as I could. Before leaving I went to downtown Indiana. I wanted to see the statue of its most famous son, Jimmy Stewart. The

light of daybreak was still thin, but there he was, right in the
middle of town, striking a pose that could have been from any
of the dozens of movies in which he etched himself forever in
the American imagination. How appropriate it was, I
thought, that this quintessentially American figure should
have been born in a small town in the Mid-Atlantic, a town
named for a state in the Midwest. You couldn't get much
more American than that.

I released the brake, made a U-turn, and nosed my way
over to U.S. 119. I was going fifty miles due north, headed
once again deep into my own past. I wanted to see the town
of Brookville. That was where, in the summer of 1959, I had
tasted my first Rolling Rock and my first Utz. It was also
where for three months I had gotten out of my own world and
into that of people quite unlike me. It had been a good summer that I remembered with fondness. I wondered what
Brookville looked like now.

It was my mother who got me there. During the Depression
the legal services of her father had been engaged by a small
mining operation in the Alleghenies that, like so much else in
those days, hovered at the edge of extinction. His labor on its
behalf was by all accounts heroic; he kept the firm out of
bankruptcy until it could get back on its feet, and maintained
a friendly relationship with it thereafter.

As the summer of 1959 approached I was eighteen years old
and had never had a genuinely demanding job. I'd always
worked in the summers, but as a farmhand at Chatham Hall
or a counselor at a day camp in Rhode Island. My parents
knew that I was headed for a life in which my mind would get
more exercise than my body; they thought, properly, that I
needed a real taste of real labor. So my mother wrote to her
father's old client and asked if a place might be found for me
somewhere. The answer was in the affirmative: Not merely did
he have a job for me, he also had one for my Chapel Hill
classmate and close friend, John Colescott.

We got there in early June. We had been assigned to a
section gang on the railroad, known as the Pittsburgh &

Shawmut, which ran coal from the Alleghenies down to the
company's headquarters in Kittanning. We were scared very
nearly to death. We weren't spoiled boys, but we'd lived
protected and insulated lives in which manual labor was a
matter of choice, not necessity. Furthermore we were college
students, come to a part of the country where few went
beyond high school and where suspicion of our kind ran fairly
high, by no means without reason. We knew we'd spend the
summer in a room rented to us by an older widow and that we
would make what seemed to us a terrific amount of money—
around $100 a week, I believe—but beyond that we knew
nothing at all.

The crew to which we reported consisted of about a half
dozen men. They were, as we came to understand, exceptionally honest and decent men, but in their eyes we were freaks.
Their teasing wasn't mean, but it certainly was to the point.
We were "college boys"; whether we could muscle up to the
demands of the job struck our fellow workers as highly doubt-
ful. Beyond that there was the foreman, a gruff, pithy old man
named Walter Reitz. In time I came to have a deep admiration for him, but most of the summer he had me in a state of
terror. He could laugh at a joke or tell one, but his glare could
slice your neck in half and his bite was every bit as sharp as
his bark.

Early each morning we all climbed aboard a hand trolley
and pumped our way along the tracks to whatever section of
rail was in need of raising and aligning. Nowadays this work
is done by machines, but then it was all done by hand. Mr.
Reitz—I'd have been shot on the spot if I'd called him "Walter"—bent down over the track and sized it up by eye and by
level. He told us where to go, and we went. We urged the track
into line with immense crowbars, moving in unison; we raised
the track with jacks. Then we took shovels and, with one man
at each side of a crosstie, pushed the heavy gravel under the
tie—"tamped" it—until it held firm.

We did this day after day, week after week. It was cold in
the morning and blistering by noon, especially in the ravines

through which parts of the track passed. When lunchtime came we collapsed, wolfing down the lunches we'd packed—the other men had far more appetizing ones than we did—and gulping water. By day's end we were utterly exhausted, too tired to do much more than go back to our room and fall into our beds.

But we didn't quit. The railroad didn't defeat us. We never got very good at our work, but the men stopped teasing us as outsiders and started teasing us as equals. They got on us about our love lives, which were nonexistent until I somehow burst out of my shyness and found, for a few weeks, a girl-friend. They asked us about what we studied in college, what we hoped to be in life, how we thought we'd remember them twenty or thirty years hence. They took an interest in us that bordered on the paternal. Even—no, especially—Walter Reitz.

We ended up having a very good time. I can speak only for myself—poor dear John died suddenly, in his mid-thirties, before he'd had a chance at a real life—but I think it fair to say that we came to love Brookville. Any distance we may at first have felt from its railway, coal, oil, and lumber workers was soon dispelled; we admired their grit, their good humor, their forbearance, and we came to look up to many of them. We also found a few friends our own age who introduced us to the low life in Punxsutawney, twenty miles to the southeast, where we consumed not merely Rolling Rock but also potions far more potent. We were fascinated by our landlady's son, a man in his forties who worked—when he worked at all—as a professional gambler. He was a figure of legend for most of the summer; when at last he appeared, he turned out to be a mild-mannered fellow who was happy to talk baseball with us.

I'd be lying if I said we were displeased when the summer ended; I did stay on until the last of August—John packed it in two or three weeks earlier—but that was more out of a sense that I should finish what I'd begun than out of any desire to keep on heaving that crowbar. I was in the best physical shape of my life and was proud that I'd risen to a

challenge the exact dimensions of which I'd scarcely understood when I undertook it. I had learned a lot about what it's
like to do hard work with one's hands, and what I'd learned
imbued me with a respect for those who do such work that I
maintain to this day. But I'd also learned that whatever the
shortcomings of my wits, it was by them that my life would
be lived; it was time to get on with that life.

Now I drove into Brookville at about eight in the morning.
The SHO had never been there, but it seemed to know exactly
where to go. I stayed straight, rode up a steep hill, turned
right, and there I was: right in front of the little house, near
the intersection of Barnett and Jefferson streets. The neighborhood looked more modest than I'd remembered it, but the
house was exactly the same: square, yellowish brown brick, a
covered porch to one side and a small one at the front door.
One night John and I came back from Punxsutawney and left
much of the night's carousing on the floor of that side porch;
the next morning our landlady was patient, and mildly
amused, but very, very firm in her disapproval.

I was amazed at how easy it was; if I could find the house
that quickly, finding the railroad would be a snap. I drove a
couple of blocks down the hill, parked on the main street, and
went in search of breakfast. I found it at a place called the
American Hotel. The name was different but the place was the
same. This was where, once John and I had fit into the local
ways, we used to come for dinner. There was an astonishingly
beautiful young woman who worked there, a year or two our
senior but light-years beyond our reach; we stared in desperate longing, savoring each word she bestowed upon us as she
took our orders and cleared our places. When she was on duty,
we could make a hamburger last two hours.

Breakfast was fine, certainly far better than I'd have had
back at the Best Western. I ate slowly, read the local papers,
then wandered out to the street. I was going to walk to the
railroad—I quite clearly remembered the route we'd taken—
but first I thought I'd look around. What I saw was another
classic American small town: handsome, not beautiful in the

manner of New Castle, but sturdy and self-sufficient. The lettering on McCabe's Rexall Drugs looked as if it had been there at least thirty-five years, and the red-brick courthouse at the center of town was just as quietly dignified as I'd remembered it. Of course there were changes—the Video Shop, the Meeting Place, All of My Favorite Things: A Collectible and Consignment Shop—but they were purely cosmetic. Brookville was the same as ever: a hard place to work and a good place to live.

Now it was time to see the railroad. I swung confidently down the hill. I walked several blocks, looked as far as I could, and realized there was no railroad there. I walked back to town and went down another hill; no railroad there, either. Finally I went into a store and asked directions. I was given an exceedingly complex route that took me several minutes to cover, by car; at its end I had gone two and a half miles. For all those years that walk from our lodgings to the railroad had been a figment of my fancy. Obviously someone gave us a lift. I think his name was Bill.

The railroad looked precisely as I remembered it. A couple of locomotives and several coal cars sat on side tracks. SHAW-MUT LINE, they said; whatever happened to Pittsburgh & Shawmut? The work shed where we'd assembled each morning and parted each evening was long, low, cluttered; pieces of equipment were scattered here and there, inside and out.

It was after nine by now and the place was deserted. I felt as though I were an intruder. I was just about to leave when I saw what looked as if it were an office. I pushed the door open and went in. A man in his forties was sitting at a desk. He looked up and gave me a friendly, quizzical smile. I doubt that he saw many middle-aged men wearing Bermuda shorts and carrying notepads and cameras.

"About thirty years ago I worked here for a summer," I said. "Do you mind if I look around?"

"Help yourself. What kind of work did you do?"

"I was a section hand. We used to go out and tamp all day."

"No kidding. We haven't done that here for years. Now it's all automated."

I stood there for a moment. "Just out of curiosity," I said, "do you remember my foreman? His name was Walter Reitz."

"Walter Reitz." He turned that over in his mind. "No, I never met him, but I heard about him. He was one of our best men."

"Oh," I said, "he was a good man, all right. But let me tell you this. If you were eighteen years old, all he did was scare you half to death."

The man shook his head and laughed. I thanked him and left. I had permission to look around, but I'd seen all I needed to see. I'd given new life to old memories, and gotten a glimpse of the boy who had lived them.

16

MOUNTAINEERS

I was three hours west of Baltimore, in the far western panhandle of Maryland. A few minutes earlier there had been signs for Deep Creek Lake; now I passed over the Youghiogheny River. Ahead I could see another sign: WELCOME TO WILD, WONDERFUL WEST VIRGINIA. I couldn't have been happier, not to leave Maryland but to be rid at last of its fifty-five-mile-an-hour speed limit. I'd been driving an edgy seventy; now I could hold that speed and relax, knowing that it was within legal reach of the sixty-five that sensible West Virginia had adopted.

Think of West Virginia and you think of mountains. But here, at its northeastern corner, the terrain was more hilly than rough, more rolling than angular. With the occasional exception of a weathered farmhouse or shack, the only sign of habitation was U.S. 48 itself, snaking gently through the hills on its way to Morgantown and the junction with I-79. Traffic was light, and most of the few cars I saw had Maryland tags; for the people of far-western Maryland, Morgantown must be the place to shop and perhaps even to work.

A billboard advertised the Ponderosa Steak House; another, the Stone Crab Inn. I wondered, What's going on here? The ponderosa is a pine of the American West, the stone crab

a delicacy of Florida. What connection could either possibly
have with West Virginia? Was this an effort to import glam-
our, or just another small instance of American roadside incongruity?

It was a clear, lovely morning, but the closer I came to
Morgantown the thicker and dirtier the air became. I never
saw smokestacks or any other sign of industrial activity, but
this clearly wasn't nature's doing. In fact, I never saw Morgantown at all. It was an oddity; the highway passed within
a couple of miles of one of West Virginia's major cities, the site
of its state university, yet on neither U.S. 48 nor I-79 was
there a single sign that urbanity lurked nearby.

South of Morgantown the air got even dirtier; the sun was
barely visible. But at least it was a quick, uneventful thirty
miles from Morgantown south to Clarksburg, where I turned
due west on U.S. 50. Now the air began to clear and the land
started to resemble what I'd expected. The hills slanted down
to the road at steep angles, thick with trees. Every once in a
while I passed a hamlet so tiny it couldn't be found on my
AAA map, approached by a road—usually unpaved—called
Dog's Run or England's Run or Wilhelm Run or Cabin Run.

It was land of incredible beauty, but I couldn't help thinking that its beauty was exceeded only by its uselessness for
human habitation. I tried, with not much success, to imagine
the struggles of the settlers crossing these forbidding mountains, one after one, in what must have seemed a process
without hope of end. Here I sped through it at sixty-five miles
an hour, thinking much about the beauty and little about how
hard and unforgiving that beauty was.

It served as backdrop to human flotsam and jetsam. Pushing right up to the edge of the road were trailers and shacks
with dead automobiles suspended on blocks or foundered on
the ground. On the tumbledown porch of one tumbledown
shack sat a figure out of Al Capp or Erskine Caldwell, an old
gent on a rocker, pipe in his mouth, idly watching the race of
man pass by. A few miles later there was another cliché: a
lean, erect farmer at the wheel of his pickup truck, his prim

wife seated beside him. *American Gothic* may have lost its edge decades ago, but a scene such as that showed exactly how right Grant Wood had got it.

Progress had come to the tiny town of Sandyville; in its center was "3-D Video—One-Stop Party Shop." How did they like that nearby at the Mud Run Church of Christ? Not much, I suspected. The same video stores that had invaded the crossroads of Tidewater Virginia were up here in the hills of West Virginia, bringing the glittering icons of contemporary America—Madonna, Cher, Prince—to the grim precincts of Appalachia.

Just east of Parkersburg I went south on I-77 for a mile, exited at State Road 47, and worked my way along the banks of the Little Kanawha River to State Road 6, a thoroughfare unacknowledged by the mapmakers at AAA. I stayed on that, the banks of the river not far to my right, until I saw the sign: LITTLE KANAWHA NURSERY. WHOLESALE ONLY. I turned in and followed directions to a double-wide trailer hard by a man-made pond. I got out of the car, knocked at the door, and was given a welcoming hug by my sister Jane.

How did Jane Yardley, then forty-nine years old and still in the prime of her youth, find her way to a trailer in a nursery by a river in West Virginia? It is one of my favorite stories.

In the late 1950s and early 1960s, when Jane was a student first at Chatham Hall and then at Sweet Briar, her closest friend was a girl from West Virginia named Mary Amos. In the course of various visits back and forth between the girls' residences, Jane came to know Mary's older brother, John, whom she regarded as something of a hero; once John escorted her to a fancy ball—they were photographed there, Jane looking stunned at her good fortune—but that was as far as things went.

John got married and stayed in West Virginia, practicing law; Jane got married and moved to Maine, where her husband, too, practiced law. Then, in the mid-1980s, Jane and Rob Page divorced. Jane started a new life. She went back to

school for a year, polished up her credentials in teaching and
school administration, and got a job at a private school in
Minneapolis. She became head of its lower school, bought a
town house near the center of the city, made new friends, and
was as happy as ever she had been.

Then one day she had a telephone call from John Amos. He
was in town on business. Would she like to have dinner? Of
course she would. She liked it even more when she realized
that John too was at loose marital ends. It had taken them a
quarter century to get together, but things moved fast once
they did. On a sunny day in July 1989, they were married in
our backyard in Baltimore, next to the swimming pool we had
at last constructed. It was one of the happiest days my family
has known.

Jane quit her job in Minneapolis and moved with John to
Parkersburg; she did so knowing that she was giving up a
great deal, but confident that she was gaining a great deal
more. John by then had quit his law practice and was devot-
ing his full energies to running the nursery, which he and a
partner had started several years before. For a year the newly-
weds lived in John's house, but they wanted one of their own,
so when a good offer came along they sold. The problem was
that they hadn't yet found a new place of their own; they
solved it, temporarily, by moving into the vacant trailer at
the nursery.

If you doubt that appearances can be deceiving, come with
me inside this double-wide trailer. However unprepossessing
it may have been on the outside, on the inside it was a comfortable and ample dwelling. It had three bedrooms, a couple
of bathrooms, a full kitchen, and a substantial living room, as
well as an enclosed porch large enough to contain the two
rambunctious young Dalmatians to which Jane and John
had, inexplicably, become ardently attached.

John was off meeting with bankers. Running a nursery is a
hard, risky business. By the fall of 1988 John thought he had
Little Kanawha well in hand, but then disaster struck. On

September 22 the area was hit by a hard freeze; the temperature went down to twenty-two degrees, with devastating effect on the rhododendrons and azaleas that are the nursery's chief wares. Overnight, John was transported from a state of modest prosperity to one of near-penury. The nursery became dependent on the kind attentions of banks, whose officers extended loans warily and with the usual strings attached.

I had not realized it until I got there, but today's meeting was crucial. If the bank refused to give Little Kanawha the money it needed to survive, everything that John and Jane owned could be at risk, from the farm at the other end of the state that had been John's parents' to the house he and Jane had just bought in Parkersburg. So when the telephone suddenly rang, Jane could be forgiven for starting nervously and hurrying to answer it.

The news was good. Whatever it was that John had said to the bankers about his plans to reorganize the nursery—to make it more efficient and to bring its managerial practices up to speed—they clearly had liked. Not merely had they bailed Little Kanawha out for the moment, they had assured it a financial pillow against which to rest in the future. John and Jane—she had stepped into an active role in the firm's business office—could now turn their attention to running the daily affairs of the company and, though it would take years, to retiring the indebtedness that had been run up in the aftermath of the big chill.

So the mood that evening was celebratory. John and Jane had a treat in store for me. We packed a picnic and drove to Parkersburg, where their small powerboat lay at anchor near the junction of the Little Kanawha and Ohio rivers. John cranked up the motor and we eased our way to the Ohio, headed on a northeasterly course. We were in the spot described by *West Virginia: A Guide to the Mountain State* as "the valley of the beautiful Ohio, beloved of the Indians and important in the early development of the Northwest." This is how it was in the valley a half-century ago:

Agricultural customs of 100 years ago are common in the back country: grain is harvested with horse-powered threshers, and fodder for livestock is ground in hand mills. Neighbors gather for all-night vigils at maple-sugar camps; out from the morning mist blanketing the hillsides, men and boys emerge, plodding toward the syrup stills, their shoulders bent under the weight of buckets of sugar-water suspended from wooden beams.

There were no signs of horsepower or maple sugar, but the valley was beautiful even now. At Parkersburg a few houses of surprisingly nondescript character lined the riverbank— you'd think the local aristocracy would fall all over itself for river views—and farther on there were the usual signs of industrial activity. But there weren't many of them. We took the right fork of the river past Neal Island, then rejoined the mainstream as we continued toward Marietta, Ohio, a dozen miles upriver from Parkersburg.

As we neared Marietta there were a couple of old riverboats lashed to the bank, now at permanent anchor and functioning as restaurants or nightspots. At Marietta we swung briefly north onto the Muskingum River, then turned around, killed the motor, and floated idly—there was almost no traffic on the river—while we ate our picnic and drank our wine.

The setting bordered on the idyllic. I had been absolutely unprepared for it. Ignorant outlander that I was, I'd never associated West Virginia with the Ohio, though even the briefest glimpse at a map could have told me that the river defines the state's entire western border. But sometimes ignorance really is bliss; knowing nothing, I was in a condition to be startled, and thus to be reminded that the surprises this country holds in wait for the traveler are infinite in number and glorious in nature.

In the morning I got a shorter tour. For a couple of hours John walked me around the twenty-six acres occupied by the Little Kanawha Nursery. He is a tall, easygoing man with an instinct for the irreverent and a calmness—at least on the exterior—of which I am passionately envious. His father was a self-made man who came out of the countryside, established himself as a lawyer, and for a while in the 1950s and 1960s was one of the most influential political figures in a state that takes its politics with intense seriousness. Though John absorbed a lifetime's worth of political knowledge from his father, to whom he was close, in the end he decided to make his own life, in Parkersburg rather than Charleston, raising plants rather than trying cases.

In the 1970s, when the nursery got under way, it was little more than a patch of ground. Now it had a hundred twenty-five greenhouses and an inventory valued at more than $2 million. A map in the office was dotted with pins, showing the places to which Little Kanawha ships its azaleas and rhododendrons; all the states of the Mid-Atlantic were amply represented, but so too were places as far west as Kansas City, as far northeast as Boston, and as far south as Alabama. Rated against the competition, John said, Little Kanawha is "significant but not major"; its biggest account to date had been K Mart, with which it had substantial if not grand dealings.

On this midsummer day the nursery was quiet. The shed across the road where its homegrown potting soil is mixed was shut down. The workers hired by the day to pot cuttings and infant plants weren't needed that day. In the greenhouses the plants sat unattended, in various stages of growth—doing their own thing, just like the beer in Latrobe's vats a hundred and fifty miles to the east.

The nursery was orderly and clean, but you could hardly call it beautiful. The greenhouses were of metal frames wrapped in clear plastic, more pleasing to the plants inside than to the eye. The paths between them were gravelly, with hoses wandering in different directions and puddles here and there. Someday the shrubs would be replanted in suburban yards in Charlotte and Harrisburg, Charleston and Richmond, Pittsburgh and Baltimore, and would lend much color

and beauty to them. But it takes work to make beautiful
things, and Little Kanawha was strictly a working place—"a
ton of hard work," as John put it.

After my tour of the nursery I put my bag in the SHO and
prepared to leave. John and Jane had insisted that I could not
visit them without also visiting the Amos family place—The
Farm, as the family calls it—a four-hour drive to the south in
the hills near Lewisburg and White Sulphur Springs. They
also had insisted that I drive not the back roads but the two
interstates, I-77 south to Charleston and I-77-64 southeast to
Lewisburg. The previous night John had talked about the
tremendous pride that West Virginians take in their interstates, and reminded me that they have John Fitzgerald
Kennedy to thank for them; in exchange for West Virginia's
votes at the 1960 Democratic Convention, he promised to
break the logjam that had kept the state out of the interstate
system, and he delivered.

So I drove back to I-77 and turned south. Immediately
ahead of me was a car, being driven badly, with Ohio plates.
John had told me that in the eyes of West Virginians, Ohioans
are hillbillies and never to be trusted on the road; I told him
that Marylanders feel precisely the same way about Pennsyl-
vanians. But John then laughed and qualified his statement
by confessing, "We may look down on Ohioans, but we look
up to just about everybody else."

I reached Charleston in a hurry. The first eighty miles of the
trip were notable more for efficiency than beauty. I didn't
stop off at Charleston, but I did observe that precisely the
same was true there as at Morgantown: The approach gave no
evidence that a city lay ahead, though once Charleston finally
came into view the highway cut almost through the center of
town and provided a panorama of it.

Now the highway turned to the south. I was on the combined I-77 and I-64, the West Virginia Turnpike, a toll road
and thus a direct descendant of the Pennsylvania Turnpike.
For a few miles the road followed the Kanawha River, but

then it cut away and raced along beside mountains. Clearly
the highway was an engineer's dream, carved so efficiently out
of harsh territory that the motorist could give scarcely a
thought to its dangers and concentrate instead on its majesty.
At Beckley I exited for a late lunch and a look around. Its
downtown was, like those of so many other small cities, pretty
much bombed out; an attempt had been made to fabricate a
center-city mall with bricked streets and other contrivances
calculated to create an effect of old-fashioned charm, but it
was more pathetic than charming. The city's traffic engineers
seemed determined to keep as many people away from it as
possible, for the streets were designed to get cars through
town lickety-split—though this day their design had been
thwarted by traffic jams so intense as to bring the place to a
halt. I couldn't help wondering if the rest of West Virginia
seemed so sparsely populated because everybody had come to
Beckley.

I had the usual fast-food lunch and then worked my way
over to the city's chief tourist attraction, the Beckley Exhibi-
tion Coal Mine. "Beckley, West Virginia," read its brochure.
"The City With a Mine of Its Own." For decades it had been
a working mine; now it was a mini-theme park, complete with
a gift shop hustling "homemade cream and butter fudge and
'Coal Candy' from down in the mine!"

I paid my $5 and sat down to wait for the car that, visitors
were assured, was "guided through the mine by veteran min-
ers for an authentic view of low seam coal mining from its
earliest manual stages to modern mechanized operation." At
the entrance to the mine a "Fire Boss Report" declared that
the mine was safe and that the temperature inside was fifty-
eight degrees. Finally the little line of cars chugged out of the
mine, discharged its load of tourists, and took on ours, which
now numbered about two dozen.

Our guide was a septuagenarian gentleman, a pleasant fellow who had been cursed with a congenital inability to shut
his mouth. The tour took about forty-five minutes; he chat-
tered throughout, sometimes inanely and sometimes not. He

told us that he was one of five members of his family who had
worked in the mines and the only one who was neither dead
nor dying of black lung. He had "five per cent black lung," he
said, and thought himself lucky; he'd been an engineer rather
than a miner and thus had spent comparatively little time
inhaling coal dust. He loved working in the mines but acknowledged that it was "a very, very hard and dangerous
business"; this drew a sympathetic murmur from his retinue,
many members of which had by now identified themselves as
from mining families.

We didn't go very deep into the mine. Given the tendency
to claustrophobia from which I suffer, I was just as glad. It
was cold—all of us had brought sweaters or jackets—and
moist and dark. Only a very small person could have stood
upright. In order to gain access to many of the corridors that
branched off the main one along which we slowly rode, it was
necessary to lie down on a low cart and propel oneself into the
equivalent of a long, dank coffin. That people could not
merely tolerate such an existence but take pride in it was more
than I could comprehend; but West Virginians are strong,
doughty people who have learned to live with hard labor and
privation.

Back on I-64, and into the most spectacular stretch of road I
had seen anywhere along the thousands of miles I had by now
traveled. The road was mine alone; I scooted up to eighty and
held steady there, delighting in the car's power and its smooth
passage through the highway's gentle curves. The forests
alongside the road were incredibly thick and, as at the state's
northern edge, impossibly green. A bridge carried me over
what was identified as Glade Creek, though I could not see it
through the deep ravine below. I looked up at one mountain—high, *high* above the road—and was astonished to see
an auto junkyard near its crest: How on earth had they gotten
the wrecks up there, and *why*? But patches such as this of
what passes for civilization were rare, and when they did come

along it was hard not to admire the tenacity of those who inhabited them.

Not far from Lewisburg a sign beckoned me to Sam Black Church. It was tempting to pull off and take a picture or two, see how picturesque the place no doubt was, but in the instant I had to make up my mind I decided to stay put. The last thing the souls of Sam Black Church needed, I thought, was someone from Baltimore poking around in their privacy, condescending to them with his city ways. So I left Sam Black Church alone, but later I looked it up in the WPA guide:

> A small bell tower rises above the hipped roof of the rectangular Sam Black Church, a white frame structure erected in 1902 in memory of the Reverend Sam Black, an early Southern Methodist circuit rider. His name is written in large letters across the doorway of the building. On his horse, Shiloh, Black traveled through Greenbrier, Fayette, Clay, Nicholas, Webster, and Kanawha Counties, organizing congregations and building churches with money obtained by selling gloves and socks made by women of the church.

I got off at Lewisburg; the Greenbrier was six miles away. Just like that I was in a whole new West Virginia. A store calling itself the Hitchin' Post advertised tack, boots, and apparel for the horsey set. It was a pretty little town with historic houses, many of them identified on a map offered to visitors, but I wasn't interested; what I'd seen and heard at Beckley was still on my mind, and I wasn't in the mood for anything quaint. So I drove south a few miles, turned onto a singularly narrow country road, and found The Farm precisely where it was supposed to be. I opened the gate, drove up to the handsome hilltop house that John's parents had constructed, and parked the car. I'd barely had a chance to look around when Jane, John, and their infernal Dalmatians drove up. As we entered the house I glanced at the guest book in the front hall. The first entry—I could scarcely believe my eyes—was dated June 1–10, 1956, and read: "Jane Yardley, Chatham Hall, Va. No comment for fear of being sent home."

I spent one night at The Farm, a spread of three hundred fifty acres that John's father had bought for what seems a pittance; it is worth a substantial amount now—enough, perhaps, to purchase a pretentious house on a half acre of land ten miles outside Washington or Baltimore—but in the depressed real estate market of 1991 its potential market value had taken a beating. This was a matter of concern, though not urgency, to John. He loved The Farm but wondered if the family used it enough to justify holding on to it; he had thought off and on for years about selling it.

He loaded me into a four-wheel-drive vehicle and we lumbered across the rough countryside to another hill, about a half mile from the house. The machine clawed its way to the top, where John had constructed a handsome picnic area. We could see for miles, a view that included in the near distance a BF Goodrich plant; the inevitable intrusions of growth—however ugly, it meant jobs for West Virginians—were inching toward The Farm, another reason why John wondered if it was time to let the place go and put the money it would bring to some other use.

The subject was gnawing at John's mind; Jane said, half jokingly, that he loved to worry about it. He kept returning to it during the evening, eventually winding his way to one of the strongest reasons for holding on: his deep love for his native state and his reluctance to part with an inch of it that was his. He told me about what he called the "chip-on-their-shoulders" quality characteristic of West Virginians, the inflated pride they take in being Mountaineers. The rest of the country may think West Virginia is depressed and forlorn, he said, but West Virginia itself is stubborn, defensive, ready to take on all comers.

I had an early departure scheduled for the morning, but held it back an hour to baby-sit one of the Dalmatians while Jane and John took the other, which had come up lame, to the veterinarian. As coowner of several city animals I was im-

pressed at the country courtesy of the vet, who told them to
come right in at seven-thirty and who doubtless would have
made a house call had they asked her to. In the city they don't
make house calls; they let you make an appointment, a week
or two in advance.

By nine I was on the road, passing a sign announcing a
reunion of the Ratliff family; I thought at once of V. K.
Ratliff, the amiable, laconic itinerant peddler through whose
eyes we see the comings and goings of the Snopes family in
William Faulkner's great comic novel *The Hamlet.* It's a long
way from West Virginia to Mississippi, but this had the look
of Snopes country: hardscrabble and demanding.

In little more than an hour I was in Bluefield; the last miles
of the drive, on U.S. 460, had been especially pretty, winding
through steep, emerald hills. I found the Holiday Inn, shuddered to see that it would add yet another chapter to the
guidebook of uninhabitable motels that I was assembling, and
checked in. I had nothing to do until seven that evening; I
decided to see what I could see.

Bluefield calls itself "Coal City." Eight miles away is the
gigantic Pocahontas coal field, fourteen hundred square miles,
mined since 1892 yet *still* holding two billion untouched tons
of coal. Coal mines, as I knew from painful experience, need
railroads. Bluefield came into being to provide them. Now, as
fifty years ago, it is a railroad town:

> For four and a half miles of its length Bluefield is split by the
> 21 tracks of the Norfolk and Western Railway yards, always
> filled with hundreds of loaded coal cars and switching engines.
> The business district is separated from the yards by a four-foot
> stone wall, topped with concrete flower pots—an esthetic ges-
> ture in the midst of much smoke, steam, and noise. The noise,
> however, is an index to local prosperity; when the mines are
> active the valley is filled, night and day, with the clink of
> heavy car wheels passing over the maze of switches and the
> whistles of yard locomotives as they shuttle the heavy coal
> gondolas from track to track.

The yards were quiet that day, and so was Bluefield. It was Saturday. Downtown was dead. The only hot spot was a parking garage, hard across the street from the rail yard, in which a flea market had been set up. Everyone in town seemed to be there. In front of me a sedan poked along, the two young couples inside all dressed up as if for church or a party; they hung a hard right and pulled into the flea market.

Almost every other place of business was shut tight. Lampposts along downtown streets had been rigged up with small banners proclaiming the city's renewal, but there was little sign of it. I was ready for lunch, but couldn't find a restaurant—not even a snack bar—that was open and serving.

I ended up a few miles out of town at the Mercer Mall. It could have been anywhere—old folks creaking along, teenaged girls flouncing around in their Farrah Fawcett hairdos, idle boys eyeing them hungrily—except for one startling exception: Right in the heart of the mall stood a statue of a coal car, with a plaque beside it declaring that it was in memory of John L. Lewis. It was hard to imagine that the businessmen who erected this mall had permitted a monument to this most intransigent and truculent of labor leaders; it was even harder to imagine that any of the Valley Girls mincing past had any notion of who he was.

The place to eat at the Mercer Mall, at least for those of a certain age, clearly was the K&W Cafeteria. It put me back into another time warp; it could have been the S&W in Greensboro a quarter century before, with the same food and the same customers. At fifty-one I seemed to be the youngest person in the place, except for the girls who dashed about the dining rooms refilling iced tea glasses. I went through the line, ending up at the cash register with chopped steak and mashed potatoes suffocating under gravy, a salad with an indeterminate dressing, a blueberry muffin and a biscuit, a few chunks of watermelon, and a glass of tea. The check came to only $5.30, but hold your envy: The meal wasn't worth a penny more.

I spent the afternoon driving around the mining country to

the northwest of town. I went about a hundred miles; the roads were such that it took four hours. Besides, there was plenty to look at. On U.S. 52 North—the federal designation makes the road sound far more grand than it actually is—I was startled to see how many black communities there were; but I had managed to forget that West Virginia existed because of its opposition to the Confederate cause and that after the war, in the WPA guide's account, it "was spared the Reconstruction evils of carpetbag government, which brought ill-feeling and hatred between Negroes and whites in states farther south." One such community was called Maybeury. A brief paragraph about it in the guide succinctly characterizes all these little settlements:

> In Maybeury, a mining center, rows of houses, monotonously alike, radiate up narrow hollows into the hills. Near the store is the tipple, from which rise clouds of coal dust to settle on houses and yards. Life for the miner's wife is a continuous chore of dusting and washing; few of the yards are brightened with flowers.

Maybeury was small, poor, and patriotic. The adventure in the Persian Gulf had ended a few months earlier. Obviously Maybeury had sent some of its sons and daughters there. WELCOME HOME TROOPS signs were displayed in windows, tacked up on doors. In the era of the volunteer army, the Maybeurys of America are where the troops come from.

A few miles farther on, the Kimball Garden Club welcomed me to Kimball. I could see no evidence of its handiwork. It was another little red-brick village huddled by the street; most of its storefronts were closed, though the branch library was open and so was the A. P. Wood West Virginia Grocery.

Everywhere I went there were trains. I saw more trains in forty-eight hours in West Virginia than I'd seen in a decade. The road ran parallel to the tracks, right into the famous old mining town of Welch. "On Saturday nights," the guide told me, "thousands of operators from dozens of operations de-

scend upon the town to shop and find amusement; among
them are Negroes, Japanese, Chinese, and Europeans of every
nationality. Race prejudice is conspicuously absent." Today,
people were conspicuously absent. Welch must have gone to
Bluefield for the day. Except for the sight—startling in these
surroundings—of a jogger huffing along the roadside, the
town was empty.

At Welch I turned onto State Road 16 and wound north to
Pineville, through Woosley and Wolf Pen. I looked up a hill
and saw that its strip-mined sides had been replanted and
restored; a couple of miles farther along another hill was still
raw, ugly, and bare. On my left I saw a magnificent stone
building, once the headquarters of a nearby mine, its facade
forbidding and harsh; a sign still identified its personnel office,
but the building was boarded up and deserted.

Right on Route 10, headed back to Bluefield through—the
temptation to read off the roll is irresistible—Itmann, Tralee,
Alpoca, Bud, Herndon, Covel, Arista, Springton, Hiawatha,
Giatto, Matoaka, and Kegley. For a while I drove along the
north bank of the Guyandotte River; it looked clear and cool.
The drive had been easier than I'd expected, but around
Springton the road instantly turned narrow and nasty. I had
to stop looking at the countryside and keep my eye on the
road, which at a couple of spots threatened to veer off into the
void. But I didn't have much chance to do myself harm
because every car in front of me was going ten miles an hour
under the speed limit. I found my way back to the motel and
plunged into the pool.

At six o'clock I was too itchy to wait around any longer. I got
directions from the clerk at the desk and drove about three
miles to Bluefield's substantial recreation and entertainment
complex: a municipal auditorium, a huge swimming pool, a
small football stadium, and, at the very end, the new Bowen
Stadium, dedicated by the Baltimore Orioles to the Bluefield
Orioles on June 25, 1975, "in commemoration of a highly
successful relationship originating in 1958."

The Orioles were what had brought me to Bluefield. For thirteen summers I had sat in the grandstand at Memorial Stadium in Baltimore, watching the major-league Orioles play and developing an emotional relationship with them that was more intense than a grown man in his right mind should countenance. The Bluefield Orioles were at the very other end of the line, a team in the Appalachian Rookie League, as low as you could go in the Baltimore organization and still be inside it. Theoretically Bluefield was where a youngster started on the long climb to the big club; in actuality it was where cold reality introduced itself to all but the most fortunate, as was attested by the presence of only three Bluefield alumni on the twenty-five-man Baltimore major-league roster.

Tonight the Bluefield Orioles were playing the Martinsville Phillies; when I was a boy minor-league teams had their own names, usually reflecting some distinctive local characteristic, but as the minors became appendages of the majors instead of self-sustaining entities, the teams started to assume their identities, and their names, from on high. It was also cheaper that way; the Bluefield Orioles used hand-me-down Baltimore uniforms and equipment, and many of the souvenirs they sold were knockoffs of those to be had at Memorial Stadium.

The parking lot next to Bowen Stadium looked as if it could have handled a crowd of two or three thousand, but there clearly weren't to be that many tonight, even though it was Saturday and a sign on the shuttered box office window read, ADMISSION 'FREE,' SPONSOR HUMANA HOSPITAL. This was a beneficence I hadn't counted on, so when I saw a sign right inside the gate for a raffle to benefit a local charity I handed the girl selling tickets a $5 bill. Then I went to the concession stand for what would have to pass as dinner. I got two large slices of pizza—not bad pizza, either—plus a Diet Pepsi and a program, for $3.75; back in Baltimore that would have gotten me one beer.

Beer wasn't for sale here; fans brought their own. Bowen Stadium was that sort of place. Its concrete stands had no built-in seats, only wide rows along which fans planted folding metal chairs wherever they liked; I picked one up and moved it to the first-base side near home plate, my regular location in Baltimore. I unfolded my chair, took a seat, and looked around.

What I saw pleased me. The stadium itself—*field* or *park* would have been so much better than *stadium*, with its inappropriate evocation of football—was nothing much, though it served its purpose without frills or fuss. The atmosphere was casual; Don Buford, who'd been a star in Baltimore in the 1970s and now worked for the club as director of minor-league field operations, wandered through the stands, saying hello to fans, before taking a seat at the screen behind home plate. A couple of rows behind me two youngsters, one white and one black, had a running mock argument about the ownership of the bat they'd brought.

But what really impressed me was the park's natural setting. Behind the left-field and center-field walls a small mountain rose precipitously to the sky, so sharply it seemed almost perpendicular to the playing field. It was thick with the same astonishingly green trees I'd noticed all over West Virginia. From where I sat it created the illusion that we were in a large bowl; as the evening darkened the mountain seemed to grow closer and closer, higher and higher, enclosing us in shared intimacy.

At 6:59, one minute before game time, the lights came on; someone here was watching his nickels and dimes. It didn't take long for me to realize that I'd picked a bad place to sit. A few feet away was a belligerently loudmouthed woman who delighted in spouting her opinions, every one of them misguided. When a Martinsville player got a hit she jumped up to cheer, realized her mistake, and tried to cover it by shouting, "Wrong team! Wrong team!" I was appalled to discover, a couple of innings later, that she too had come down from Baltimore.

Bowen Stadium looked like a hitters' park, with short shots to center field and the power alleys in left and right, but such hitting as was being done this evening was unimpressive. So were the pitching, the fielding, and the baserunning. Fifteen years before, while living a mile from the campus of the University of Miami, I'd attended the home games of its baseball team with some regularity; they were played at a higher level, and on a better infield, than was this one. The players on both clubs were hustling and enjoying themselves, but accomplishing little; the notes I made about their performance were littered with words like *poor* and *disaster*.

The fans were more interesting. A foul ball got stuck in the screen; a boy climbed the screen and, with what clearly was practiced artistry, extracted the ball. The public-address announcer said, "We have guests here tonight from California. Let's give them a *warm* Bluefield welcome," which is just what the crowd—it looked to be about three hundred—was happy to do. A little boy came through hawking peanuts for the ridiculous price of fifty cents; in Baltimore they're $2.

In the middle of the fifth inning, the announcer said, "Tonight's drawing is worth sixty-five dollars. The number is six four seven nine seven six. I'll repeat that: six four seven nine seven six." I looked at the clump of tickets I'd stuffed into my pocket. The one at the top read: 647977. I looked at the one underneath it. I looked at it again. I turned to the man seated next to me. "Good God!" I said. "I *won!*"

I'd never won anything in my life. I tossed $20 or $30 down the slot machines thirty-two years ago on Route 301 and $55 more down the slots in Atlantic City six months before. I went to the Preakness once and lost my $50 stake before the eighth race had been run. I bet Sonny Liston over Cassius Clay and the Colts over the Jets. All my life I'd been a loser, but on this balmy night in Bluefield, West By-God Virginia, I'd *won.*

I clutched the winning ticket in my right hand and walked down to the aisle. The fans nearby gave me a friendly hand. I went over to the third-base stands and climbed up to the public-address booth. A couple of old parties were sitting in front of it.

"Is this where I turn in my ticket?" I asked.

"Yup," one of them said. I handed it to him. He looked it over carefully. "Looks like you got a winner," he said. He reached into his pocket and pulled out a small roll of bills. He slowly counted them out: three tens, six fives, five ones. Sixty-five dollars. "Thanks a lot," I said, and started to leave.

"Whoa there," he said. "Fill out this here ticket and maybe you'll win that car come August." He pointed to a bright red Geo Metro, parked just inside the main entrance to the park. It looked nice to me—no, I didn't win it—so I filled out the card, thanked him again, and went back to my seat.

I lasted one more inning. The Orioles were ahead 7–4, but it had taken three hours to get that far. Three hours was enough bad baseball for me, that night and almost any other. So I got my gear together and headed out of the stands. Just as I left the public-address announcer spoke again, sending me home thoroughly chastened.

"The winner of the sixty-five dollars," he boomed into the night air, "came all the way from Baltimore, Maryland—Joe . . . Nathan . . . *Yortley*."

17

HOME GAMES

My last journey began early on the afternoon of October 6, 1991, except that it wasn't much of one and it really didn't begin exactly then. It was a journey only if the five-mile round-trip between Hawthorne Road and Venable Avenue can be considered one, and as for when it began . . . that could have been any one of a number of times. It could have been one unknown afternoon in the early 1960s, when I looked at a television set and saw for the first time the row of white houses along 36th Street. It could have been Friday, April 6, 1979, when for more than three hours I sat in an icy wind that chilled my bones right through to the marrow.

Let's say, though, that it began early in the morning of Monday, April 8, 1991. Shortly before six I drove the SHO west on Cold Spring Lane, south on St. Paul Street, southeast on Ellerslie Avenue. At Venable Avenue I turned right and, just past Frisby Street, parked the car. Sue was right behind me. I locked the SHO, jumped into her car, and got a lift to the train station. I did my business in Washington as speedily as decency permitted, then got back on the train and went right back to Baltimore. The first day of my New Year had arrived.

What a day it is. Each year I start worrying about it a

month or more in advance. I consult long-range forecasts, hover over the Weather Channel, cast my eyes to the sky. Will there be rain? (One year there was.) Will there be high winds? (Several years there have been.) Will there be snow? (Once, incredibly, there was.) But this year there was nothing to worry about. This year I stepped out of Penn Station in Baltimore into a blast of heat more typical of July than April. The temperature was eighty-nine degrees; a couple of hours later it climbed into the low nineties.

I could have taken a bus, but traffic on North Charles Street already was dense; in any event, the walk was part of my ritual. I slung my jacket over my shoulder, took off my tie, and headed up the street. By the time I'd worked my way over to Calvert Street, a couple of blocks to the east and several to the north, I was sweating. In the block on North Calvert where my father had participated in fraternity events during his years at Johns Hopkins, a group of men stood in front of a row house in short sleeves. They were grilling hot dogs and drinking beer.

On 33rd Street I turned right, headed east. Now traffic measured its progress in feet and inches; all four lanes were eastbound, and all were packed. The bus I'd thought about riding was nowhere to be seen, presumably still bumper-to-bumper on Charles Street. The sidewalks were packed, too. Vendors were waving pennants and souvenirs. A man was sitting at a card table, chanting over and over, "Peanuts! Get your peanuts! Dollar a bag! Dollar on the outside, two dollar inside! Peanuts! Get your peanuts! Dollar on the outside, two dollar inside!"

I walked over to Venable Avenue and opened the trunk of the SHO. Into it I tossed my jacket, my tie, and my briefcase. From it I extracted two foam-rubber seat cushions and two pairs of binoculars. I closed the trunk, turned around, and headed down the street to Memorial Stadium.

Opening Day. Of the three hundred sixty-four days of my year, there is none to match this one. You can have Christmas, Thanksgiving, the Fourth of July. Give me Opening Day. A long time ago I wrote that the year has only two seasons, Baseball and the Void, and that Opening Day is New Year's Day; a lot of people wrote to say that they agreed, so I must have touched a previously undetected chord.

Let the reader beware. Years ago I promised to stop trying to wax lyrical or rhapsodic about baseball, but I can't say with absolute certainty that the promise will go unbroken here. It is true beyond doubt that far too much saccharine verbiage has been committed in the name of baseball by persons masquerading as poets and novelists, journalists and pundits; I pray not to add to the slag heap. But as I contemplate Opening Day 1991, more than just baseball courses through my mind. The first day of any baseball season is enough to stir the blood, but this day was more than that. It was the last Opening Day at Memorial Stadium, to be followed six months later by the last game ever. A place that had been witness to some of the best baseball in the history of the game was about to close its doors; with them would close a small part of Baltimore and a large part of my life.

I elbowed my way through the crowd at Gate W-2, handed my ticket to the usher, and walked inside. I turned right and started up the dingy ramp. At the field-level concourse the crowd could barely move; I was on the third-base side and had to press all the way around to first. It seemed to take forever, but probably I made it in five minutes. The crowd was immobile but good-natured; there was nearly an hour until game time and nobody seemed in much of a hurry. Just before turning into our section I was appalled to see a new concession stand called "Memorial Stadium Memories"; it seemed that the Orioles, whose previous owner had cowed the state into building them a new ballpark at public expense, were determined to cash in on the same public's affection for the one they were abandoning.

Finally I reached Section 39. Mike the usher was there, at his usual post. We shook hands, then he ran his towel over my seat: Row 16, Seat 7. I sat down, leaned back, and soaked it

all in. It is, to me, the best moment of all on this best of all
days. For six months the sights and sounds everywhere
around me had existed only in memory; now they were back,
and I was there. The flag atop the left-field stands that read
simply, "HERE"; that's where Frank Robinson hit the only
fair ball ever to leave Memorial Stadium. The Orioles' grimy
dugout on the third-base side; that's where Earl Weaver used
to scream expletives at the umpires. The seat in Row 20,
Section 4; that's where I sat during the 1979 World Series.

A few minutes later Sue arrived; she'd walked down from
her offices at a building called the Rotunda, a mile and a half
away. We didn't need to say anything about it: We knew that
for us, Opening Day would never again be the same. Memorial
Stadium is only two and a half miles from our house. We knew
all the tricks about parking on side streets within a half mile
of it; even in the largest of crowds, it was no more than fifteen
minutes from our front door to our seats. Both literally and
psychologically, Memorial Stadium was part of our neighborhood; the new downtown ballpark that was to replace it,
however lovely it might be, was in another part of the planet.
We were losing a lot more than a place to watch baseball
games.

Just before the National Anthem was played, John and
Debbie Ware slipped into the seats immediately to our right;
over the years of sitting next to each other they had become
our partners in an elaborate ticket-swapping scheme, and our
friends as well. A woman wearing an army sergeant's uniform
walked onto the field to sing the "Star-Spangled Banner."
The Gulf War had just ended and saber rattling was much in
vogue; Richard Cheney, the secretary of defense, was in the
owner's box, and so too was Dan Quayle, the vice president,
who was to throw out the first ball. That's the bad side of
Opening Day: the self-important bigwigs from Washington
who fly over in their helicopters, preen for photo opportunities, and leave in the third inning. They don't belong here.

The sergeant sang. In the outfield a large color guard stood
at attention, holding the flags of the states and territories;

these ruffles and flourishes would have blended in nicely at a
football game, but they didn't belong here either.

At last it was over. The soldiers marched away and the
umpires took command. They weren't major-league umpires
but scabs brought up from the minor leagues; the regular
umpires were on strike, in one of their periodic disputes with
the lords of baseball. Say it for the replacements, though, that
they did their jobs; once the game got under way, nobody
knew they were there, which in baseball lore is the mark of
good umpiring.

The players for the visiting team, the Chicago White Sox,
were introduced, then the Orioles. The cheers, though loud
and heartfelt, were nothing out of the usual until Mike Flanagan's name was called. Now our souls were stirred and our
cheers came from deep within us. Flanagan, a left-handed
pitcher, had been the heart of the last great Oriole teams,
those of the late 1970s and early 1980s: a gritty competitor
and a smart, witty man, loved and admired with equal intensity by players and fans. Then in 1988 he was traded away, to
the Toronto Blue Jays, for two young pitchers. He looked
utterly out of place in his new uniform. For two seasons he
pitched well, but in 1990 he had arm trouble and Toronto let
him go. He came to the Orioles' camp in 1991 as a non-roster
player, thirty-nine years old, and pitched his way onto the
staff. To say that Baltimore was glad to have him back only
hints at the emotions aroused by his return.

It was, as things turned out, the day's last cheer. We left at
the end of six interminable innings with the Orioles down by
8–1; the final score was 9–1. The club was promoting this as
"A Season to Remember," but it quickly became a season to
forget; if you read those words once in the sports pages, you
read them a million times, so dreary was the Orioles' year.
Watching them play was painful; it was much more pleasant
to dwell on the past.

Nineteen seventy-nine. Whenever I think about Baltimore
and the Orioles, I think about 1979. If, as I wrote many pages

ago, I cannot say with utter certainty that my four years at
Chapel Hill were the happiest of my life, I can say this without a moment of hesitation: In no single year have I been so
happy as I was in 1979.

You never would have known that from its prologue. On
December 1, 1978, we drove in from Florida and took possession of the house on Hawthorne Road. It was a sobering day;
we saw that many of the house's cosmetic flaws had been
papered over with furniture and draperies and that we faced
a far more tedious and expensive rehabilitation job than we
had anticipated. Then I reported for work at the *Washington
Star* and discovered that Time, Incorporated, its owner, had
given its unions an ultimatum: Accept our terms by December
31 or we'll shut the paper down.

Christmas was ghastly. Had the move from Miami to Baltimore been an indescribably stupid mistake? For three weeks
we fretted and stewed. Then, at the eleventh hour, the unions
caved in. The *Star* was saved—for two and a half years, as it
turned out—and so were we. Life would go on; now we could
start to live it.

That the Orioles would become so important a part of that
life was then beyond my reckoning. To be sure we had seen
them often in Miami, where they trained in the spring, but
both of us had been Red Sox fans and both of us assumed that
Boston's visits to Baltimore would be what drew us to Memorial Stadium. I had seen the ballpark on television for years
and was curious about it—the white houses past the center-
field fence had always struck me as both unique and fetching—but curiosity was about as deep as my emotions went.

Now that I think about it, this was odd. I was a child of the
Mid-Atlantic, and the Orioles are the Mid-Atlantic's team.
The region's other major-league clubs, the Pittsburgh Pirates
and the Philadelphia Phillies, somehow have always seemed
more Northern in orientation; but the Orioles are situated
near the heart of the region and their radio broadcasts can be
heard just about everywhere in it. Surely I must have listened
to Orioles games as a boy. Why wasn't I enticed by them to

adopt the team as a fan and thus satisfy my lifelong yearning
to have a major-league team to call my own?

I have no idea why. But slowly, in the late winter and early
spring of 1979, the Orioles began to insinuate their way into
my heart. Local television news broadcasts showed tapes of
Orioles games in Florida and gave breathless reports on the
progress of a team that the previous year had finished at the
unwontedly low level of fourth place. I made the acquaintance of Ethel Hogan, in the ticket office, who steered us to a
thirteen-game season ticket plan and, as the year progressed,
unfailingly found us the best seats available. I read the city's
sports pages with ever-increasing interest, and urged my colleagues at the *Star* to increase their coverage of what had
become, by default, Washington's team as well.

Opening Day that year was brutally cold but exhilarating.
Entering Memorial Stadium for the first time, I was en-
tranced. It was a large, horseshoe-shaped concrete structure
of no particular beauty or distinction, yet it had an air about
it. Those white houses obviously were part of its appeal, but
so too was an unexpected intimacy. I'd spent a fair amount of
time in that most celebrated of all ballparks, Fenway Park in
Boston, but even though Memorial Stadium was substantially
larger it seemed to me every bit as snug in its own way, and
a far higher proportion of its seats had relatively clean lines
of sight.

There was a crowd of just under forty thousand that day,
nearly fifteen thousand shy of capacity but large by Orioles
standards. Baltimore's failure to support what for some years
had been the best team in professional sport had been one of
the enduring mysteries of the game. The Orioles had never
drawn more than 1.2 million fans, and that was thirteen years
before. There were rumors that the team's owner, a local
brewer named Jerold C. Hoffberger, was losing the patience
that had long distinguished him and was preparing to sell the
club, possibly to someone who would move it elsewhere.

The more I followed the Orioles, the more this prospect
worried me, but I must admit that when the excitement of

Opening Day had worn off and the crowds dwindled to under
ten thousand, I wasn't complaining. It was wonderful to walk
up to the box office a half hour before game time and come
away with an excellent seat. I vividly remember one spring
night when Jim and Bill were in town. We got unreserved
seats and sat in the fifth row of the upper deck, right behind
home plate. We had the section all to ourselves. We stretched
out, put our feet up, and relaxed; baseball clubs may need big
crowds, but baseball fans love small ones.

The on-field particulars of that 1979 season aren't pertinent
here. Suffice it to say that although people in the know had
predicted that the Orioles would finish no higher than fourth,
they—*we*—took over first place on May 6 and held it the rest
of the way. We beat the California Angels in the American
League play-offs and went the full seven games before losing
the World Series to the Pittsburgh Pirates. A Baltimore-
Pittsburgh series? I thought I was watching "This Is Your
Life."

The baseball of 1979 seized me and shook me and then left
me in a state of blissful exhaustion. But baseball games are
baseball games; if you've seen as many as I have, after a while
all but the most memorable of them dissolve into a blur. I'd
thought, for example, that the night game I saw with my sons
was a doubleheader against the Milwaukee Brewers; a look at
the records of the 1979 season makes clear that it couldn't
possibly have been. It was just another ball game, if a very
happy night.

What really mattered about 1979 wasn't baseball but Baltimore, and what baseball did for it. The city when we moved
there was in trouble; it still is, but this was trouble of a
different and in some ways deeper order. Whatever civic self-
confidence Baltimore once had enjoyed had taken a beating
over the years. It was a stop on the railroad between Washington and New York, nothing more, and an ugly stop at that:
All the passenger saw of it was street after street of dilapi-
dated houses and empty factories. Washington in the postwar

years had grown fat and arrogant; it loved to turn up its nose
at Baltimore, which hadn't the poise to laugh at the insult.

Downtown Baltimore was a disaster area. My colleague at
the *Miami Herald*, Edwin Pope, had warned me not to go
there at night; when he went to Baltimore to cover games
between the Miami Dolphins and the Baltimore Colts, he said,
there were guard dogs outside downtown hotels, while customers inside shivered in fear. The City Fairs brought people
downtown for one weekend each September, but otherwise
people stayed away, taking their business to the shopping
centers and malls that ringed the city.

The sense I got was that it was a city without a center.
People walled themselves off in their neighborhoods. The
city's old Wasp power structure had, like Wasps elsewhere,
long ago retreated into its clubs and drawing rooms; Jewish
leadership was essential to the city's cultural affairs but less
assertive in civic ones; a strong black leadership existed, especially in the formidable person of the legendary Clarence
Mitchell, but its influence was more communal than civic.
More and more outsiders were coming to this insular, hermetic
place; the city feared them, fretted that they were "taking
over."

As the summer of 1979 unfolded, the embodiment of the
outsider became Edward Bennett Williams, the celebrated
attorney who on August 2 completed his purchase of the club
from Jerry Hoffberger. That the new owner might be from
Washington had been the subject of frenzied rumor for weeks,
rumor abetted by extraordinarily arrogant editorials in the
Washington Post to the effect that, itself having twice failed to
hold on to baseball clubs, Washington now somehow was
entitled to the Orioles. Baltimore had been scared all summer;
the arrival of Williams, the very embodiment of the phrase
"Washington lawyer," reduced the city to a bizarre mixture
of obsequiousness and fury.

What Williams's real intentions were at that time, I have
no idea. I have been told by people who knew him well that

he really did intend to move the club to Washington, but that the great leaps in attendance it enjoyed in the 1980s cut the ground out from under him; eventually, I am told, he became fond of the city, and before his death in 1988 he had arranged the club's affairs in such a way as to assure the Orioles' long-term commitment to Baltimore. I met Williams once and found him unspeakably charming; all the hostility I had accumulated over the years washed away in one fifteen-minute conversation.

But the only thing Baltimore knew in the summer of 1979 was that it faced a very real possibility of losing the team that it was only now learning to love. In any previous year its response almost surely would have been to whine and pout and stay away from the ballpark as it always had. But in 1979 it stepped out of character. It was as though the entire city had read a pop psychological treatise on assertiveness training: Baltimore got mad, and it got off its duff. Beginning in midsummer 1979, Baltimoreans went on what was, for them, an attendance toot of astonishing proportions. Crowds of thirty and forty thousand, once miraculous, became routine. In August of 1980, the Yankees came to town and drew a total of 249,605 fans, to this day the largest five-game attendance in baseball history; when the record was announced during the fifth game the entire crowd rose and jabbed its fists toward Williams in his box, roaring in defiance.

One afternoon, riding home from Penn Station on the bus, I found myself sitting opposite an elderly woman of evident wealth. She had all the trimmings—blue hair, tweed suit, stockings rolled up to just below her knees—except that she had a tiny radio pressed closely against her ear and a worried look on her face. I watched, puzzled, until suddenly she burst out, "Oh, come on, Palmer, get the ball over the *plate!*" I smiled, and she smiled back. Thanks to the Orioles, I had crossed the rich-old-lady gap.

Thanks to the Orioles, a lot of gaps were crossed. I used to think the notion that a team can unite a city was malarkey. I was wrong. The Orioles of 1979 brought Baltimore together so tightly that it seemed one small community. Oriole bumper stickers blossomed like black-eyed Susans, eventually to be joined by others announcing, "The Birds Belong in Baltimore." Oriole displays were set up in store windows. Banners saluting the team went up across downtown streets. On the commuter train, everybody seemed to be reading the sports pages. The Orioles were the talk of the town.

To an extraordinary degree, the Orioles of 1979 reflected the city in which they played. They were scrappy. They were unknown. They were underdogs. They had a lot of pride but not much money. They were "the home team" in ways that professional clubs, with their itinerant stars, can rarely be. The Orioles were Baltimore, which is why the city loved them so.

Of course it mattered a lot to the city that they were very good at winning baseball games, and not for a moment should that aspect of their importance be overlooked; but Orioles teams had been winning for years. What the 1979 team really did was to wrap a band of adhesive tape around a city that had been on the verge of losing its heart. It was pure coincidence, but their summer of triumph was followed a year later by the stupendously successful debut of Harborplace, the bazaar on the city's waterfront, and soon after that by a succession of developments that dramatically altered downtown. None of these managed to make much of a dent in the city's most definable problems—rotting infrastructure, a shrinking middle class, appalling infant mortality, crime, drugs, underfinanced schools, underfinanced *everything*—but cumulatively, with the Orioles in the lead, they accomplished one heroic task: They got rid of the malaise.

In a quite different way, the Orioles were every bit as good for me. They gave me a welcome distraction from work— every boy should have a toy—and, of far greater moment, a firm connection to friends old and new. Thanks to the ticket-swapping arrangement with the Wares, we had four seats for almost every Saturday and Sunday game. From April until October, the Orioles became our principal means of socializing. Friends came from as close as next door and as far as California. We served them Saturday dinner or Sunday brunch, then made the quick trip down to Waverley, the pleasant row house neighborhood to the stadium's west; we parked—now it can be told—on Barclay Street, then walked the short distance to the ballpark. It was a ritual in which dozens of our friends took part, one that enriched and deepened those friendships. It was one of the most important reasons why I cannot imagine Baltimore without the Orioles; that we can no longer take our friends to see them play in Memorial Stadium has left me with almost as great a sense of loss as would the departure of the Orioles themselves.

The last game was played on October 6, 1991. The games of the final week themselves, *qua* games, meant absolutely nothing; appalling deficiencies in starting pitching had dragged the Orioles into the netherworld of sixth place, with only the Cleveland Indians between them and the Slough of Despond. This was to be a weekend about baseball past and baseball future—and, inescapably, about Baltimore past and Baltimore future.

I gave a visiting friend a look at the latter early on Sunday morning, while most of the city was still asleep. We drove downtown, parked the car, and walked over to the new ballpark. That was what everybody called it then, because an official name had yet to be chosen. William Donald Schaefer, the governor, whose constituents were the park's real owners, wanted—properly, in my view—to call it Camden Yards, in commemoration of the site's previous history as a rail yard; Eli Jacobs, the club's owner, wanted to call it Oriole Park, for obvious reasons. Finally, well into the fall, they settled on Oriole Park at Camden Yards, one of those unhappy compromises that succeeds in pleasing nobody.

Call it what you will, it was an impressive sight even in its incomplete state. We could only walk around the outside and peer in through the outfield fence, but that was all one needed to sense the intelligence and integrity of the park's design: its fidelity to the red-brick ambience of downtown Baltimore, its adroit use of the immense old warehouse behind the right-field wall, its expert blend of modern convenience and old-fashioned atmosphere, its inherent good taste. I had been given a tour a few weeks earlier and was able to tell my friend the simple truth: It was going to be one hell of a ballpark.

But if the new ballpark is a civic treasure, it is also emblematic of changes in the city that I do not regard as for the better. The protestations of the Orioles to the contrary notwithstanding, Camden Yards is a rich-people's ballpark. Apart from architectural distinction and suitability for baseball, a chief consideration in its design was the care and feeding of the comfortable few who have acquired the "Private Suites"—the local euphemism for skyboxes—that ring its middle tier and the "Club Seats" immediately in front of them. Except for those holding tickets in these locations, the middle tier is out of bounds. Admission to the skybox level is controlled by guards, masquerading as ushers, who stand at its entrances; the concourse of the skybox level is enclosed and air-conditioned, with concession stands serving the ballpark equivalent of *haute cuisine*—not, by many reports, half so good as what you can buy from vendors near the cheap seats—and, astonishing though it may be, a concierge standing behind a pretentious desk, ready with fax machine, hotel-reservation services, and all other basic ballpark necessities.

Camden Yards radiates money; were it not so lovely, it could be said to stink of money. It is divided into two worlds: the privileged in their aeries and the customers in their seats. Even the latter are, by the standards of Memorial Stadium, privileged. Ticket prices at Camden Yards are among the highest in the league, and the stadium was designed to include as many high-priced tickets as possible, field boxes and terrace boxes most particularly; even with the very modest 5 per cent discount offered to season ticket holders who pay early, it cost Sue and me $1,846 for our two terrace boxes for the 1992 season.

In 1979 a fan could walk up to the gate at Memorial Stadium and get a reserved seat for $3.50, a general admission ticket for $2.50; all of the upper deck was available at these prices—21,077 seats, 40 per cent of Memorial Stadium's capacity or 44 per cent of Camden Yards's. In the new park the cheap seats are restricted to far left field and, in the outfield, a token bleacher section holding fewer than two thousand. No matter where in the park you happen to be sitting, you can't miss the elite behind the glass doors of their skyboxes, pouring drinks at their private bars, doing deals in their easy chairs— even glancing from time to time at the game below.

This is not—or at least not necessarily—what the Orioles would most like their new park to be. It is a reflection of the specific economics of baseball and the broader ones of post-Reaganite America. In August 1992 the Orioles signed their nonpareil shortstop, Cal Ripken, Jr., to a long-term contract worth more than $6 million a year; with a promising young pitching staff waiting to receive its due, their payroll surely will be well over $30 million before long, perhaps much higher.

The players deserve what they can get. But where is the money to come from? Revenue from contracts with the television networks is likely to be static or even to decline; for a club such as the Orioles, in a market that is small by comparison with those in New York and Los Angeles, there are limits to what local broadcasting rights can bring. So box office receipts have to go up, yet only so much can be extracted from the pockets of working people, or even from relatively well-to-do members of the middle class such as me. The money must come from those who can afford to pay: corporations willing to underwrite the cost of skyboxes in order to enhance their business, individuals willing to pay for them in order to enhance their vanity.

It makes perfect economic sense. Still, as the 1992 season approached I found myself thinking gloomy thoughts, worrying that whereas Memorial Stadium was the place that brought Baltimore together, Camden Yards might prove to have less salubrious effects: drawing all too visible lines between the very rich and the rest of us, which would be wholly out of character in an old working-class city such as Balti-more. I worried that, once the short-term benefits of the stadium had been collected, its long-term influence on rela-tions among Baltimoreans might be less benign.

I think now that I was wrong. The rich in their aeries *are* an incongruous presence—"Private Suites" in a ballpark!—but no one in the huge, happy crowds at Camden Yards seems to pay them much attention. Baltimore's response to the new park has been one of joy and gratitude, and that may well prove to have richly revitalizing effects on the center city; certainly Camden Yards is bringing people there in unprece-dented numbers, and thus is making old downtown Baltimore a more vivid part of the region's identity than it has been in years. If an excess of creature comfort for the privileged few is the price to be paid for that, perhaps over the years it will prove a bargain.

On Sunday, October 6, we had an early lunch and then drove to the ballpark. I had hoped, for sentiment's sake, to park on Barclay Street, but my secret had gotten out; we settled for a spot a quarter mile farther away. The previous day had been warm, almost hot, but overnight a cold front had come in from the northwest; we were amply supplied with sweaters and winter jackets. We crossed Greenmount Avenue and, for the last time, passed an agreeably seedy bar called the Sta-dium Lounge, its raffish clientele hanging around outside, drinking beer and eating pit beef. There were going to be too many last times today. I didn't want to think about it.

When we entered the stadium, the ushers returned our tickets without tearing off the stubs: souvenirs. We learned later that for a few minutes the ballplayers greeted fans per-sonally as they arrived at the gates. Inside, the concourse was crammed to the rafters; passage to our seats was laborious, so once we got there, we stayed put. Mike the usher was at work; he said he didn't know if he'd stay on at the new park, though in the end he did. All around me I could see my fellow fans, few of whose names I knew, many of whose faces were as

familiar to me as my neighbors'; as fellow residents of Section
39, neighbors are just what they had been.

The game itself was like the season itself: bad. The Tigers
took an early lead and cruised; the final score was 7–1. But
there was one scene that for the rest of my life I will treasure.
Mike Flanagan had let it be known that he wanted to throw
the last pitch; John Oates, the manager, had promised to
accommodate him should circumstances permit. They did.
With one man out in the bottom of the ninth, Oates called
him in.

Flanagan started to walk in from the bull pen in left field.
IIe was walking directly—slowly, deliberately, clearly wish-
ing this could never end—toward our seats. The grass seemed
to shimmer under his feet; I thought of Omar Sharif riding
toward Peter O'Toole in *Lawrence of Arabia*, the desert glimmering beneath him. The crowd stood and roared, a deep,
echoing sound that reverberated far beyond baseball. I could
see through my binoculars that Flanagan was close to tears;
I had the same problem.

Oates handed him the ball, gave him a pat, and went back
to the dugout. Flanagan took his warm-up pitches. Then he
followed the script: He struck out the last two batters. Did he
get a little help from his friends, the Tigers? I wondered that
at the time, and still do. But that is of no moment at all. This
was the way the last game at Memorial Stadium *had* to end;
no other conclusion was permissible.

The field was cleared. The crowd was on its feet; the air was
thick with anticipatory tension. Something was going to happen, but none of us knew what. A couple of weeks earlier my
friend and former *Washington Star* colleague Dan Shaugh-
nessy, now a sports columnist for the *Boston Globe*, had passed
through town; he told me that the finale would involve
"about a hundred former Orioles," but that was as much as
I knew.

Suddenly the gate next to the left-field bull pen opened and
an immense limousine raced through, a police escort howling
ahead of it. It was the biggest, whitest, ugliest stretch limo I'd

ever seen. It tore around the outfield track and screeched to a halt right at home plate. The doors flew open—and out dashed a half dozen members of the Orioles' grounds crew, spiffily dressed in white tuxedos, orange ties and orange cummerbunds. While music blared frantically in the background, they raced to the plate and began digging: Their mission was to remove the plate and then transport it to Camden Yards.

It was a wonderful comic set piece, stirring memories of the routine—clowns pouring out of a miniature car—that I'd seen at the circus forty-five years before. The crowd shouted its pleasure and gave the crew a huge hand as it sped back through the gate.

Now the stadium grew quiet. Soft music began to play over the public-address system; later I learned that it was the theme music of *Field of Dreams*, a movie I'd declined to see on the grounds that baseball is to be enjoyed, not sentimentalized and exploited. Never mind. It sounded fine in that place at that time.

Then the crowd began to murmur. Something was happening in the Orioles' dugout. In a moment we realized what it was, and this time the cheers were thunderous. Brooks Robinson, the most beloved player in the history of the team, a man whose name means "Baltimore" to Americans everywhere, appeared on the top step of the dugout. He was wearing his old uniform. He trotted slowly out to third base and took his accustomed place there.

Moments later Frank Robinson followed him. He loped—fifty-six years old, and he still loped—out to right field. Boog Powell, all Lord knows how many pounds of him, lumbered to first base. Jim Palmer, tears pouring down his famously handsome face, walked slowly, head down, to the pitcher's mound.

On and on the procession went. By the time it was complete more than a hundred Orioles, past and present, were on the field. If you aren't a Baltimorean, aren't a baseball fan, the names will mean nothing to you. They mean everything to me. Some of them were before my time, but most had played on that field before my eyes. I had never met a single one, yet they were integral parts of my life. They had given me pleasure beyond measure. I did not know how to thank them; all I could do was clap, so that is what I did.

There was other business, all of it touching and exactly right; the Orioles were going to walk away from Memorial Stadium with class, that was clear. I watched it through a mist. I wanted to hold forever in my eye the picture of those players—first standing in happy clumps at the positions they'd played, then forming a circle for a panoramic photograph, then clustered together at the center of the field, waving to the crowd and embracing each other. I realized what those of us in the stands too often fail to understand: We had meant something to them, too.

I didn't want to leave but it was time to go; I'm not one for lingering. In the crush I shook Mike's hand, took one last look at the field, then beckoned to Sue and plunged down the runway. As we left the stadium for the last time I said a sad, silent farewell. It was time to go home.

18

MY MID-ATLANTIC: II

Going home. It took me a year to figure it out, but that was what I had been doing all along. From first day to last—from Philadelphia to Memorial Stadium—my journey through the Mid-Atlantic had been a search for the home place that throughout my life I mistakenly thought had eluded me. In the end I found it, but it was not at all what I had expected.

It turned out to be not a single home but a succession, or a conglomeration, of homes. The little town in Pennsylvania where my distant ancestors had started my family's life in America; the great city a few miles away where my grandparents lay buried; the bleak, stark land on the banks of the James River where lonely settlers struggled to plant English roots; the city where I was born; the two schools, one where I lived as a boy and the other where I began my real life; the shingled community by the sea; the little neighborhood within the big city where I live now—individually and collectively, all of these are my home places.

Quite apart from the deep feelings they arouse in me, these places are noteworthy for a single salient characteristic: All are in the Mid-Atlantic. You can get from any one to any other in a single day's drive, though if you're going from Pittsburgh to Duck you'll want to have your foot on the floor most of the way. The Mid-Atlantic is a tight little region, larger than New England but far smaller than the South, the Midwest, or the West; it is compact enough so that a person can plant many roots there, all of them close enough together to be tended and nurtured more or less simultaneously.

My conclusions about this place are much the same at journey's end as they were at its outset. If they don't call it Mid-*Atlantic* for nothing, neither do they call it *Mid*-Atlantic for nothing. It is, in every sense, a place in the middle. To be sure it has irrational moments, as the voters of North Carolina persist in reminding us every six years, and its foolish ones as well: The decline of its old cities is a terrible waste of human resources and physical assets, not to mention history and tradition. Mostly, though, the Mid-Atlantic is as temperate and benign as its weather: "The Land of Pleasant Living," indeed.

It is at once a distinctly American place and a place all its own. That it is the nation in microcosm seems to me as self-evident now as it did before my journey began. Spacious skies, amber waves, mountain majesties, fruited plains: You'll find it all here, in a mere seven states and one federal district. If you wanted to introduce an alien visitor to these United States and had only a week in which to do it, you could do far worse than to spend that week driving the Mid-Atlantic.

Yet no one will confuse the Mid-Atlantic with any of the nation's other regions, however much it may look or feel like them. The beach at the Outer Banks bears little resemblance to any in California; the cityscape of Baltimore looks not in the least like that of Houston; the campus at Chapel Hill will never be confused with that of Ann Arbor; Route 29 as it winds through Virginia is only a distant relative of Route 2 as it crosses Massachusetts.

We may have no definable regional cuisine, but our place has its own flavors. Except in the mountains our land slopes gently; by contrast with those of the West, even our mountains are gentle. Except for the violent turns it occasionally takes near Cape Hatteras, our seacoast is mild and subdued.

Our cities are substantial but not gigantic; even in Philadelphia it is possible to maintain a human scale. Our unpredictable winters may borrow a bit from New England and our steamy summers a bit from the South, but in no place except the Mid-Atlantic can one find the blissful spring and fall that we enjoy.

We don't have a clearly definable human character, but then neither does any other region. The crusty Yankee is as much a creature of myth as the hospitable Southerner or the quick-triggered Westerner; even the smallest of American regions is too large to permit facile generalizations about its residents. But, again, the notion of middleness is based in reality. In politics, society, and culture, we prefer compromise and accommodation; our history of relations among the races and other disparate groups is far from perfect, Lord knows, but just about everything in our history suggests that we'd rather talk than fight.

Perhaps I see in the region what I want to see. However blunt and contentious I may be in the journalistic pulpit from which it is my privilege to preach, in my private life I prefer harmony to confrontation and alleviation to aggravation. I have spent most of that life in the Mid-Atlantic and I have found exactly what I want. The word for it is *home*.

Bibliography

Although this book draws primarily upon my own observations and memory, I made use of numerous publications. I am a daily reader of the Baltimore *Sunpapers*, the *New York Times*, the *Washington Post*, and the *Wall Street Journal*, and herewith express my gratitude for the assistance I found in the pages of these estimable newspapers. I found certain magazine articles helpful; these are acknowledged in the text as they occur. So too are the tour books and maps published by the American Automobile Association, the comprehensiveness of which needs no testimony from me. These book-length works were helpful:

Alcamo, John. *Atlantic City: Behind the Tables*. Grand Rapids: Gollehon Press, 1991.

Allcott, John V. *The Campus at Chapel Hill: Two Hundred Years of Architecture*. Chapel Hill Historical Society, 1986.

Beard, Gordon. *Basic Baltimorese II*. Baltimore: 1990.

Birnbach, Lisa, ed. *The Official Preppy Handbook*. New York: Workman, 1980.

Brugger, Robert J. *Maryland: A Middle Temperament 1634–1980*. Baltimore: Johns Hopkins, 1988.

Cupper, Dan. *The Pennsylvania Turnpike: A History*. Lebanon: Applied Arts Publishers, 1990.

Deetz, James. *In Small Things Forgotten: The Archaeology of Early American Life*. New York: Anchor, 1977.

Delaware: A Guide to the First State. New York: Hastings House, second printing, 1948.

Farmer, Fannie Merritt. *The Original Boston Cooking-School Cook Book*. 1896. Facsimile. New York: Weathervane Books.

Fee, Elizabeth; Shopes, Linda; and Zeidman, Linda, eds. *The Baltimore Book: New Views of Local History*. Philadelphia: Temple University Press, 1991.

Jackson, Michael. *The Simon and Schuster Pocket Guide to Beer*. New York: Simon and Schuster, 1986.

Key, V. O. *Southern Politics in State and Nation*. New York: Knopf, 1949.

New Jersey: A Guide to Its Present and Past. New York: Hastings House, second printing, 1946.

Papenfuse, Edward C.; Stiverson, Gregory A.; Collins, Susan A.; and Carr, Lois Green, eds. *Maryland: A New Guide to the Old Line State*. Baltimore: Johns Hopkins, 1976.

Pennsylvania: A Guide to the Keystone State. New York: Oxford University Press, 1940.

Roberts, Bruce. *Plantation Homes of the James River*. Chapel Hill: University of North Carolina Press, 1990.

Robinson, Blackwell P., ed. *The North Carolina Guide*. Chapel Hill: University of North Carolina Press, 1955.

Schoenbaum, Thomas J. *Islands, Capes and Sounds: The North Carolina Coast*. Winston-Salem: John F. Blair, 1982.

Stewart, George R. *U.S. 40: Cross Section of the United States of America*. Boston: Houghton Mifflin, 1953.

Stilgoe, John R. *Borderland: Origins of the American Suburb, 1820–1939*. New Haven: Yale University Press, 1988.

Tyler, Anne. *The Accidental Tourist*. New York: Knopf, 1985.

Virginia: A Guide to the Old Dominion. New York: Oxford University Press, fourth printing, 1947.

Waesche, James F. *Crowning the Gravelly Hill: A History of the Roland Park–Guilford–Homeland District*. Baltimore: Maclay and Associates, 1987.

Washington, D.C.: A Guide to the Nation's Capital. New rev. ed. New York: Hastings House, 1968.

West Virginia: A Guide to the Mountain State. New York: Oxford University Press, 1941.

WPA Guide to Philadelphia. Philadelphia: University of Pennsylvania Press, 1988.

Wise, David. *Spectrum.* New York: Viking, 1981.

Yardley, Jonathan. *Our Kind of People: The Story of an American Family.* New York: Weidenfeld and Nicolson, 1989.

ABOUT THE AUTHOR

Jonathan Yardley is book critic and a columnist for the *Washington Post*. In 1968 he was awarded a Nieman Fellowship at Harvard University and in 1981 he won the Pulitzer Prize for Distinguished Criticism. He lives in Baltimore with his wife, Susan Hartt Yardley.